Always Music in the Air
The Sounds of Twin Peaks

WRITTEN BY SCOTT RYAN

SCOTT LUCK STORIES
(2014)
THIRTYSOMETHING AT THIRTY: AN ORAL HISTORY
(2017)
THE LAST DAYS OF LETTERMAN
(2019)
BUT, COULDN'T I DO THAT? ANSWERING YOUR QUESTIONS ABOUT SELF-PUBLISHING (WITH ERIN O'NEIL)
(2021)
MOONLIGHTING: AN ORAL HISTORY
(2021)
FIRE WALK WITH ME: YOUR LAURA DISAPPEARED
(2022)
LOST HIGHWAY: THE FIST OF LOVE
(2023)
MASSILLON AGAINST THE WORLD
(WITH BECCA MOORE)
(2024)
THE LAST DECADE OF CINEMA
(2024)

EDITED BY SCOTT RYAN

THE BLUE ROSE MAGAZINE
(2017-2025)
THE WOMEN OF DAVID LYNCH
(2019)
THE WOMEN OF AMY SHERMAN-PALLADINO
(2020)
TWIN PEAKS UNWRAPPED
(WRITTEN BY BEN DURANT & BRYON KOZACZKA)
(2020)
MASSILLON TIGERS: 15 FOR 15
(WRITTEN BY DAVID LEE MORGAN, JR.)
(2020)
MYTH OR MAYOR: THE SEARCH FOR MY FAMILY'S LEGACY
(WRITTEN BY ALEX RYAN/AFTERWORD BY SCOTT RYAN)
(2021)
BARBRA STREISAND: THE ALBUMS, THE SINGLES, THE MUSIC
(WRITTEN BY MATT HOWE)
(2023,2025)

Always Music in the Air
The Sounds of Twin Peaks

A BOOK BY *Scott Ryan*

TUCKER

PRESS

Always Music in the Air: The Sounds of Twin Peaks
©2025 Scott Ryan

All Rights Reserved.
Reproduction in whole or in part without the author's permission is strictly forbidden.
All photos and/or copyrighted material appearing in this publication remains the work
of its owners. This book is not affiliated with *Twin Peaks*, Lynch/Frost Productions,
New Line Cinema, or CBS. This is a scholarly work of review and commentary only,
and no attempt is made or should be inferred to infringe upon the copyrights of any
corporation.

Cover design by Scott Ryan
Cover photos courtesy of CBS
All photos/screen captures from *FWWM* are courtesy of New Line Cinema.
All photos/screen captures from *Twin Peaks* are courtesy of CBS.
MP3 Covers courtesy of Russ Dudle or Dean Hurley
Author photo by Faye Murman

Edited by David Bushman
Book designed by Scott Ryan

Published in the USA by Tucker DS Press
Columbus, Ohio

Contact Information
Email: TuckerDSPress@gmail.com
Website: TuckerDSPress.com
BlueSky: @scottryanfmp.bsky.social
Instagram: @Fayettevillemafiapress

*This book is dedicated to Katie Edgin,
who is right now having coffee with
the Log Lady,
Albert,
and the Major.*

CONTENTS

Foreword by Brad Dukes...viii

Prelude/Angry Young Man...1

1. "Moving Through Time," 1989...15

2. "Falling" *Floating into the Night*, 1989..22

3. "Freshly Squeezed" The Music Editor's Duet.................................43

4. "Laura Palmer's Theme" *Soundtrack from Twin Peaks*, 1990.................60

5. "The Bookhouse Boys" The Director's Trio....................................80

6. "Sycamore Trees" *Twin Peaks: Fire Walk With Me*, 1992...................97

7. "Just You" *Twin Peaks: Season Two Music and More*, 2007.................116

8. "I'm Hurt Bad" Dean Hurley...137

9. "Black Lodge Rumble" *The Twin Peaks Archive*, 2011-2012.................145

10. "The Fireman" Dean Hurley (Reprise)..247

11. "Shadow" *Twin Peaks Music from the Limited Event Series*, 2017.............256

12. "Heartbreaking" *Twin Peaks Limited Event Series Soundtrack*, 2017.....276

13. *The Voice of Love*, 1993...295

Special Thanks...306

FOREWORD
BY BRAD DUKES

LIGHT YOURSELF ON FIRE

Writing a book about *Twin Peaks* requires a certain sense of lunacy, which is why I was delighted to hear that my friend Scott Ryan was writing this book. I've spent years myself documenting this world cocreated by David Lynch and Mark Frost, and I'm excited to uncover even more of the story of this wondrous soundtrack through Scott's perspective. And who better to write a book about the music of *Twin Peaks* than someone who has written and composed his own darn song about how much he loves *Twin Peaks*?

> "I can't believe this place
> The smile upon my face
> Mountains surround, this sleepy town
> Guess what I found?
> I think I'm home"

I hum Scott's song to myself often, then I chuckle and smile and text Scott to say hey. *Twin Peaks* is the gift that just keeps on giving. *Twin Peaks* stokes creativity. You watch the show and you want to make art of your own. Drawings, music, mittens, candles, tarot cards—I've just about seen it all. All this art, made by interesting people invested in this fictional world. And *Twin Peaks* friends make the best friends. When Scott asked me to write a foreword for this book, I kept gravitating to a visceral core memory.

It was getting late on a Friday night, twelve or so years ago. About to turn in, I got a Facebook message from the Roadhouse singer herself, Julee Cruise: "Can you talk now?"

My eyes widened as I typed back a very calm, understated "yep." I'd been hounding Julee for months to talk with me for an interview on a now-defunct blog. Every attempt at pinning her down had failed. I sent her my phone number, readied my recorder, and within moments had corralled the voice of love to ask all my burning questions regarding *Twin Peaks*.

"I haven't eaten in three days," she claimed as a delivery man buzzed her New York apartment. A racket hummed in the background. Rustling papers, another voice in the background, and a dog barking. Julee's voice didn't resemble the ethereal, angelic notes that emanate from the Roadhouse stage.

Ravaged. Blunt. Racing. Erratic. Descriptive. Above all, Julee was New York: "I have a big, huge butcher knife in my purse." I'm not sure what question I led off with, but that first bone I threw out was gnawed on, chewed up, and spit back at me. Julee was all over the place, dragging me by the collar with her through the phone. Back in 2012, *Twin Peaks* fans wanted a third season—and I was living *The Return* myself a few years early, grasping to make sense of it all. I was fascinated, captivated, bewildered by everything I heard. Julee didn't just have hot takes. She had plans. She had spoken to David Lynch the night prior about working on some new material. She had agreed to put on a one-woman show in Russia: "When I sing now, I cry, and it freaks people out a little bit, but they love it. They want to see you light yourself on fire and slit yourself open and spill your guts, and that's exactly what I do." She cursed Lynch for abandoning her in the same breath she thanked him and Angelo Badalamenti for the big break they gave her back in the days of *Blue Velvet*. Memory lane was all beautiful, all muddy, and everywhere in between. Such is life, such is *Twin Peaks*.

Eighty minutes later, I hung up the phone and let out a deep exhale. It took me weeks to figure out how to package Julee's words into a story. Julee had to be heard to be comprehended. This wasn't just work she reflected upon. Rather, her life, legacy, and what someday would be her epitaph to the masses. Julee's role in this artistic landmark was never going to fade, and she embraced the good and bad with both arms. The work Julee made with Lynch and Badalamenti is just too damn good to ever be forgotten, rather discovered and rediscovered in perpetuity. And

Julee knew that.

Julee is but one captivating character in the music hall of *Twin Peaks*. Al Regni on saxophone, Grady Tate on the drums. Kinny Landrum laying down that sweet, sweet "Falling" synthesizer—which I call the one true signature of all things *Twin Peaks*. These incredible talents swirl together, forming all these incredible sounds. The dark, dreamy water that Laura Palmer, wrapped in plastic, floated upon.

A few years after I talked to Julee, I attended one of her final live performances in the same room *Twin Peaks: Fire Walk With Me* had premiered to American audiences. She wasn't just fashionably late, but fraught and dramatic, preceded by rumors of a straight up no-show. And then she appeared. Each sustained note of "Rockin' Back Inside My Heart" seemed to take a little bit more life out of her tiny frame. Downtime between songs was silent, void of banter. I couldn't call it a concert. Maybe a farewell. Tears squeaked from the corners of her eyes as she peered around the room, her own voice reverberating through the audience, off the walls, then returning to her. She left the stage with a dissonant gait. Reaching toward the wall to stay on her feet. I don't know if it was an act, or if this rare return to the stage was bringing her to her knees. I do know she relished in lighting herself on fire one more time. Spilling her guts while she still could.

If you immerse yourself in *Twin Peaks* and its music, you will feel it all, just as Julee did.

Allow "Blue Frank" to pulverize your senses on a lonesome night's drive.

Crank "The World Spins" and submit yourself to the red curtains of the world that will one day consume you.

Do not skip the James and Evelyn scenes or you'll deny yourself a real luxury—Badalamenti's most evocative jazz of the series. (Seriously, "Trail Mix." Damn.)

Do pour a cup of damn good coffee before proceeding any further.

Light yourself on fire. Slit yourself open and spill your guts.

"Gotta rocket,
In your pocket,
Keep coolly cool, boy."
"Cool" from *West Side Story*, Stephen Sondheim

"Baby, you are more like a three stage rocket—a pocket rocket."
Bobby Briggs, *Twin Peaks*

PRELUDE/ ANGRY YOUNG MAN

Part A: Prelude

On March 10, 2011, on the Dugpa internet forum, which covered the 1990-1991 series *Twin Peaks*, long-time poster under the alias Jerry Horne wrote this:

> **Subject: "Deer Meadow Shuffle" now available at Davidlynch.com!**
> **Post: OH MY GOD!! More unreleased tracks from the series and**
> ***FWWM* soon!!**

Let's Rock! It would be next to impossible to explain to a viewer who just discovered *Twin Peaks* what it was like to be a hardcore fan of the series during the lean years of 1993-2007. Being a fan was lonelier than Harold Smith's apartment on New Year's Eve. It was colder than an anniversary dinner between Catherine and Pete Martell. Norma Jennings would have better luck getting flowers from Hank on their anniversary than a *Twin Peaks* fan would have of getting any new information on the series.

Twin Peaks premiered on April 8, 1990, and became that year's biggest moment in pop culture. "She's dead, wrapped in plastic" had the same impact on a generation of television watchers as when Ed Sullivan proclaimed, "Ladies and gentlemen, the Beatles" in 1964. Both iconic quotes were broadcast on television screens, back when television was consumed live and was a shared communal experience. The show's history and its effect on pop culture have been covered and recovered in a ton of books. Most books look to explain the other worldly Red Room or theorize on what role the atomic bomb played in the birth of supervillain Bob. The author wants to tell readers just exactly where Phillip Jeffries is, tell them they know what year this is, or explain just how Annie is doing. Here is a (not-so) secret confession from one of the people who's had a hand in well over twenty of those publications: I don't really care about any of those answers or theories. For me, it's always been about the music that played on the foreground or in the background of *Twin Peaks*.

"Where we're from, the birds sing a pretty song and there's always music in the air," warbled the Man from Another Place in Episode 2. But anyone watching up to that point had surely figured that out by then. The music of the series, more commonly known as the score, was turned up louder than a traffic jam in front of the Double R diner. The score wasn't just a by-product of the series; it was as much a part of the story as the ceiling fan, the dangling stoplight, or Laura Palmer herself. I watched said Pilot episode live on ABC in the summer of 1990, and while I was haunted and moved by the incredible piece of art that it was and still is, it was the music that grabbed me from the get-go. The script for the Pilot was written by Mark Frost and David Lynch and directed by Lynch. The truth is just about every aspect of the series was so different from everything else that was airing on television at the time. Frost and Lynch were already known names in the world of film and television: Lynch from directing *Eraserhead* (1977), *Elephant* Man (1980), and *Blue Velvet* (1986), Frost from being a writer on *Hill Street Blues* (1981-1987). But that wasn't the name I was staring at during the credits and trying to figure out how to pronounce. Who the heck was Angelo Badalamenti? Since when did credits on a television show tell viewers who "composed and conducted" the music? Today, I can say it and spell it as easily as Andy quotes French suicide notes.

"The Norwegians Are Leaving"

The funny thing about me falling in love with the music so quickly is that it wasn't any of the three famous musical themes from the Pilot that I was taken with. I mean of course I loved "Laura Palmer's Theme." I was a piano player, and the middle section of that piano coming to life in the very moments of the news of Laura's tragic death made me want to find the sheet music for that song right away. I eventually did find it, and scans from that 1990 piano book are used in the chapter on that song to explain the musicality of Badalamenti's composition. I don't remember having any immediate feelings about the main theme song or Julee Cruise's performance of two songs during scenes at the Roadhouse in the two-hour premiere episode. It wasn't even the third major theme, "Dance of the Dream Man," which was used to introduce Agent Cooper as he first drove into town, that had me wishing for a CD of the music. While all three cues made me take notice that the show I was watching was doing something new on television, none of those was the track that burned into my musical memory.

No, the song that I specifically remember from the Pilot was a cue that we now know as "The Norwegians." Audrey Horne walks into the conference room where a group of Norwegian businessmen are going over the Ghostwood contracts, and she just stands there pouting. This slow-bouncing music of bass notes on a keyboard bumps along as each businessman's head turns from the paperwork they were reviewing to Audrey Horne. She tells them that her friend was murdered and looks sad, but we know she has no sad feelings about the death of Laura Palmer

because Angelo's music is so silly and comical that we are smiling at her mischief. She is only doing this to ruin her father's business deal.

The musical cue is brought back moments later when the Norwegians are checking out of the Great Northern hotel en masse and the clerk repeatedly hits the bell, screaming over and over, "The Norwegians are leaving! The Norwegians are leaving!" The bass of the music is still bouncing along, but the melody is playing a fun waltz that honestly sounds like the future theme of *Curb Your Enthusiasm*. This playfulness perfectly captures Audrey's adolescent desire to mess with her father's business and the kinetic energy of people exiting a hotel in droves. The music, the tone, the comedy are in stark contrast to everything else we had seen up to this point in the episode. The Norwegians-are-leaving scene is sandwiched between two serious investigation scenes with Agent Cooper. The before is Cooper interviewing a belligerent Bobby Briggs and the after is Bobby and Mike in the hallway and then Cooper talking to a crying Donna Hayward while she watches a video of her picnic with Laura. That is a neck-snapping change in tone. How can a director make sure he doesn't lose his audience by placing a comedy scene in between these back-to-back scenes? How can a series, in the beginning minutes of its existence, communicate that this show will have sudden changes in tone? The only way a film can pull off that change is with a musical cue that directly communicates to the audience one simple fact: it's okay to laugh.

Angelo Badalamenti nails this assignment with a cue that is under a minute and a half in length. And the track is virtually never used again in the entire series. (Three notes of the bass are used in Episode 2, but the main cue is never played again.) Most series back then would have used this cue EVERY time something mischievous happened. I knew in that first moment that this little track would be a song I would need to own. But television series rarely released their scores. There were series that would have soundtracks, but they were always filled with pop songs that played during critical episodes, and maybe the theme song. One can take a look at the *Moonlighting* television soundtrack, which had the track "Limbo Rock" by Chubby Checker but not the instrumental piano piece known as "Maddie's Theme." Those kinds of soundtracks just were never released. But as I stated, *Twin Peaks* was different.

That September, the soundtrack to *Twin Peaks* was released on CD. The soundtrack was released a few weeks before Season 2 hit the airways. I bought it from my local music shop the day it came out. I still have the CD longbox it came in. (If you don't remember what a longbox is then I bet you never carried a metal lunchbox to school either.) I was careful to pull the top of the box apart so I could slide the CD out without damaging the box. My plan was to pin that useless, environmentally wasteful box of cardboard, which I still own, on my basement bulletin board. It had the beloved "Welcome to Twin Peaks" sign on the cover. It would allow me to feel that the room had a piece of my favorite town in it. I was so excited to finally have all my favorite music tracks from the first season. I was ready to own that beautiful opening song that made every other nighttime soap theme sound like it had been plucked from a Mike Post grab bag. I was wondering what it would be like to own that crazy jazz ditty that the little man danced to in Cooper's dream, but mostly I wanted to hear that fun Norwegians song, plus the number that Leland broke down and danced to at the Great Northern after Laura's funeral.

I popped the CD into my player, and I listened from start to finish. I experienced something for the first time that as a die hard *Twin Peaks* fan I would come to recognize as a familiar feeling: I noticed everything that was missing. I was crushed that the tracks I wanted the most were—I don't know what to call them—let's maybe call them "missing pieces"? Yeah, that sounds about right: missing pieces of music. There is no doubt that I was enthralled to hear the crisp perfection of the full recording of "Laura Palmer's Theme" and "The Bookhouse Boys," but where the hell were the songs I wanted? Oh well, I guess I'd just have to wait till the Season 2 soundtrack came out the following year. Wrong, again. Not only would the Season 2 soundtrack not come out the following year, it wouldn't come out for *seventeen* more years. And when the SOB did come out, it would NOT have either the "The Norwegians" or the "Great Northern Big Band" cue. All of this made me feel like somebody taped my lips to the tailpipe of a bus. I started to wonder if maybe it was going to be difficult to be a *Twin Peaks* fan. Nah, I'm sure it would all be as easy as preparing a pig's head with an apple in its mouth for dinner.

Part B: Angry Young Man

In the fall of 1990, I was twenty years old and attending college. The *Twin Peaks* soundtrack was an aberration in my music collection. Before *Twin Peaks* came around, I wasn't listening to soft, angelic music from artists like Julee Cruise, or the smooth jazz of Angelo Badalamenti. My favorite musician was Billy Joel. I was listening to his new CD *Storm Front* and his number one single "We Didn't Start the Fire" on repeat. I was into R.E.M.; Indigo Girls; the Traveling Wilburys; 10,000 Maniacs; and Madonna. I modeled my college self after Billy Joel's song "Prelude/Angry Young Man." I was there to fight the world and everyone in it. I was angry at the missing music on the soundtrack. I wasn't sure that the CD needed to have "Laura Palmer's Theme" and the "Love Theme from Twin Peaks." They were virtually the same song. "Freshly Squeezed" and "Dance of the Dream Man" were also versions of the same tune. Obviously, the only difference between "Theme from Twin Peaks" and "Falling" was one had lyrics, one didn't. I loved the soundtrack and I listened to it on repeat, but I also was baffled by the lack of variety in the song selection.

Part of the problem was that I had purchased Julee Cruise's album *Floating into the Night* before the soundtrack was released. That album contained the exact versions of "Falling," "The Nightingale," and "Into the Night" that were on the soundtrack. More repetition for me. There were so many music cues from that first season, and while I understood that they couldn't fit all of them on one CD, I was young and still hopeful, and I wanted more. Wanting more, and being angry about not getting everything you want, are what being an original *Twin Peaks* fan is all about. We wanted more episodes, we wanted more Cooper in *FWWM*, we wanted the deleted scenes from *FWWM*, we wanted more of *Twin Peaks*, and then, when they released *The Return*, we went right back to wanting more Cooper. (I actually wanted more Sheryl Lee, but it's the same point.) Through it all, what I really wanted was more music and my "Norwegians" cue.

This leads us back to that post from "Jerry Horne" on the Dugpa website in 2011. Twenty-one years after the series aired, the music was finally being released on DavidLynch.com for download. This was, and still is, my favorite thing to ever happen with *Twin Peaks*. By that point, we had three official soundtracks. The *Twin Peaks* soundtrack (1990), *Fire Walk With Me* (1992), and *Season Two Music and More* (2007). Today, we can add to that total the two releases from *The Return* in 2017, plus the two Julee Cruise solo albums on which she sings some songs from the series. But in 2011, so many tracks were still missing. This online release, titled *Twin Peaks Archive* (*TPA*), finally included my "The Norwegians" track as part of a year and a half long odyssey that would total 212 MP3s that listeners could download to their computers and iPods. When you add those 212 tracks to the five official soundtrack releases, you get a total of 290 tracks that have been released. Those are the tracks I will be covering in this book. I will not be covering tracks that have been bootlegged or have not been released under the *Twin Peaks* brand.

Part of the reason *Twin Peaks* fans had such a strong desire to own all this music, besides the fact that they are about as mentally stable as Johnny Horne on a day when his Teddy Bear is out of batteries, is because the music is a huge part of the original series and *FWWM*. I was curious to know just how many minutes of a typical episode of the original series was filled with music. So I did an unscientific Scott-study to find out. Using the same instrument that Sam Stanley used to crack the Whitman case, I discovered the first hour-long episode of *Twin Peaks*, directed by Duwayne Dunham, has twenty-one minutes of music, which means 46 percent of the episode is scored. This coincides with the Season 1 finale, directed by Mark Frost. Forty-six percent of that episode too is backed with Angelo's music. In Season 2, the music really starts to take over. Episode 16, directed by Tim Hunter, uses twenty-four unique music cues (according to Ross Dudle's *Twin Peaks* Soundtrack Design website), totaling thirty-five of the episode's forty-four minutes, which comes out to 79 percent. You might think that would make it the most scored episode, but Episode 29, the final hour of the original series, directed by Lynch himself, wins that prize. There is a whopping forty-two minutes of music in the fifty-minute episode. That means that 87 percent of the episode is scored. With that much music being played, plus the impact of that music on scenes in the series, what else could a fan do but get swept up in desire for these tracks, like an old mayor falling in love with Lana?

When the series came back in 2017, the episodes weren't as heavily scored. I didn't test how much any particular "part" was scored in the new series because there is so much ominous whoosh going on, I don't really know how I could distinguish the music from the whoosh. Some tasks are beyond even Agent Stanley's contraptions. But music still played an important aspect in *The Return*, just in a different way. Almost every part ended in the Roadhouse with a different band singing a song on screen to wrap things up. (Well, not to wrap up the plot, just the part. We never wrap up plot.) When it was announced that *The Return* would have two soundtracks released, one score based and one song based, I was elated. So why am I still angry? (How much time do you have?)

Badalamenti's Blue Rose

This "Angry Young Man" has turned into an "Angry Old Man." Yes, we have been given five official soundtrack albums. But that means only 25 percent of the cues used in the series have been released on vinyl or CD or are commercially available to stream. It kills me to even include streaming in that threesome, but I am aware that streaming is how 99 percent of music listeners are consuming music today, whether I like it or not. I just don't like that only a fourth of Angelo Badalamenti's legacy as a composer is preserved for posterity. Would it be acceptable if only three of the Beatles' twelve albums were available? Should nine of their albums be available only to people who bought them in the past? It's a fair comparison because Angelo is the Beatles of television composers as far as I am concerned. When I mentioned how most of the tracks from *Twin Peaks* are not available to stream, my dear friend AM Starr pointed out to me that the *Twin Peaks Archive* tracks are up on YouTube. But they are NOT official. They are put up by random fans. Those tracks can be removed at any time as soon as a corporation gets involved. Also, how do we know what quality they are uploaded at? Also also, are the musicians getting paid for those tracks? No. "Birds in Hell" shouldn't be heard only as bootlegged music. It should be revered. It should be remastered. It should be preserved. I also wouldn't say YouTube is where most streamers listen to music. I hate even talking about streaming because I am not a fan of music being released on a platform whereby it can be scrubbed by any lawyer on a whim. Now might be a good time to point out that

Leland Palmer was a lawyer. Do we really want Bob in control of our music?

And before you say, "Scott, don't be such an Ernie Niles and worry about every little thing," I don't have to go far back into the past to see an example of this very thing occurring. In July 2024, Jon Stewart's original *Daily Show* run, *The Colbert Report*, and MTV News were all removed from the internet, and all of that content faded away like the white horse in the Palmer living room. Hours of art were summarily deleted by Paramount. You know why? It doesn't want you watching stuff like that for free. Paramount knows that every minute your eyes spend looking at content for free is time you aren't paying to watch its "new," subpar content. How much longer before this happens to music as well? It could remove all *Twin Peaks* music from streaming, and a new generation of music lovers would never discover the artistry of what Angelo Badalamenti created. But it could never happen, right? By the way, do you know who owns the rights to the original *Twin Peaks* series? Paramount, the same company that just scrubbed all the content from MTV and Jon Stewart. Still feel secure? No one can take my *Twin Peaks* tracks from me. I own the five albums on vinyl and listen to them weekly. I own all the music released on MP3s in 2011, and they are loaded into my phone. There isn't a bot or algorithm that even knows if I listened to "Audrey's Prayer (Clarinet Synth)" today or not.

"A Path is Formed"

My first goal for this book is to remind fans of the quantity and quality of music used in the series and let them know where those tracks can be found. I want to help the original fans who might not have taken notice, as well as assist new fans of the series who might have just discovered it on Paramount Plus and want to find all the music. Another book could be written about protecting the series, as the complete box set of *Twin Peaks* is currently out of print and sells for a price on eBay that could practically fund the Ghostwood project. I want this book to serve as a warning bell that in our haste to stream everything through corporations, we are passively allowing the art that has been created over the past century to just slip away into the Black Lodge. In going to events, I have discovered a lot of original fans of the series aren't aware of some of the music, like Cruise's second album, *The Voice of Love*. This breaks my heart because I think that album is superior to her first album. Plus, if you have not heard the David Lynch-scribed lyrics to the "Theme of *FWWM* / She Would Die for Love" or "The Voice of Love," you are truly missing out on two of Julee's most beautiful performances. My hope is that once I have pointed out all that Angelo Badalamenti composed while on this planet, others will join me in convincing the powers that be there should finally be a vinyl or CD box set that releases these tracks. It doesn't have to be every cue, but it sure as cream corn should be more than 25 percent of the total songs written for the series.

Despite the fact that the music goes hand in hand with the show, there has been only one book released about the music, and it's a short book from the 33 ⅓ book series, which covers popular albums. Written by Clare Nina Norelli, it covers only the original soundtrack. You know, the CD that made me angry because it really had only five distinct themes on it. My book covers all the music from Seasons 1-3 and *FWWM*. I have conducted brand-new interviews with the music editors for the series and the film (David Slusser, Pilot; Lori Eschler, series, *FWWM*); band members who performed the cues (keyboardist Kinny Landrum, saxophonist Al Regni); directors from the show who scored episodes (Mark Frost cocreator; Duwayne Dunham, editor; Tim Hunter); the sound supervisor on *The Return* and David Lynch's right hand in the studio since the mid-2000s (Dean Hurley); and Julee Cruise's A&R man from Warner Bros. records (Kevin Laffey).

I have incorporated interviews I conducted earlier with Julee Cruise and some of the cast members as well as archival interviews with David Lynch and Angelo Badalamenti. This book will tell the story of how the cues were created and why these songs mattered so much to the plot and aesthetic of the series. I would be remiss if I didn't mention the assistance I received from the ultimate trio of Brian "Dugpa" Kursar, Josh "Gordon Cole" Eisenstadt, and Steven "Little Nicky" Miller. These three helped me in huge ways, and are such "Green Butt Skunk" friends to me. Brad Dukes came through by writing a wonderful foreword to this book. Great *Twin Peaks* books happen when the conversation is lively among friends you met in the trees. Speaking of trees . . .

The "Sycamore Trees" Mystery

My second goal was to answer a question I had had for well over thirty years. This became the central mystery of this book. If the series was built, ostensibly, around the mystery of "Who killed Laura Palmer?" this book is built around the puzzle of when the song "Sycamore Trees" was written and recorded. One question I've always had was born from the lore surrounding the filming of Episode 29, the final episode of the original run, directed by David Lynch. It is known that Mark Frost, with an assist from Harley Peyton and Robert Engels, finished the first draft of the final episode on February 14, 1991. David Lynch started shooting the episode on March 4, 1991, and the episode he shot was nothing like what was written. Many of the actors have commented in interviews how Lynch was just improvising as they went along. If you ever have a chance to read the original script, you will see that most of the last twenty-five minutes is quite different from Frost's script. It has been covered many times how Lynch improvised the dialogue in the Red Room section of the episode. But there was one thing that just never sat well with me about this idea. In the Red Room, "Sycamore Trees" plays in its entirety, sung by legendary jazz artist Little Jimmy Scott. [Below.] I get that someone can improv lines in a fixed set of red curtains, but how does someone improv an orchestration, lyrics, and a studio recording

and then pull Little Jimmy out of one's own butt? That is too great of a magic trick for even the great and powerful Oz, I mean Lynch. For years, I have asked anyone and everyone involved in that episode if they know the answer to the "Sycamore" question. The writers had been developing the sycamore trees plot point for a while. The map from Owl Cave shows the Giant and the Man from Another Place standing around the twelve trees that Windom Earle finds in the woods with Annie. So this is a connection that couldn't have been made up that same day. No matter whom I asked, no one knew when the song was written, when Jimmy Scott was cast, or when the song was recorded. I mean I get how you can call a casting agent and say "Ask Sheryl Lee if she can come in and play Laura and Maddy tomorrow" or "Get me the Giant." But a full song that is lip synched to on set? No.

Later in the book you will read full interviews that I conducted with Dean Hurley, who is David Lynch's studio guru, sound designer, mixer, and cocomposer. But to set up this mystery, I want you to read his answer when I first asked him my question about how Lynch could have just improvised this song:

Dean Hurley: You are thinking about all of this in a singular dimensional way. You have to understand the essence of the show. You hear the nugget that he threw out the script and rewrote it. Yes, the way you were presented with "Sycamore Trees" made it seem like it was integral to the episode, but that's not how stuff comes together. What probably happened, and I have no idea how this actually happened, but I've seen other things like this happen, where David has a song idea that he wants to do, it's not FOR anything, but he does it because that is how he lives his life. He is constantly doing things.

So when he is in a hot seat, where he needs to manufacture something, he is looking at things in terms of "What pieces do I have? Well, I have this song. What if I bring Jimmy Scott back and we do a whole performance integral to this episode?" This is his code to living.

It makes sense what Dean says, but it still is a lot to pull out of nowhere. There's also the fact that the lyrics to the song were written in the late seventies. How do I know this? Because they are in Lynch's original script for an unproduced film called *Ronnie Rocket* that he was working on right after *Eraserhead*. So are we really to believe that in 1991, during the few days between Frost finishing a script and Lynch directing the episode, he went back to some lines of dialogue that were in the first draft of *Ronnie Rocket?*—dialogue that was cut from the next version of the script—and he just plopped them onto a tune that Angelo had written for that episode? Who am I to argue with Dean Hurley? But I wanted a more substantial answer, and I wanted dates to back it up. You will see throughout this book that I will offer up the "Sycamore Trees" question to everyone I interview, and astonishingly, everyone will have a small piece to add to the puzzle. In order to track down the story of the "Trees," I employed deductive technique, Tibetan method, instinct, and luck. I encourage you, my dear reader, to read this book in order so that story will unfold for you without spoilers. It is a fun journey, and just like in a David Lynch movie, you will get answers, and you will be left with new mysteries.

In the end, it will be up to Warner Bros. records, and David Lynch and Angelo Badalamenti's estates if they want to let my first goal of this book be achieved. They will decide if a box set will be released to protect this music from the hands of the lawyers and the Bobs of this world. And if you think my quest to save beautiful, moving pieces of music that exist only on a few hard drives across the world is a futile battle that will only end up being a "heartbreaking" endeavor, I will return to Billy Joel, who wrote these lyrics the same year that Lynch was finishing up work on *Eraserhead*.

"And there's always a place for the angry young man
With his fist in the air and his head in the sand
And he's never been able to learn from mistakes
So he can't understand why his heart always breaks."

And if you are asking yourself, "Why does this writer keep coming back to some Billy Joel song I never heard of?," I will let you dip in on the end of a different interview for the book. Here is one of my calls with keyboardist Kinny Landrum, who played the piano on "Laura Palmer's Theme" and many other tracks. As Cooper so famously said, "Gentlemen, when two separate events occur simultaneously pertaining to the same object of inquiry, we must always pay strict attention."

Scott Ryan: So what are you up to now?

Kinny Landrum: I play in a Billy Joel tribute band. His stuff is good. While it may look on the surface as simple, it's not that simple. I use "Allentown" as an example. It sounds simple, but it is complex.

Scott Ryan: This is so much fun for me. We are talking about Billy Joel, Stephen Sondheim, and Angelo Badalamenti. You know Sondheim and Angelo have the same birthday. Not sure what that means, but I like it.

Kinny Landrum: I didn't know that until right now.

Scott Ryan: Can you play Billy's "Angry Young Man"?

Kinny Landrum: Oh, it's easy.

Scott Ryan: Easy? Hey, I've been trying to perfect that for thirty years. It is anything but easy.

[Kinny starts playing the fast piano part of the prelude to "Angry Young Man" on his keyboard over the phone. Scott hangs up the phone and sets his piano on fire.]

TRACK 1
"Moving Through Time"
1989

When you set out to the tell the story of the music of *Twin Peaks*, you realize pretty quickly that tracing the origins of the music is more complex than deciphering Part 8. There really is no way to look at just the music of *Twin Peaks*, without taking a look around at what else Lynch and Badalamenti were working on during that time period. The subtitle of this book may be *The Sounds of Twin Peaks*, but it sure could have been *Floating into Wild at Industrial Peaks*, because all of these projects are more intertwined than Scotch tape on Deputy Andy's hands. When it comes to studying the music that Angelo Badalamenti composed under the direction of David Lynch for *Twin Peaks*, you have to study the genealogy more carefully than Donna Hayward trying to fill out a form at 23AndMe.com. Four distinct projects were floating around in Lynch's unified field in 1989, all with a lot of music in them and all connected. I know there are fans of David Lynch's film work who are not fans of *Twin Peaks*, and vice versa, so I break down the four major projects he was working on in 1989 and provide a rudimentary explanation in case any of these projects have been forgotten by readers.

Floating into the Night
This is an album's worth of songs released by Warner Bros. Records. Lynch wrote the lyrics, Badalamenti wrote the music, and Julee Cruise sang the

songs. The album contains ten tracks and was released in September of 1989. The backing band included Kinny Landrum and Badalamenti on keys, Vinnie Bell on guitar, Eddy Dixon on electric guitar, and Al Regni on sax. Most of the songs were written and recorded in 1988 (outside of "Mysteries of Love," which was the end-credits song for Lynch's 1986 film, *Blue Velvet*). At the beginning of 1989, Lynch was putting the final touches on the album. He believed at that point that the album would be released in April 1989. But after *Twin Peaks* wrapped in March, Warner Bros. decided to push the release of *Floating into the Night* to September 1989 to capitalize on the upcoming television series. By the end of the year, the album had been released to the world. It got positive reviews, but had lackluster sales and almost no radio airplay. This would dramatically change in April 1990, when *Twin Peaks* premiered on television.

Industrial Symphony No. 1

Floating into the Night spawned a two-night live performance at the Brooklyn Academy of Music, which Lynch named *Industrial Symphony No. 1: The Dream of the Broken Hearted*. It was performed and filmed in November 1989 and released on homevideo in 1990. This is a "live" performance of the songs from the Julee Cruise album, starring Julee Cruise. I use the quotes because the entire performance was lip-synched to recorded tracks. The show began with a filmed monologue between Laura Dern and Nicolas Cage. It also costarred Michael J. Anderson, the Man from Another Place from *Twin Peaks*, who was on stage as a woodsman and reperformed the beginning Dern/Cage monologue live. At the beginning of 1989, Lynch didn't even know this performance was a possibility, and by the end of the year it was completed—never to be performed again. It was released on VHS and on the Lime box set release in the UK, but has never had a full-on American Blu-ray release.

Twin Peaks

As for *Twin Peaks*, if you have never heard of that project, you have been suckered into buying this book by mistake, and we don't take returns, so you might as well stream the show and then come back and finish the book. The show aired on ABC from April 1990 through June 1991. David Lynch wrote the Pilot with Mark Frost and directed it along with a few other episodes through the series's run. Angelo Badalamenti wrote the score for the series, which also used a few tracks from *Floating into the Night*. The Pilot was viewed by over 34 million people, became a cultural phenomena, and spawned a 1992 feature film titled *Twin Peaks: Fire Walk With Me* (*FWWM*). The series was resurrected on Showtime in 2017 under the title *Twin Peaks: The Return*. In the beginning of 1989, Lynch had yet to film the Pilot of the original series, and he and Frost had no idea if ABC would even pick it up. They had no idea when or even if it would ever come out. By the end of the year, the Pilot and the first seven episodes had been filmed, and the series was slated for release in 1990.

Wild at Heart

Wild at Heart (*WAH*) is a film that David Lynch wrote and directed starring Laura Dern and Nicolas Cage, based on a novel by Barry Gifford. Angelo Badalamenti wrote the score and a song, "Up in Flames," with lyrics by Lynch. Many of the instrumental pieces were recorded with the same backing band from the other projects of that year. This film premiered at the Cannes Film Festival in May 1990, winning the *Palme d'Or*. By the beginning of 1989, Lynch *might* have read the book, but he had no idea he would adapt it into a movie until May. He had no cast, no script, and no thought about this being his next major motion picture. By the end of the year, he had written the script and filmed the entire movie and was in the process of editing the film.

Those are the four projects that Lynch/Badalamenti were involved in during the calendar year of 1989 that required music. But how did they accomplish all that, and when did they even have the time? Before we drink full and descend into each track from *Twin Peaks*, it is important to understand how all of this music was born. I have never understood how all of this music could possibly have been created in such a short time. Because of all the cross-pollination involved in the projects in which these songs appeared, figuring this out can be stickier than a Horne family reunion. I was determined to at least map out the year 1989 to assist me with this undertaking. With a major contribution from Dean Hurley, Lynch's sound designer, I have been able to figure some of it out. Hurley was kind enough to track down recording dates to try to figure out when certain songs were completed. I also turned to, with no offense to Mike Nelson, Josh Eisenstadt, who is "the man" when it comes to all dates concerning the filming of *Twin Peaks*. I also was able to tap the memories of Duwayne Dunham, who edited the Pilot and *Wild at Heart,* and Mark Frost, who corroborated the timeline. All of these dates will be discussed in the interviews contained in the book, but before we get there, just trust me that I have checked and double-checked Lynch's schedule for 1989. I think it's important to lay it out like it's a spread of donuts on the sheriff's conference table.

January

The year starts with Lynch, Badalamenti, and Julee Cruise finishing tracks for *Floating into the Night.* They complete "Floating," "I Float Alone," "I Remember," "Into the Night," and "The Swan" on January 30.

February

On February 21, Lynch starts filming the Pilot episode of *Twin Peaks.* On February 28, Angelo recorded the initial demos for the score of *Twin Peaks,* including "Laura Palmer's Theme," which was called "Love Theme Slower and Darker"; "Slow Cool Jazz," which became "Audrey's Dance"; and "Chinese Theme," which doesn't become anything of consequence in the world of *Twin Peaks.* All of the tracks were recorded on Angelo's solo Rhodes synth that bounces between the left and right speakers, producing a sound that I have never enjoyed. Luckily, this sound effect isn't used much on the finished music.

March

On March 20 or 21, Lynch finishes shooting the *Twin Peaks* Pilot. Most likely he wraps on the twentieth, after shooting the interiors of the Great Northern at Kiana Lodge. It is fascinating to me that the single best shot in all of Lynch's directing career is filmed on the final day. (Fight me.) This is the scene where Leland Palmer gets the call from Sarah and then Sheriff Truman's car pulls up behind him. Harry walks into the "Great Northern" (though actually it's in the Kiana Lodge, which is over an hour away from the Salish Lodge, which is just the exterior of the Great

Northern) as Leland realizes his daughter is dead. We know they filmed there that day, but Josh Eisenstadt has a call sheet for March 21 that mentions Cooper and Truman filming on a boat. One can imagine this was to check out the large log by where Laura's body showed up. This was never used, and possibly not even filmed at all. My guess is filming wrapped on the twentieth.

April

The first official studio music sessions occur for the scoring of *Twin Peaks*. Angelo, Kinny, Vinnie, Grady, and Al record "Slow Cool Jazz" ("Audrey's Dance") and "Fast Cool Jazz" ("Dance of the Dream Man"). *Floating into the Night* is scheduled to be released but is pushed back to September. Duwayne Dunham begins editing the Pilot.

May

Duwayne Dunham and Lynch finish up editing the Pilot, and Lynch finds out Monty Montgomery (the cowboy from *Mulholland Drive*) has the rights to the *Wild at Heart* book. Lynch decides he is going to direct the adaptation and says he will write the script over the next six weeks. He asks Barry Gifford, the book's author, to cowrite the film with him, but Gifford turns him down because he is in the middle of writing the sequel to the novel. Lynch begins the script alone. On May 22, ABC greenlights Season 1 of *Twin Peaks* as a midseason replacement and orders seven one-hour episodes. Mark and David start writing Episodes 1 and 2.

June

Final touches are completed on "The World Spins" and "Falling" for *Floating into the Night* on June 21.

July

On July 3, Lynch films what would become known as "Cooper's Dream" with Kyle MacLachlan, Sheryl Lee, and Michael J. Anderson. He also films the Lucy and Andy apartment scene and Leland calling them on the phone. All these scenes will be used for the closed ending for Spelling Entertainment because of a clause in the contract that says the Pilot must have an ending that Spelling can release in Europe on VHS. Cooper's dream will end up in Episode 2 of the series, but the other scenes filmed that day will come to be known as components of the European ending. On July 7, a party is held at the studio to celebrate the pickup of *Twin Peaks* and to welcome everyone as they prepare to get to work on Season 1. Writing begins on the rest of Season 1.

August
On August 10, David Lynch begins shooting *Wild at Heart*. Mark Frost continues to prep the series.

September
Yale Evelev asks Kevin Laffey, Lynch/Badalamenti/Cruise's A&R man at Warner Bros., to pitch the idea of a two-night performance at Brooklyn of Academy of Music. On September 12, the album *Floating into the Night* is released in America. On September 29, Mark Frost goes behind the camera to film all the episodes of *Invitation to Love* that will be edited into multiple episodes throughout Season 1.

October
October 11 is David Lynch's final day of shooting *Wild at Heart*. On October 17, filming begins on Episode 1 of Season 1 with Duwayne Dunham directing. He wraps on October 25. At that point, Lynch and Dunham begin cutting *WAH* as well as Episode 1 of *Twin Peaks*.

November
On November 10 at the Brooklyn Academy of Music, Lynch, Badalamenti, and Cruise stage *Industrial Symphony No. 1*. It is performed twice that day, at 8:15 pm and 9:30 pm. Both performances are captured on film.

December
December 4 might be the most exciting *Twin Peaks* filming day ever, as Mark Frost, David Lynch, and Caleb Deschanel shoot scenes from three different episodes. Episode 2: Ben and Jerry order double Scotches on the rocks, see Blackie, and flip a coin for the new girl. This means Lynch, director of Episode 2, shot this scene while the rest of the cast and crew was working on Episode 6; he wouldn't "officially" begin shooting

Episode 2 for another three days. Frost shoots a scene from Episode 7: Jacques and Cooper have drinks and Jacques talks about Waldo (the "bite the bullet" scene). On December 6, the crew shoots at Malibou Lake, which stands in for Easter Park, with Maddy dressed as Laura. On December 7, Lynch officially begins directing Episode 2 of *Twin Peaks*, even though the cast has just finished Episode 6. On December 8, the Pilot episode with the closed, European ending is released on home video in the United Kingdom. Lynch finishes filming Episode 2 on December 14. On December 15, Mark Frost steps behind the camera to finish out the first season of *Twin Peaks*. He wraps Episode 7 and the first season of *Twin Peaks* on December 22.

December 31, 1989: David and Angelo take a nap.

And what have you done this year? Thank goodness there weren't smart phones in 1989 or Lynch and Badalamenti would only have had time to doom scroll Instagram all year. They created all those projects, and all were music intensive. The focus of this book will be on the music that ended up in *Twin Peaks*, but many of those songs will have connections to these other projects. So that's the setup, tracing the backstories of all this music. Now what do you say we spin a bunch of great vinyl, fire up the old iTunes, and play some MP3 tracks? Let's not waste anymore time in silence, and in the words of Laura Palmer at the Roadhouse, "Okay, Donna. Let's go."

TRACK 2

"Falling"
Floating into the Night, 1989

In the winter of 1988, Kevin Laffey braved the cold weather and seediness of Times Square to head to Art Polhemus's Excalibur Sound studio to hear the first tracks of *Floating into the Night*. The album was scheduled to come out in April 1989. He loved what he heard that day, which was reassuring because he was the one who had signed David Lynch and Angelo Badalamenti to a Warner Bros. record deal with the sole purpose of creating an entire album built around Julee Cruise. Like many other moviegoers, Laffey had trouble leaving his seat once *Blue Velvet* ended. There was much to contemplate when the robin returned to Lumbertown. But Laffey had another reason to stay behind. He was mesmerized by the end-credit song, "Mysteries of Love," and he just had to know who sang it. He saw the name Julee Cruise and thought she might be a good artist to bring to Warner Bros. records. Laffey was an A&R man for the label, so it was his job to find and develop new talent. There was nothing quite as new as the sound Lynch, Badalamenti, and Cruise had created for the one song in *Blue Velvet*.

Kevin Laffey: You know the world that Lynch creates. It's kind of one foot in the past and another in the unknown.

That just may be the best description for the music this threesome created over the next few years. Laffey wanted Cruise but knew he would have to go through Lynch to get her. Lynch had exploded on the scene in the late seventies, and Laffey was well aware of him as a filmmaker. Angelo Badalamenti wasn't a household name yet. He had taught music and English for five years and was writing pop songs during that time. He was a classically trained musician; French horn was his instrument. He was hired as a vocal coach for Isabella Rossellini on *Blue Velvet*. Angelo was also tasked with finding someone to sing the end-credits song; he enlisted Cruise to help find a singer. She found herself, and the results were magical. "Mysteries of Love" is the perfect ending song to a film that is part love, part obsession, and way creepy. Before singing "Mysteries of Love" in a breathy, airy voice, Julee Cruise was on the path to being a Broadway baby. Once I heard that, I had to ask her about my favorite Broadway composer, Stephen Sondheim.

Julee Cruise: *Gypsy* and *A Little Night Music* are my favorite shows of his. I played Petra and stopped the show singing "The Miller's Son." It's not high Sondheim like *Sunday in the Park with George*. I can go up to a high D, but it sounds like an opera singer. I got a job in the theater right away.

Strangely, Julee, just like Angelo, studied the French horn in college. She had never sung a song like "Mysteries" before. She was only belting out showtunes. She learned how to hold back the power and make it sound like she was singing with a high soprano voice, but she told me that wasn't what she actually was doing.

Julee Cruise: My voice sounds high, but the keys are not high. Angelo writes beautiful music. If you have a great friend that you are playing golf with, you're going to play a better game. I knew when I met Angelo that he was great. When I met him, I told him to call me. Three years later, he did.

Kevin Laffey: I was interested in Julee Cruise. David called me about that, and he told me that she was an artist in her own right, and there was a whole album of songs written, which I didn't quite believe, and I still don't believe. I think they only had the one song, "Mysteries of Love" from *Blue Velvet*. But I can't prove that. He wanted a production deal for him and Angelo, which is more like signing a label rather than an artist. He said Julee was signed to their production company. I don't think there probably was any ambition to make an album with her. Up to this point, David was only known as a filmmaker. So him having a full blown artist with an album was not something he'd been doing. I pitched that idea to my superiors. David Lynch would be a crown jewel for Warner Bros.

Scott Ryan: Did they give you any idea what kind of songs they had? Did you get to hear any?

Kevin Laffey: Once we finally got the deal done, I asked David about the songs, and he kept it pretty close to the vest.

Scott Ryan: When you say you made a deal, did you sign Julee Cruise, or you signed David and Angelo, or you signed all three?

Kevin Laffey: Well, a production deal is a business in itself. So David and Angelo had a partnership, and they were the owners of the production company. They really had control of Julee, which ultimately was not ideal for her as an artist in her own right, with ambitions and looking for a path forward.

Scott Ryan: I have heard they finished almost all of the songs in January 1989 for an April release. Why did the release get pushed back to September?

Kevin Laffey: It was finished by March or April, and it was held to anticipate the release of *Twin Peaks*. It was frustrating for Julee because a production deal with David and Angelo's production company doesn't make you independently wealthy. *Twin Peaks* was not even an idea that David had at the time of beginning the project.

Scott Ryan: The sound is so different. When you heard the tracks in New York, were you worried about a single?

Kevin Laffey: I couldn't imagine anything on that album being like Top 40. The one song that we thought had the biggest chance to cross over would be "Rockin' Back Inside My Heart." We released a twelve-inch remix.

Julee Cruise: It was really hard to get these songs on the radio. The Warner Bros. radio people worked their ass off. The artist better have a good personality and get along with the DJs at KCRW and K-Rock. Most of the songs didn't have a beat, but "Rockin'" did. It was something different. The music was strange. It wasn't fifties. It wasn't nineties. What was it?

"Rockin' Back Inside My Heart"

"Rockin' Back Inside My Heart" was the lead single from the album. The song would eventually play a pivotal role in Episode 14 of *Twin Peaks*, but that wouldn't happen until November 1990. In January 1990, the song was released as a music video on VH-1. This is corroborated in the *Detroit Free Press* article called "Video Play" on January 22, 1990. Other new videos for VH-1 that week included songs by Soul II Soul, Eric Clapton, Bob Dylan, and Michael Penn.

I specifically remember seeing the video at the time because I was recording VH-1 on VHS tapes so I could get a copy of Billy Joel's "We Didn't Start the Fire" music video. (Yes, I was always an obsessive fan about the music I love.) This was actually the first Julee Cruise song I ever heard. The video clip was in heavy rotation on the music channel. Julee sings the song from the inside of a car trunk while multiple video screens are filled with tight shots of her face as she sings the song. I remember thinking how nutty the video was and how strange the song sounded, but I also could never look away. The song, which is probably the most uptempo song in her entire catalog, has such a catchy fifties feel to it. The lyrics in the bridge get a little Lynchian, but the overall chorus of "I want you rockin' back inside my heart" is a typical love song refrain. This video was lifted directly from *Industrial Symphony*, but I wouldn't learn anything about that for many months. Same with *Twin Peaks*, which I wouldn't see till that summer. Strangely, even though I had watched this video many times, I didn't recognize Julee when I first saw the Pilot. She looked quite different as the biker bar singer from how she does in the video.

Despite the memorable music video, this song will always be associated with Episode 14 of *Twin Peaks*. Agent Cooper, the Log Lady, and Sheriff Truman head to the bar because there are owls in the Roadhouse. I don't know about owls, but James and Donna are sitting in a booth. Bobby Briggs and Senior Drool Cup are sitting at the bar, although not together (what would that conversation be like? "Do you like warm milk?" "Only when I drink it out of an empty football"). James and Donna might be a controversial love story. It can be hard to root for them, as they have lots of ups and downs as far a cohesive storyline goes, but I think the moment of Donna lip-synching, "I want you ... rockin' back inside my heart" to James as she sways, shimmers, and smiles is the single greatest Lara Flynn Boyle moment in the entire series. It is the one true time that she captures the innocence of the Donna Hayward character. Also, I have always loved how she hides her cigarette under the booth when the sheriff comes in. That is a delightful piece of directing. A teenager would naturally fear getting caught smoking. One of the things that I love about getting to interview cast members is learning small details about my favorite moments. This is what Julee Cruise told me about Boyle lip-synching that moment:

Julee Cruise: David said, "You moved too much in that scene." I said, "Why didn't you tell me?" That is why Lara is mouthing that line, because David said I was moving too much. I think it worked out fine.

One way to know if a song is an everlasting classic is if bands are still performing it decades later. Devery Doleman is the lead singer in a Lynch-tribute band called Fuck You, Tammy! The band performs songs not just from *Twin Peaks*, but all of Lynch's films. I caught a performance at the

Mahoning Drive-In Theatre in Lehighton, Pennsylvania, when I hosted a panel there; Fuck You, Tammy! was the house band. I talked to Devery about singing these songs, and her quotes are peppered throughout the book. Here is a great story she had to tell about performing "Rockin' Back":

Devery Doleman: One of the most surreal moments in my life is from the Eraserhood Forever soundcheck. The Saturday event was at this beautiful speakeasy space called the Ruba Club–the stage is upstairs and has an old auditorium feel, and there's a beautiful painted forest backdrop on the stage. We were sound checking with "Rockin' Back Inside My Heart"—since my bandmate Julie Rozansky and I both sing on it, it's a good song for checking vocal levels. As I'm singing "Tell your heart, it's me/ I want you, rockin' back inside my heart," I see a man enter the dark auditorium, backlit from the stairway. He slowly walks toward the stage and sits down on a chair against the wall and watches us play. I realize: it's James Marshall. We made a band because of a show, and I'm singing a song from that show, and then James, from the show, walks into the room where I am singing onstage–but it's me, not Julee Cruise, and instead of the Roadhouse, it's the Ruba Club. It was wild. James was so kind and modest. He is also a musician, and when we asked him what he wanted to play, he wanted to jam some Jimi Hendrix with the band, and on my phone, I still have ten minutes of everyone jamming with James Marshall during soundcheck.

"Falling"

The second single from the album was "Falling," and that was due to the track becoming the instrumental theme song to a little show called *Twin Peaks*. Not only did the tune open every episode, but Julee Cruise shows up as a singer and performs the song, this time with lyrics, toward the end of this two-hour episode. "Falling" would become the most popular song that the Lynch-Badalamenti-Cruise threesome would ever create. Cruise even performed it on *Saturday Night Live* in May 1990.

Julee Cruise: I have a hard time associating it with *Twin Peaks* until I see how beautiful David shoots the credits. I think the song is beautiful and gorgeous. It would be hard at my age to pull it off. But sixty-year-olds fall in love too. It is my song. [Laughs.]

Julee does such a great job of repeating "Don't let yourself be hurt this time" throughout the song. It is one of my favorite parts of this song. As a lyricist, Lynch has a propensity to overrepeat lyrics. For me, if a lyric is repeated, there better be a good reason. Just like Julee, I am a disciple of Broadway, where songs are written to tell a story and meant to be acted. In the case of "Falling," the singer is making one of the most dangerous decisions human beings can make—the decision to fall in love again. We know with those opening lyrics that the last time didn't work out so well. So the singer is repeating it to themselves, "Don't let yourself be hurt this time," just like a TM mantra. It is good advice for all of us. That is the singer's mindset at the moment. What is the next word? It is the most important word in the entire song, and it is also why I believe this song is the height of Lynch as a lyricist. The next word is "then."

We know so much from that word. So the singer is going about their life with one idea: don't get hurt again. But "THEN I saw your face." The best laid plans of mice and men can go right out the window when you see someone who makes your heart skip a beat. Lots of information is delivered with that one little word. This lyric truly is one of the best love songs ever written. Because it tells us the backstory and the current story at the same time. The bass is repeated throughout the entire song, when Cruise sings the "Don't let yourself." I actually produced a version of this song where I had my cousin sing those lyrics every time that bass played through the song. (Honestly, Fuck You, Tammy! should steal that idea from me; it really works.)

Speaking of Fuck You, Tammy!, I asked the lead singer of the David Lynch cover band, Devery Doleman, to tell me what it is like to interpret "Falling" as a cover band:

Devery Doleman: "Falling" is a very emotional song to sing, and when we were first learning it as a band, way back in 2017, I watched a lot of videos of Julee Cruise performing it live. There's a particular way, when she's older, where she's sort of shaping the verses with her hands, and you can tell she's just so full of emotion when she sings. During a live performance of "Falling," I always feel the "Don't let yourself be hurt this time" part is as if I'm holding a shield in front of myself. And then the fully sung part of "Then I saw your face. Then, I saw your smile" is what lets the shield fall away. I'm giving myself to the audience–we're both falling towards each other.

When we played at the Mahoning Drive-in 2021, it was really extraordinary to sing "The sky is still blue / the clouds come and go" to a whole crowd of people in that mountain clearing, looking at the actual blue sky overhead and seeing clouds and mountains and smelling all that honeysuckle. The lyrics are very simple observances in real time, and to sing that while really taking in that actual scene made me cry during that song.

I was at that performance, and it was what made me a fan of the band. It is so interesting to hear from a band that is interpreting this song today. But none of it could have happened if it weren't for the group of studio musicians who first brought this song to life. Every note (outside of a few cymbals added later by Grady Tate) that you hear in "Falling" was played by keyboardist extraordinaire Kinny Landrum. He was kind enough to give me an interview, and his quotes are spread throughout this book. He was absolutely crucial to what "Falling" became, and to what this book became. Here is our discussion about the song:

Scott Ryan: How did you get connected with Angelo Badalamenti to work on the music of Julee Cruise?

Kinny Landrum: Art Polhemus called me saying, "There is a client of mine named Angelo Badalamenti. He needs a synthesizer player who knows how to use these machines." Angelo came to talk to me and then booked me for a studio session at Art's studio for Julee Cruise.

Scott Ryan: Was that for "Mysteries of Love," for *Blue Velvet*, or *Floating into the Night*?

Kinny Landrum: I really don't remember. One of the things about being a studio musician, something that I always liked, is that you never know what you are gonna play until you walk in the door. It might have been the song "Falling," but I don't honestly remember what song it was.

Scott Ryan: But you did play on Julee Cruise's first album?

Kinny Landrum: Yes, this was all for her album. This was way before there was a *Twin Peaks*. I am the keyboard, synth, and piano player on *Floating into the Night*. It is either me or Angelo. I always got into programming synthesizers. For me, it goes back to the days of Herbie Hancock, Joe Zawinul, and Jan Hammer, who were not only brilliant piano players but also brilliant synthesists and had their own unique style on the instruments.

Scott Ryan: What kind of keyboard did you use?

Kinny Landrum: The Yamaha DX7 was used extensively in *Twin Peaks*. In fact, that is what you hear on "Falling" and many other songs. This was the first time that you could play on one keyboard and have it connect to another with a MIDI cable. This was a big deal. You could play them all from one keyboard but have multiple synthesizers.

Scott Ryan: When you are recording "Falling," are you all together or was it just you?

Kinny Landrum: On almost all of the Julee stuff on *Floating* it started as just me, Angelo, David, and Art, who was the engineer in his studio. Angelo would come in with a lead sheet. Do you know what that is?

Scott Ryan: Yes, it is the piece of paper with the chords and the melody.

Kinny Landrum: Yes, that's correct, not a fully written-out part. I would then work with that. We would decide on a tempo. My drum machine would sync to the tape machine, and we would put a click track down. I would play the main keyboard part. Julee was not even there. I can play it for you right now if you want.

Scott Ryan: Heck yeah.

[He starts up his keyboard and plays the chords that are so recognizable from what is known as the theme to *Twin Peaks*.]

Kinny Landrum: I probably then added some string parts to it. It's difficult to add the left hand and right hand at the same time on those string pads, so I did them separately. Drums weren't an issue on "Falling." After we finished the strings and keyboards, David turned to me and said, "Can you put something on this that sounds like the fifties?" I thought, You can't do the fifties piano playing the triplets in the upper register, which is fifties but wouldn't sound good on "Falling." I said, "David, I have a twangy guitar sound that sounds like Duane Eddy." I played it on my Emulator II. It was an earlier sampler. Here, I'll play it.

[He plays that oh-so-famous "Boom. Boom boom," the iconic bass sound famously associated with the beginning of *Twin Peaks*. I can't lie. My eyes immediately fill with water. I am sitting here listening to the exact sound from the exact Emulator being played by the exact person who added the sound to the greatest theme song of any show ever. How is this my life?]

Kinny Landrum: I played those three notes with that sound, and David said, "That's it. Put it down." David didn't ask for what else I had. I think we did it in one take. When I thought about it, I realized there was no real bass line for this song.

Scott Ryan: What is that sound called?

Kinny Landrum: I'll tell you how I obtained it. In the early days of the Emulator II, we would often swap floppy disks, and I mean the old disks that were actually floppy. I got this disk from someone somewhere that had a guitar sound, and it was only playing one note. I liked the sound, so I recreated a preset where I mapped it, so it could play higher and lower. It was like a baritone guitar that Glen Campbell plays the melody of "Wichita Lineman." That sound went out of favor in the sixties. So it is associated with Duane Eddy and the fifties.

Scott Ryan: Since you have that sound up, can you play beyond the three notes and play the "Don't let yourself be hurt this time" part? I'd love to hear it.

Kinny Landrum: No. That's not the right sound for that. This sound only plays those three notes. That is a DX7 sound, like a Fender Rhodes.

[He changes the sound and plays the "Don't let yourself be hurt this time" part on an electric piano, and it sounds just like the song.]

Scott Ryan: I play this song on piano, and to me that is all in the left hand, so it's all bass to me.

Kinny Landrum: No, it's another electric piano sound, from the DX7. It is overdubbed. Technically, there are two overlapping piano parts. The one that has the chords is probably doubled with some synth string sounds too. Angelo never really liked sampled string sounds. He preferred analog synth-type string sounds.

Scott Ryan: So how many "Kinnys" are playing on "Falling"?

Kinny Landrum: There are at least six to eight tracks of me. The chord part, which may be doubled. The "Don't let me hurt" part. The twangy thing. There are at least two string pads. There are different synthesizers playing those parts.

[He plays the "Then I saw your face" part in the strings.]

Scott Ryan: What would you call that sound?

Kinny Landrum: I used the Prophet T8, and I used a particular synth that I don't even have anymore. There are low notes that I am playing.

Scott Ryan: The song is now considered a classic, but back in 1989 that was a pretty strange song to just hear. What did you honestly think of it?

Kinny Landrum: I'll be honest. I thought it was slow and lugubrious, and I didn't think it was gonna do anything. I told my wife when I got home, "It is just kinda slow and sits there. It doesn't go anywhere." Now that I think about it, I think that was actually the point. [Laughs.] I was not that impressed. I am a studio musician. I am hired to make something sound as good as I can make it sound. I didn't write it. I don't even know if I heard Julee sing it. She would have had to overdub it. I don't know when I first heard Julee sing. There just wasn't any oomph behind it.

Oomph or not, it became a hit once it played on television. Julee sings a minute and fifteen seconds of "Falling" in the Pilot, but I'm not sure it really is the same version. It is most definitely not the mix that is on the CD. There is a lot more percussion on the soundtrack version. When I compared them back-to-back, I heard a prevalent cymbal on the CD version. The track that they would have filmed to would not have been the final master of the track, since the album wouldn't come out until fall. Either way, Julee Cruise appeared onscreen and lip-synched the song, along with "The Nightingale."

Julee Cruise: I'm an actor, and it's musical theater. I just had to bring my acting down for the camera. I was not used to acting in front of the camera. I took four years of acting classes with William H. Macy. It was the David Mamet method.

Kevin Laffey: The "Falling" video was on MTV and VH-1 all the time with clips from *Twin Peaks*. Getting a song in a show was huge, and it was like running an ad on MTV when the video played. I think the song wouldn't have been played on MTV without *Twin Peaks*.

Julee Cruise: *Rolling Stone* was never behind us, and we didn't get a good review, but of course now they are.

"The World Spins"

The third song from *Floating into the Night* that plays a huge part in the series is "The World Spins." This was the track chosen to end the album in 1989, and it was also picked as the last song on *The Return*'s Roadhouse soundtrack. It also is the last song performed on the series from the Roadhouse stage in Part 17. While Part 17 may evoke emotions from fans who were worried that the limited series wrapping up, it's the use of the song in Episode 14 that turned "The World Spins" into the

most important song with lyrics in all of *Twin Peaks*. Bold statement? Nonsense. It is just fact.

Episode 14 is the episode in which viewers find out who killed Laura Palmer. The song plays as Cooper and the Log Lady know something is wrong in the air. Sheriff Truman wants to feel it, but he can't. His feet are planted too firmly on solid ground. Julee Cruise sings the song as the Giant appears to Cooper and says, "It is happening again." After we watch the brutal killing of Maddy, we return to the Roadhouse and silence as Cooper stares at the Giant, who fades away. Julee and the band return as she finishes singing "The World Spins." [See photo above.] Viewers have just watched one of the most violent sequences ever shown on network television up to that point, not to mention that a beloved character was just revealed to be the killer. The music and vocal performance exude pain and sadness. Senior Drool Cup knows it, Bobby Briggs knows it, Cooper knows it, Donna knows it. James . . . well, maybe he hasn't always been cool. The red curtains fade over Cooper as he looks up for an answer. The music soars as the synth plays the apex of the melody. This is the culmination of what viewers have waited for since the question of who killed Laura Palmer was first posed. We know who did it, but Cooper doesn't. He is no longer our guide; we are ahead of him, and it makes us feel unsettled. What does all this mean? Had the song been able to play to completion, we would have heard Julee's vocals which could represent Lynch's ambivalent answer to the secret of life: "The. World. Spins." The way Julee emotes these lyrics leaves no protection between the artist and the listener. She isn't holding anything back. She is giving everything in this moment, and it didn't come easily to her.

Julee Cruise: I did that alone with David in one day. Angelo was gone, and we worked all day long on that one song. We took it phrase by phrase. I was in total darkness in the studio. I have a special feeling about that song. I can't really tell you what I was thinking, but it's a song that's devastatingly stark, alone, and almost peacefully numb. I don't want to tell you what I was thinking while I was singing (*Gavin Report*, 1990).

David Lynch: I wrote the lyrics to that in a restaurant. I was having lunch with my daughter and I wrote this certain kind of five line poem (*Gavin Report*, 1990).

Bad things happen; love comes and goes. People are born; people die. The world just spins along, insensitive to all of the drama. Uninterested in its effect on you. The depth of Lynch's lyrics on *Floating into the Night* is truly impressive. This also happens to be Julee's favorite of all her songs.

Julee Cruise: "The World Spins" has the most powerful lyrics. He always likes to bring in a little circus freak, which is sad. When I talk about creative stuff, sometimes people think I am a little scattered. You can rarely say lyrics out loud and they stand on their own. Those lyrics, he nailed. He is a bonafide lyricist. They drive the song. Angelo just lets him do it by making it simple.

The Rest of the Album

The track list of *Floating into the Night* is as follows: "Floating," "Falling," "I Remember," "Rockin' Back Inside My Heart," "Mysteries of Love," "Into the Night," "I Float Alone," "The Nightingale," "The Swan," and "The World Spins." The songs are all credited as being written by Angelo Badalamenti and David Lynch. The first song they wrote together was "Mysteries of Love," which is also on the *Blue Velvet* soundtrack.

Angelo Badalamenti: He wrote six lines. No rhymes, no meter. No hooks as we know hooks. It was a six line sonnet. I looked at it and said, "What am I gonna do with this?" I called David and he said, "Make it very beautiful, and very sustained, and very cosmic, and make it like the wind, and the oceans, and the waves" (Warner Bros.).

Julee Cruise: The music had no meter. It was just this spacious vast melody without any breath without anything, just kind of ominous" (Warner Bros.).

Angelo Badalamenti: We worked in my office and she positioned her voice in a specific place and we went into a studio and did it. David heard it and flipped out (Warner Bros.).

David Lynch: She's got a great voice. When she sings soft and pure, it is just what the doctor ordered (Warner Bros.).

The songs on the album are romantic and sad. "Mysteries of Love" really doesn't fit the sound of the full album. It probably should have been left off and replaced by "Up in Flames" or one of the other songs they wrote, and saved for later. "Mysteries" doesn't have the fifties sound that Lynch enjoys so much. The entire album evokes such feelings, and while the description is overused when applied to the work of David Lynch, it is actually very dreamy. "Into the Night" and "Nightingale" are both used in *Twin Peaks*, and I will cover them in the chapter about the television soundtrack, but there is one other track that is technically used in the series. That is "The Swan," which plays for such a short time that it is easy to miss. I will be completely honest and say that I never knew it was in the Pilot until Dean Hurley told me. At the end of the episode, when Sheriff Truman shows up to see Josie outside of the Packard house, an instrumental version of "The Swan" plays for a few seconds. It is hidden, but once you notice it, you can hear it. The rest of the album is filled with songs that could have been used but never were. The musicians on this album also created most of the music used in the series. I interviewed Al Regni, who played all of the woodwinds on *Floating into the Night*. He told me how he got the job working on the album.

Al Regni: I knew Angelo from back at Eastman School of Music way back in 1954, when we were students together. Then I met David Lynch through Angelo, probably on *Floating into the Night*. I played any woodwind sound: clarinet, bass clarinet, flute, alto flute, tenor sax. Those are the instruments I played throughout the series. I did three or four tracks on the Julee Cruise album.

Besides the songs contained on this album, Lynch and Badalamenti wrote several other songs, some of which we still haven't heard. In 1990, Lynch said in *David Lynch Interviews*, "We created forty songs, and we made an album with Julee Cruise. All these activities—writing the script, the visual composition, the music—they're all connected for me, and each one gives me ideas for the others. So working on the music can inspire me about the visuals."

Some of those songs will pop up throughout *Twin Peaks*, sometimes when you least expect it. The album is still in demand, with Sacred Bones rereleasing the vinyl recently, with a limited edition cassette tape that had these tracks on it.

A Mixed Tape of Julee Cruise

SIDE A
Beginning Is a Very Delicate Time
Mysteries of Love Overture
Rockin' Back Inside My Heart (A Cappella)
Into the Night (Instrumental)
Theme from Twin Peaks: Fire Walk With Me (AM Radio Broadcast)
Pluramon (featuring Julee Cruise): Time for a Lie
Artificial World (Ambient Remix)
The Swan (Instrumental)
Pinkie's Bubble Egg (Industrial Symphony No. 1)

SIDE B
Floating (Demo)
Never Again (Demo)
My Blue Yonder (Drumless Cassette Mix)
Moodswings (featuring Julee Cruise): Into the Blue
Angelo Badalamenti: Farewell

There's also a twelve-inch single of "Rockin' Back Inside My Heart" that includes a dance mix of the track. The single was released after Episode 14 aired, and the dance mix is called the "Tibetan 12 Inch Mix." While dance mixes can sometimes be a little annoying, this one is actually pretty sweet. A different 2018 Sacred Bones release of the album came with a bonus record that included demos of Cruise singing "Floating," "Falling," and "The World Spins." None of these releases happens unless an album truly becomes a classic. These artists would collaborate again on a track called "Summer Kisses, Winter Tears" in 1992 and the full album *The Voice of Love* in 1993, but it was this collection of ten songs that would be known as the pinnacle of their work.

Angelo Badalamenti: Some of my finest moments have come from my long-term professional association with David Lynch. And the music for *Twin Peaks* is probably the work I'm most proud of. David and I have just an unbelievable relationship. That kind of relationship is a marriage made in heaven (Uncut).

Industrial Symphony No 1: The Dream of the Broken Hearted

Six months before *Twin Peaks* would blast songs from *Floating into the Night* into just about every home in America, Lynch, Badalamenti, and Cruise decided to try another project to support the album. They put together a stage show that would be performed twice and filmed for home video release. *Industrial Symphony No. 1* is like a live concert of the songs, but lip-synched to prerecorded vocals and music. This project also started with Warner Bros. A&R man Kevin Laffey.

Kevin Laffey: There was a guy named Yale Evelev who was working with the Brooklyn Academy of Music. He pitched the idea of David doing something for them. I didn't think David would do it. I figured between *Floating into the Night* and *Twin Peaks*, he was too busy. But he said, "Yes, I have something called *Industrial Symphony No. 1: Dream of the Brokenhearted.*" He had that title in his head. I could be wrong again. Maybe I'm not giving him enough credit, but I think he had the idea in his head but didn't put it into fact until he had a venue for it. [Program on next page. Courtesy of Laffey.]

For those of you who are unfamiliar with this piece or have never seen the video release, here is a brief synopsis of the show. It begins with a prefilmed piece in which Laura Dern, who is basically playing Lula, from *WAH*, but is billed as the Heartbroken Woman, is on the phone with Nic Cage, who is basically playing Sailor but is billed as the Heartbreaker. Both actors are dressed in the same wardrobe as their *WAH* characters and use the same accents. Cage breaks up with Dern, and this starts the live show. "Up in Flames," sung by Julee Cruise, who is billed as the Dreamself of the Heartbroken Woman, starts. This song is not included on *Floating into the Night* but was eventually released on Cruise's *The Voice of Love* album. The song was released on the *WAH* soundtrack, but performed by Koko Taylor. This song must have been written during the time Lynch claimed to have written forty songs with Angelo for Julee. She didn't sing it on the album, but he did put it in *WAH*. The song's bass walk is similar to that of "Dance of the Dream Man."

The next song is "Floating," performed as Julee is lowered onto to the stage à la the Good Witch (Sheryl Lee) in *WAH*. Next up, Michael Anderson, billed as a Woodsman, enters the stage, dressed exactly like the Man from Another Place in Cooper's dream. (Remember that even though that scene hadn't aired yet, it was filmed on July 3, 1989. This was performed on November 10, 1989.)

Anderson saws a log for longer than a guy can sweep a floor in Jean-Michel Renault's bar. "Into the Night" follows as Julee is brought down again from the ceiling. At the climatic moment, as the music gets really loud, she appears to fall to the stage. For anyone sitting in the audience, this probably seemed very scary. Then men in black masks and helmets

---

BAM Opera House
8:15 & 9:30 pm

DAVID LYNCH AND ANGELO BADALAMENTI
Industrial Symphony #1

JULEE CRUISE *vocals*

Produced by DAVID LYNCH *and* ANGELO BADALAMENTI
Music by ANGELO BADALAMENTI
Lyrics by DAVID LYNCH

Industrial Symphony #1 is a triple-exposure dream. A dream of the broken hearted. A dream about floating and falling and rising upwards.

Industrial Symphony #1 was commissioned by the Brooklyn Academy of Music 1989 NEXT WAVE Festival.

Special thanks to: Patricia Norris; John Wentworth; Margaux MacKay; Kevin Laffey; Steven Baker; Anne Militello; Art Pohlemus; Nicholas Cage; Laura Dern; Monty Montgomery; Walter Laff; Dean Jones; Roma Baran; Robin Danar; Melody London; John Huck; Donna Gregory; Special Effects Equipment by Jauchem & Meeh, NYC; Flying By Foy; The Staff of the Brooklyn Academy of Music; Warner Bros. Records, Inc.

come out and run lights around her (very similar to the scene in Part 8 in which the Woodsmen heal Mr. C), and a deer-looking monster appears as the track "I'm Hurt Bad" plays and Anderson shines a light on the monster. "I'm Hurt Bad" is the song that Bobby Briggs plays on the jukebox in the diner when he tells Norma he will see her in his dreams. All of these songs are connected in so many of these projects. The deer man is on stilts. According to Kevin Laffey, at one of the performances the actor fell on stage and the deer head just lay on the stage. Josh Eisenstadt told me Michael Anderson thought this is where Lynch got the idea for the deer head on the table at the bank in the *Twin Peaks* Pilot, but in fact the Pilot had been filmed before this event happened. Next, a spoken-word story called "Pinky's Bubble Egg" plays while men in work hats run across the stage under a roaming spotlight. Julee gets in the trunk of a car, and Anderson comes out to recount the opening scene with Laura Dern and Nic Cage while André Badalamenti plays "Up in Flames" on a clarinet. "Rockin' Back Inside My Heart" is next; this section is eventually lifted from here to become the music video that will play on VH-1 over the next few months.

The wind starts to blow, a siren goes off, and naked babies on strings descend from the ceiling. "The World Spins" begins, and Julee comes down from the ceiling again, ending the show with her favorite song. This show really is the intersection of *Twin Peaks* and *WAH*. The show was performed twice that day.

Julee Cruise: David was just making up the show as he went along. He didn't understand why you can't just use big flames of fire in the theater. [Laughs]. That was such a drama getting that done. David was busy doing *Wild at Heart*. They were busy with that. I'm not bitter. [Laughs.] I went to CBGB and picked out guys to go on tour with me. Warner Bros. gave me no money, and this was before *Twin Peaks*. David turned to me and said, "The tour was a failure. You were a failure."

"Come Back and Stay"

Floating into the Night and *Industrial* both became hits, but they didn't make Julee a millionaire. Many artists struggle to make a living from the sales of their product because so much of that money goes to other people.

They need lots of radio airplay, and a huge tour to make money. Julee ended up having a difficult relationship with Lynch and Badalamenti. They—not Warner Bros.—owned her contract.

Julee Cruise: *Industrial Symphony* went gold. I got to go to a film festival and have breakfast with Clint Eastwood, Sissy Spacek, and Daniel Day-Lewis.

Kevin Laffey: Julee went on the road. She was loved by our artist relations and marketing people. She was just really charming and gracious when she would do in-stores. She was a pro.

Julee Cruise: I met a couple of fans in Poland, and they told me I was the soundtrack to their life. I went back to the hotel, and I was so depressed. I had a bad show that night, and I felt like I didn't deserve that and they deserve better.

Kevin Laffey: Behind the scenes, she was very frustrated and at times upset with David. Angelo would just go with the flow. Sometimes Angelo could be a good middleman. But just getting them all to go back to the studio was difficult.

Julee Cruise: The best concert I ever did was with Anita Rehn. It was at the *Twin Peaks* Festival in 2016. I stayed at the Salish. I was an hour and half late getting on stage. They had started *Mulholland Drive*. Anita was dressing me. I got out on stage and bang, it all became clear. I had the best concert of my life. I was so happy. The key is to not think that the music is maudlin and down. We did eight songs. It was just really fun. I saw all these people crying. It was one of those things that won't happen again.

She was correct. It never did happen again. That 2016 concert was the last time Julee Cruise ever performed a full concert live in public. She passed away in 2022 after battling a painful disease. I was able to communicate with her a few times during the last five years of her life. She was just as wild and wacky as one could hope. But mostly I think of how incredibly sweet she was with me. We often talked about Sondheim, and we would sing together and make Broadway jokes. I never once brought up *Twin Peaks* with her outside of our interview. I would never claim to have truly known her or say we were real friends, but we definitely shared a bond through talking about music.

I know for a fact that her final concert happened only because die-hard *Twin Peaks* fan Anita Rehn, who is a dear friend of mine, busted her ass to be sure Julee got ready and had the courage to face her demons one last time on stage. (See photo courtesy of Anita Rehn.) All of those lucky attendants in North Bend, Washington, got to see her sing those iconic songs that she had made famous in *Twin Peaks* one last time. They had traveled from around the world to visit the town where the series had been filmed just to celebrate a canceled show from 1990 and hear the songs that they so loved. This was all back before corporations shut down that fan festival, which had thrived in obscurity for over twenty-five years. All in the fear that there was maybe fifty cents of IP

money that they weren't collecting. What they didn't get was that no one was there because of money. Especially not Julee. She was so scared that night. So afraid that she wouldn't be able to hit those notes. She hit some. She missed some. No one cared. All she received from the audience was love. And after years of being beaten up in the cruel world of the record industry, by the people whose job it was to take care of her and protect her, Julee got to have her final moment on stage in front of a group of people who had only love for her. Considering the anxiety she felt that night as Anita guided her to the edge of the stage before letting go of her hand, I know Julee must have felt those words that she sang for her final time ring truer and more clearly than ever before: "Don't let yourself be hurt this time."

TRACK 3

"Freshly Squeezed"

The Music Editor's Duet: David Slusser and Lori Eschler

Don't feel bad; I also didn't know what a music editor did before working on this book. But now I know that outside of Angelo Badalamenti, the two most important people in the world of *Twin Peaks* music are David Slusser and Lori Eschler. No two people did more to create everything that viewers of the original series experienced through music than these two. Their names came up in almost every interview I conducted. David Slusser was the music editor on the Pilot and *Wild at Heart*; Lori Eschler was the music editor on Episodes 1-29 and *FWWM*. Slusser did pop back in during *FWWM* when Lynch asked, during the editing of the film, if he could contribute a few tracks to the score.

These interviews are not exactly complete. If either music editor discussed a particular song, I have moved that to the chapter where I cover that cue. So if you want to hear David Slusser talk about composing "Deer Meadow Shuffle," you will read that in the chapter about the *Twin Peaks Archives*. Notice I didn't say skip there now. You first will want to get to know what these two editors did, how they created the library of music that we all know and love, and how they worked with the directors of the series. We start out with Slusser, since he did the Pilot, and then move on to Eschler, who is quite the unsung hero.

Verse 1: David Slusser

Scott Ryan: How did you start working with David Lynch?

David Slusser: The source of our meeting was the fact that he did the postproduction for *Blue Velvet* in Berkeley. In the eighties, that area had a very robust film industry, with Francis Ford Coppola, George Lucas, and the Sal Vance Film Center, which is also known as Fantasy Films, all within a few miles of each other. So there was a core group of editors and mixers working, of which I was one. I worked for all three companies. I hadn't heard of David Lynch. But he came up to do postproduction at Fantasy Films. The whole crew were friends and colleagues of mine. They described *Blue Velvet* to me, so I went out and watched it. You know how groundbreaking that was. So I was familiar with his work before I started working with him on a subsequent project, which was the TV two-hour *Twin Peaks* Pilot. He decided to do the post production at the same place in Berkeley. At that point, he needed a music editor, and I happened to be one of the only music editors in Northern California. Lucky me, as it turned out. I was familiar with the way he worked, which was very seat-of-the-pants, which was fine by me. David didn't want a traditional music editor anyway. He does not score his films the way Hollywood scores films.

Scott Ryan: That score changed all of television.

David Slusser: Ya think so? [Laughs.]

Scott Ryan: What was your first thought when you heard that score?

David Slusser: They did not have a score when I started. This speaks to how David works. David works with index cards. They would either have shots or whole scenes. He would shuffle and reshuffle the cards to see what different moods and trajectory you could get by mixing the scenes back and forth. So the picture was not locked in the way a Hollywood picture is. If you go back to Alfred Hitchcock, he was done with the picture when he finished the shooting script. The camera hadn't even been loaded yet. Then he would get someone like Bernard Herrmann to write his scores. With Lynch, he is shuffling scenes back and forth constantly. So you can *not* write a score till the picture is locked. With David, we would be on the mix stage in postproduction and the picture is still not locked. That is why I got involved more musically. When he went to shoot the scenes, he would have an inspiration cassette, like a mixtape, that would help him tell the story. In *Wild at Heart*, it was more about the characters and their milieu. In *Twin Peaks*, it was a combination of the innocent rural and undertones of badness. It is pop records and tunes he would resonate with. Those would be used for talking to his picture editor for how a scene would go.

Scott Ryan: Which would have been Duwayne Dunham on those projects.

David Slusser: David comes back from shooting the film, and he huddles with Angelo, and they just write songs. It will have the flavor of what he was listening to while shooting the film. They are not intentional to underscore a scene. They are just getting a sound and a mood together. That is when Angelo and David collaborate, Angelo at the keyboard and David saying, "Make it more like this." Talking in a Jimmy Stewart voice; it is hilarious. They have a great relationship, and they like that fifties nostalgic stuff. When I flew into New York, they were working in a place called Excalibur Sound off Times Square, and Times Square was really seedy back then.

Scott Ryan: Do you remember what month that was?

David Slusser: I don't even remember what year it was. I don't think it was winter time. Kinny Landrum was there, Grady Tate, Vinnie Bell, Angelo, and David. Angelo was still known for doing jingles under the name of Andy Badale. He came up as a French horn player who, like me, could play an arranger piano and play okay piano. Angelo would play a progression from the fifties, and David and Angelo would distill it into a couple of songs. So they only wrote a few songs for the Pilot. There was a prom high school song, music for the bad girl, and some of the mysterious stuff, and they had the "Falling" song. Everything else we just made up at the session when we would hear back from Duwayne Dunham for what we needed. He was an old Skywalker guy, so he's a part of the Northern California crew, so I had good communication with him.

Scott Ryan: How did you approach getting the music on the screen for the Pilot of *Twin Peaks*?

David Slusser: I was going to work on the final music in California, and whatever we didn't have, tough luck. So I was in the process of recording all the songs. I also made sure that I had a separate track. We worked with magnetic film in those days. When we left New York, I made sure that I mixed down every single track that was recorded to its own track so that I could recombine them myself as I needed to. I knew I'd need to because we only had a few songs. So we'd take one of the fully arranged songs, and I would choose the bass, or maybe Kinny Landrum's synth sounds, and that became a new cue, even though I pulled it out of other pieces. I had every combination you could have. That became the library for Lori Eschler, who happened to be married to one of my great friends, so I had a great relationship with her. I told Lori what I did and said, "Good luck."

Scott Ryan: Why did you not do the series?

David Slusser: I would have had to move to LA, and I was already doing so much as a sound designer and had a lot of clients. I was doing all these Super Bowl commercials. It was lucrative for me and Skywalker Sound.

Scott Ryan: I know you worked on a few songs for *FWWM*. Do you remember anything about the song "Sycamore Trees?" I am trying to find out when they wrote that, and how it came to be.

David Slusser: Number one, it was Koko Taylor singing it the first time I heard it.

Scott Ryan: Wait. What? This is so exciting! I have never heard of a Koko Taylor version of "Sycamore Trees." Did she sing it for *Wild at Heart*?

David Slusser: When I heard Jimmy Scott's version, I said, "Wow, that's great. I like it even more than when I heard Koko sing it." When they recorded her singing "Up in Flames," which wasn't much of a song, it was a simple song, I think they also shot her singing "Sycamore Trees." I remember because she was a robust blues singer and she sang it, "Sicky-mo Trees." I'll never forget the way she sang it. So it must have been an outtake or alternate from *Wild at Heart*. Then they choose "Up in Flames" for the film. "Sycamore Trees" is very much David's lyric. It is his imagery, and to see Koko Taylor sing it, in all her bruising majesty, with those lyrics, I wished that would have been in *Wild at Heart*.

Scott Ryan: Me too. I have never heard of this before. I am losing it. So you are saying it was filmed for the movie, not just recorded in a studio?

David Slusser: I only saw it on film.

Scott Ryan: That means they shot it.

David Slusser: That is what I'm saying. They shot her singing two songs and then chose between the two.

Scott Ryan: I want to hear that so badly. I would pay a million damn dollars to hear that. I love Koko. [Koko Taylor singing "Up in Flames" in *Wild at Heart* is pictured above.]

David Slusser: I'm an old man, so I might have a cassette of it.

Scott Ryan: I know you don't trust me yet.

David Slusser: [Laughs.]

Scott Ryan: But I keep secrets. I just want to hear it.

David Slusser: I have thousands of cassettes full of stuff like that.

Scott Ryan: Well, maybe let's put a note on them that says "In case of death, give these tapes to Scott Ryan." Do you have other stories from *Wild at Heart*?

David Slusser: We were all throwing sound into the mix. David had worked with Alan Splet. There are sounds on that movie that came from a Synclavier that was hooked into the console of the movie, and sometimes I'm playing sound effects live that sound like music. We threw all kinds of crazy stuff into that movie. They would hit record on the movie, and I would play weird string patches directly to the track. That was the craziest soundscape of any movie. We were all sitting at the console, and David had a fader, and he could just throw something into the mix. I remember he would have the sound of a train coupling and have it slowed down and play it backwards, and that would just be hanging in the mix at all times, and if he needed the sound, he would bring up his fader and put it into the film on his own. But when you're the director, you can do that.

Scott Ryan: Tell me about working with Lynch.

David Slusser: He knows how to talk to each member of the crew like he is the most important person in the world. Francis Coppola had the same thing. But David is a great guy. One of the funniest things he ever said to me was "Why does everyone think I'm so crazy?" It is because his movies are so odd. But he is very nice. He meditates every day and comes back with a beautiful attitude. He is continually fascinated with the ugliness of death and decay. He really looks at that stuff and sees things in it. He is very interested in sound design. After *Wild at Heart*, he had a sound studio built in his basement, and since then he has done his own sound design. We got so carried away with it on *Wild at Heart* that he said he would do it himself. Going back to *Eraserhead*, he worked with Alan Splet, so he was already associating with one of the pioneers of sound design. When Alan died and was cremated, they gave David his ashes, and they are sitting underneath the mixing console in David Lynch's basement. That's how much he loves sound design.

"Sycamore Trees" update: So now we have an interesting piece of information. What if David and Angelo wrote the song for *Wild at Heart* and they had Koko sing that song and "Up in Flames" but only used one song? That would mean the song was written over a year before Episode 29. But we simply MUST find this Koko version, or I will get more catty than a M. T. Wentz review of Taco Bell.

Verse 2: Lori Eschler

When it comes to the music of *Twin Peaks*, I would submit that the most important person, outside of Angelo Badalamenti, is Lori Eschler, and I bet you've never heard the name before. This is what happens when something gets as big as *Twin Peaks* did. All the glory runs to the top, and the workers who actually performed the craft get forgotten. This is why I love to do research on a topic. I didn't know who Lori Eschler was until Dean Hurley told me in the first interview I did for this book. He said that no book about the music of *Twin Peaks* would be valid without her. Facebook destroyed the fabric of kindness and decency, but it sure can help you find a music editor whom you've never met before.

Lori Eschler was the keeper of the cues. She knew what theme each character was associated with and made sure it remained consistent over the twenty-nine episodes. She assisted each director in choosing those cues, and then she mixed them together with other cues and created sonic pieces of beauty that viewers heard through their television sets. Talking to her was like was like interviewing Ron Garcia for my *FWWM* book and discovering he was the one who shot the ceiling fan in the Palmer House. There are so many unsung heroes out there. Everything I always assumed Angelo did outside of writing the songs, Lori was the one who actually did it. I love knowing this.

While Lynch gets a whole lot of praise for a whole lot of things, the one, and possibly only, thing he doesn't get enough credit for is placing women in positions of authority behind the scenes. Everyone knows he gives women a lot to do in front of the camera, despite all that pearl clutching from male critics; he is widely credited with coaxing legendary performances from Laura Dern, Sheryl Lee, Patricia Arquette, Naomi Watts, and David Duchovny. (It's just a joke, settle down my sensitive ones.) Frost and Lynch hired female directors like Lesli Linka Glatter, Diane Keaton, and Tina Rathborne. He hired Mary Sweeney to edit *FWWM* and his other films. He hired Sabrina Sutherland as the producer on so many of his most recent films. He hands a ton of power to casting agent Johanna Ray on his projects. Lynch is a true supporter of females in positions of power, and I salute Mark Frost and David Lynch for doing that with Lori Eschler at a time when that wasn't in style. Meet Lori Eschler.

Scott Ryan: How did *Twin Peaks* come into your life?

Lori Eschler: The job I had before *Twin Peaks* was on the U2 film *Rattle and Hum*. In the editing room, I was the only musical person there. So I would show them where to cut the music. I laid out all the music edits. It was just rock music; count to eight and cut. [Laughs.] When David Lynch had finished the Pilot and Dave Slusser, who was the music editor on that, didn't want to continue on to the series, he asked Jon Huck, who was the sound recordist on the Pilot, to be the music editor, and he said no. But he told David, "You should call Lori Eschler. You will love her because she is from Montana." I had just seen Jon the night before, so I was very lucky. The producer on *Rattle and Hum* was Gregg Fienberg, and he was the producer on *Twin Peaks*. So David said, "Get Lori in here; I want to meet her." Gregg said, "She's not a music editor." David loved to do the opposite of what Gregg asked him to do, so that was in my favor. I came in, met David, we hit it off, and he hired me. It was my first music editing job and one of my favorites because of the creativity. It kind of spoiled me.

Scott Ryan: Do you remember what month and year that you began on the series?

Lori Eschler: It was the fall of '89.

Scott Ryan: When did you start getting new cues, and when did you use David Slusser's library?

Lori Eschler: The library we had from the Pilot was the three basic themes: "Laura Palmer's Theme" and "Falling" and "Fast Cool Jazz" and the variations and solos. That's what I was working with for the first season. Angelo was in New York. Occasionally they would need something that didn't exist. We would talk about that in our spotting sessions. Angelo would be on the phone, and he would pull his people together, record some cues, and send them to me. It wasn't digital, so it took forever. They would send them to me, and I would transfer them to mag 35mm and add that to the library. I don't even know how we did that. It was very slow. He started doing additional musical cues by the second or third episode. I would then add those to the library and use it again if it worked in certain places. It was really fun for me because I had this vast amount of tracks to work with, and I got to do all sorts of layering and editing and looping. The second season I was gifted a digital editing system that sped it up. It was way early in the digital editing realm.

Scott Ryan: Tell me about working with the different directors.

Lori Eschler: It was really nicely scheduled because we could pretty much focus on one episode at a time. I was in the same building as the picture editor for Season 1 and just across the street for Season 2. So the director could see the picture editor and then come over and watch a scene where I added music to it. The directors loved it. Well, not all of them. Some of them wanted to score to picture, but most of them loved playing with the music. "Why don't you try delaying it by three frames?" They always have to pee on their project and make it their own. [Laughs.] They brought in this array of people that had different backgrounds, and it was really creative and fun. Most TV directors only work through production, and they don't go into postproduction. They would say, "What, I have two more weeks of work?" But the ones who got into it really loved it. Everybody seemed like they were really close friends with David, and everybody knew each other. I know some of them went to AFI together. There was a unique vernacular in how far they could push the envelope and experiment with things.

Scott Ryan: How was it for you when you have all this knowledge and then you'd get a director who wants to play "Laura Palmer's Theme" on top of Lucy and Andy?

Lori Eschler: David was really clear from the first time someone wanted to do that. He was very diplomatic, and he would explain, "No, that song is just for Laura Palmer." I think he was even in on the early spotting sessions at the beginning. The definition of *Twin Peaks* music developed over time. One time somebody brought me a piece of rock 'n' roll music for the jukebox in the Double R diner. David was like, "No. There is no rock 'n' roll in Twin Peaks." [Laughs.]

Scott Ryan: What about working with Duwayne Dunham? How was that, since he edited the Pilot and directed the first episode, which would have been your first episode as well?

Lori Eschler: I didn't remember that he directed the first regular episode. I met Duwayne on the same day that I met David. I met them in my interview. Duwayne is one of the nicest guys I have ever met. That established a dynamic where everyone was at ease. You could feel comfortable making mistakes or trying things. They always called them "happy accidents." Duwayne was so enthusiastic. He is so smart and humble. I did learn a lot in regards to editing and placement before the cut and after the cut.

Scott Ryan: What does that mean?

Lori Eschler: Like if there was a musical moment or downbeat, he taught me to put it like eight film frames after the cut. A lot of people prelap it, and it was too jarring. It is a technical thing to help the edit be more elegant.

Scott Ryan: What is the difference between working with a guest director and working with David Lynch?

Lori Eschler: [Laughs.] I remember at the end of Episode 2, after Cooper's dream, we were on the dubbing stage, and we finished. We were ready to send it off to the network, and he turned around and said, "Well, I don't know what people are gonna think about this, but I really like it."

Scott Ryan: What did you think of it?

Lori Eschler: It was scary. I was too close to it. I really enjoyed working on it because of the creative freedom and experimentation. I don't think anyone thought it was gonna be as big as it became. It was definitely something that had never been done before, and that is what everyone was aware of. I had watched David's films since college, so I knew the difference.

Scott Ryan: Did the Red Room stuff make it more difficult for you as the music editor, since everything is backwards?

Lori Eschler: The dialogue where the actors are speaking backwards had nothing to do with me, but it inspired some of the manipulations with the music. I slowed down some tracks and would play them backwards and overlap them with forward-running things. It was a technique that was used in that scene. It was unbelievable that the actors could do that. It was mind-blowing. It was fun to play music backwards in the cutting room and see what they would sound like. I was on a flatbed editing system. I would put it in rewind and see what it would sound like and then make a loop of that.

Scott Ryan: How did you go through the library to find cues?

Lori Eschler: I actually had an audiocassette that I would fast forward through. That is how I would look for songs. In the first season when we were still analog, once I found the portion of the cue, I would have it transferred to mag. I would have several cues that were set up, and we could try for the general mood. So we would audition it in the early decision time for the directors.

Scott Ryan: Did you have a cue that you really liked to use?

Lori Eschler: There was so much to work with. There were two major main themes with different instrumentation of those tracks. A lot of times we would ask Angelo to play a theme just on Fender Rhodes, and he would do it. My favorite was "Falling." It was so beautiful.

Scott Ryan: Who named the original cues? "Dance of the Dream Man" was originally "Fast Cool Jazz." Did you name them?

Lori Eschler: When I got the tracks, they were named by Angelo or David. When the tracks started to evolve, like "Audrey's Dance" is a good example, it evolved to being a part of the brand of Audrey; it would be reserved for her. Then, with the final cue sheet, I would run the names of the songs by Angelo or David, and they would name them. Angelo would call and say, "Change this to that and change this around." Sometimes he would defer to what David called it.

Scott Ryan: What about the first *Twin Peaks* soundtrack release? Most of those tracks are mixes of parts of cues. Did you have anything to do with that?

Lori Eschler: I just provided them with a digital library to work with. They did that in New York while I was on vacation in Indonesia.

Scott Ryan: Were you surprised that it went gold?

Lori Eschler: It was really fantastic. It was surreal for me because I hadn't even been a music editor when I got the job, and then I am on this TV show that everybody is talking about. In the beginning of the second season, we were working on an episode, and I'm sitting next to David, and they bring him a copy of *Time* magazine, and he is on the cover.

Scott Ryan: What about doing the music for Episode 14 when Maddy is killed? The music is so creepy in that one. Also, doesn't that mean that you knew who the killer was before the episode aired?

Lori Eschler: I didn't know until we were editing, and we saw the episode. David came to the dub stage to show it to us.

Scott Ryan: And at this point it had no music?

Lori Eschler: Yeah, no sound and no music. It was so intense without the sound and the music. I just remember the head mixer, Gary Alexander, who loved Leland so much, just turned around after the reveal and looked at David and said, "I hate you." [Laughs.] It was such an emotional, intense thing to work on. Again, David worked with subtraction. We brought all the guns, and then he would have us take out things and raise certain things. That sequence was a masterpiece.

Scott Ryan: There is a song that scores that scene called "Half Speed Orchestra 6 (Bob's Dance/Back to Missoula)." Did Angelo score that to the scene?

Lori Eschler: No, it was all edited for the scene from the library.

Scott Ryan: So you and David just picked tracks to play underneath it?

Lori Eschler: Yeah, David was pretty specific as to what he wanted because he knew the library as well as I did. I think he would oftentimes know that he was going to feature a certain piece of music, and then he would carve the sound out around it so they would work together. Sometimes we would even pitch the sound effects to clash or harmonize to the music—the metallic drones that would roll in. Boy, oh boy, it just turned out so well. It is so hard to watch that sequence.

Scott Ryan: Since you knew who did it before it aired, did they swear you to secrecy?

Lori Eschler: When they finished picture editing each episode, they would deliver it to us on three-quarter-inch tape. With that one, David brought it over and showed it to us with the understanding "Nobody says a word." It was made very clear this is not going to get out. We will find you.

Scott Ryan: What was it like working on the final episode of the series?

Lori Eschler: I was already slated to work on *On the Air*, so I wasn't worried about a job. But that episode was really intense. Everybody worked really hard on it. It was our last time to play together. I remember sleeping there on the couch in my office. It was so emotional. We had become really close. I am sure others were glad to get rid of us.

Scott Ryan: Do you remember when you heard "Sycamore Trees" for the first time?

Lori Eschler: Yes, and they said, "We will tell you when you can use this one." I didn't have it in Season 1, but it was part of the Season 2 early delivery. When we started Season 2, they delivered a bunch of new variations on existing themes, and some new tracks, and I think that is when "Sycamore Trees" came in. I was a huge fan of Little Jimmy Scott. I had seen him that year at a jazz club and was just blown away. He was amazing. So it was a big treat for me. Ron Carter played bass on that track. He is one of the great jazz bassists in my opinion.

Scott Ryan: I have recently been told it was going to be used in *Wild at Heart*.

Lori Eschler: I really thought I was going to be the music editor on *Wild at Heart* because Angelo said, "Let's get Lori on this." Then one of the producers said, "No, I need her for the Pilot of *Beverly Hills 90210.*" I wasn't in the room at the time. I was so mad because I would rather have done *Wild at Heart*. Then I got to work with Tim Hunter, who directed the Pilot of *90210*, and we became good friends. He was one of those guys who loved to play in the editing room and shift the music.

Scott Ryan: Were Mark Frost and David Lynch as involved in Season 1 as they were in Season 2?

Lori Eschler: Mark was more involved in the writing realm and above-the-line production stuff. David came to every final mix of every single episode to sign off on it. He always made a little tweak here and there.

Scott Ryan: I love hearing that because my number one annoyance is when someone writes in a book how David Lynch wasn't a part of Season 2, that he was working on *Wild at Heart*, which is nuts seeing how *Wild at Heart* premiered at Cannes in May of 1990 and Season 2 premiered in late September 1990.

Lori Eschler: Yeah, he was always around, and he came to the dubbing stage to watch the final of each episode. It was fun because it became a game for me. "What is he going to come up with to tweak on this episode?" I remember on Tim Hunter's Episode 4 in Season 1, [Picture on next page.] David said, "Tim, this is almost perfect." He told the editor to go back to a certain spot. He said, "Open a mic for me." When Audrey and Donna were talking and Audrey threw the cigarette in the sink, he made a little "tss" noise. And it's there in the episode; you can hear it. He would pull things out of closets to make sounds, and then he would record them directly into the film. They called it recording on the fly.

Scott Ryan: So how did *FWWM* come to you?

Lori Eschler: They took me to New York for the music recording. They wanted me to start as soon as the film was in the can. They wanted me to keep track of all the cues and keep up on the organization. It was really cool being in the studio and watching David and Angelo work. The thing that struck me was this was play for them. They weren't working. They had this rapport that was incredible. They were joking around.

Scott Ryan: Do you remember what songs they were working on?

Lori Eschler: I remember Buster Williams and Grady Tate were there. So it was the jazz stuff. [They play on "Theme from FWWM" and "The Pine Float."]

Scott Ryan: This is one of the questions that I have always wondered. *FWWM* begins with the saxophone version, and then it goes into the trumpet version. So it's only the first ten seconds that are different. Why?

Lori Eschler: We had different mixes of all those themes. They always kept the instruments separate so that we could mix them however we wanted.

Scott Ryan: There is so much sound in *FWWM*. There is wall-to-wall music, but also sounds. Did you mix in all of that?

Lori Eschler: It was me, and the sound supervisor was Doug Murray. We did everything on the dubbing stage. I just set up my kit right next to David because he would mix in all the tracks. I would talk to him about what I am sending him. We developed a shorthand because we weren't talking. He would make a little face, and I just knew what he meant for some reason. It was so codependent. [Laughs.] I would give him a track, and if he liked it, he would smile. There was a certain amount of trust he had in me, and that gave me the confidence to do a good job, and also, there were no mistakes

Scott Ryan: How did you decide when to use old, series music and when to use new music in *FWWM*?

Lori Eschler: We tried not to use much from the series because he really wanted it to be before the series. It is interesting to think about how much darker it is. In the series, everything is presumed innocent, but as people start to discover what went on, it gets darker and darker. While it is going on in FWWM, the music and the mood is just at the depth of darkness. It is so ethereal and wild.

Scott Ryan: A lot of people don't like *FWWM*. I think it's the best part of *Twin Peaks*. What did you think of it at the time?

Lori Eschler: It was disturbing, and even some of the people who worked on *Twin Peaks* would say to me, "How can you work on that? David is such a misogynist." I think it was a little more complex than that. The film disturbed me very much. But a lot of it resonated with me.

Scott Ryan: What do you say to people who think Lynch films are misogynistic?

Lori Eschler: I have women and men who have said it, and they were in the film business. I think it is just way more complex than that. There is a part of David that flirts with the girls, and he portrayed himself in *The Return* that way, but I think he was making fun of himself. During *FWWM*, it was because he ventured into this really brutal child sexual abuse within the family; everybody was so uncomfortable with it. All they could do was to pigeonhole the film as misogynist because it was the easiest way to deal with it, but it was way more complex than that.

Scott Ryan: How was the experience for you as a woman in a field of men?

Lori Eschler: I was the first music editor that was completely digital. So the engineers from Todd-AO would have to come in to help me. My cutting room was right next to the dubbing stage. I would go into their office, and this was back in the day when they had nude pictures all over their workspace. I brought it up to the president of Todd-AO, and he said, "Let them be. Let them have their fun." Being the only woman on a lot of jobs led to my second-favorite music editing job, which was a film that Lesli Glatter directed where she hired mostly females to do the work. That was fun. It was called *The Proposition*.

Scott Ryan: What did you think of *The Return*?

Lori Eschler: I just love *The Return*. It was so great to see Audrey Horne with baggage. I ran into Duwayne at a restaurant, and he said that I needed to come in and help them. I went in for an interview, but when they realized that I was caregiving and my plate was quite full, so I wouldn't be able to be there like their young editors could, they decided not to bring me in, which was probably for the best. When I watched it, I was just mesmerized. I watched it twice, and I don't recall hearing any old cues that were never used in the original series.

Scott Ryan: I also saw that you were the music editor on the Pilot for the short-lived sitcom from Mark Frost and David Lynch, *On the Air*. But you weren't for the series. Why did you just do the Pilot?

Lori Eschler: Yeah, I was working on *FWWM* during Episode 2 of *On the Air*. Bunny Andrews took over for me. I knew her from some work I did at Universal. She was, and still is, a very respected music editor. I liked her an awful lot.

Scott Ryan: While I can't really say that series is all that wonderful, the music in it is pretty unique and different from *Twin Peaks*. I would love for that to be released at some point because it still is classic Angelo music.

Lori Eschler: When we were recording the score for *On the Air*, we had a session with studio musicians in LA. David and Angelo were used to working with musicians who could improvise. There was a take of one of the cues that was really stiff. At the end of the take, David said, "That was really good, guys, but let's do it again, and this time play it like a Sunday school that's on fire." The musicians looked completely perplexed.

"Sycamore Trees" update: Lori remembers getting the song early in Season 2, but being told not to use it until she was given permission. But who sang it? Was it the Koko version? The Jimmy Scott version? Maybe James Marshall? Stay tuned . . .

TRACK 4

"Laura Palmer's Theme"

Soundtrack from Twin Peaks, 1990

My guess is that if you only own one *Twin Peaks* album, this is the one. It sold over a half a million copies in the States, which is a lot of donuts. Whenever I go to a record store, I always look to see if they have used copies of this CD. I rarely see it, which means people not only bought it, they kept it. This is the perfect collection for the average fan. You get the "Laura Palmer Theme." You get Cooper's dream song, the Audrey stuff, a few Julee Cruise songs, and the theme song. What more could you want? It's like getting a wonderful greatest hits album. When the album was compiled, the mixers basically made up mixes for a few of the songs to try to get in as many themes as they could. "The Bookhouse Boys" and "Nightlife in Twin Peaks" are not actual songs that a group of musicians played from start to finish. They are stems of songs put together to give listeners a taste of the music that played on the series. It is why the soundtrack is so popular; it was made for the populous.

Kevin Lafffey: I had to pitch that to Warner Bros., and it was a no-brainer. The master was owned by Lynch and their production company. So that was a separate negotiation. It wasn't a given, but it made perfect sense, and I'm sure David and Angelo thought so too. I was only involved in selling the idea to the powers that be.

The front cover [my actual longbox from 1990 is placed to the side] contained a picture of that famous bend in the road and the "Welcome to Twin Peaks" sign that viewers saw when Cooper entered town. The back cover had the Red Room curtains and floor (where the zigzags are not black and white, but dark yellow and almost brown) with little pictures of key cast members displayed like a list of suspects in little boxes. This was such a helpful thing to have back in 1990. I was still learning the characters' names. "Wait. Killer Bob? That's his name? You are telling me that this is one of the greatest mysteries of all time and one of the characters is named KILLER Bob, and he turns out to be the

killer?" They even had a picture of Diane listed as one of the characters on the back cover. No, it wasn't a young Laura Dern. It was a picture of Cooper's hand holding a dictaphone.

The album was released on September 11, 1990, about two weeks before Season 2 premiered. Four days later, *The Secret Diary of Laura Palmer*, which was written by Jen Lynch, was released. You add in Fenn, Boyle, and Amick on the cover of *Rolling Stone* and Kyle MacLachlan hosting *SNL* and you've got one hell of a *Twin Peaks* month. This would be the peak of *Twin Peaks*'s pop culture moment. Once Season 2 debuted on September 30, it would begin the slow side down to 1-1-9. But in early September, it was all cherry pie for fans like me who bought all of these items and would have bought even more. (A *USA Today* article promised me a Nintendo game; where is it Matt Roush?)

The music for the first season of *Twin Peaks* was recorded in 1989, with Kinny Landrum laying down the keyboard parts. I asked Kinny when those sessions happened and how that worked for the studio musicians.

Kinny Landrum: They all happened between 1989 and 1991. I don't think there were more than one or two sessions during the first season. But there were probably twenty for the second season. There were different directors for different episodes. Those directors would request X, Y, Z from Angelo. We would play the cue on videotape if there was an existing video tape. We would watch it, get a click track that would work, record it, and then watch it back. You couldn't fine-tune it back then. Now it is child's play to hook a computer up with video and audio.

Scott Ryan: How many times did you have sessions for scoring *Twin Peaks*?

Kinny Landrum: A lot. We probably had at least twenty. The way musicians get special payments is a once-a-year payment, and it all depends on what they collect that year. They send you a statement for a particular film. It doesn't tell you how many hours of work you put in, but it tells you your percentage of the work you did. They figure how many times you were on a contract and how much you did of the complete contracts of that project, and then they give you a prorated share. My share of *Twin Peaks* is about 33 percent. Angelo would have been on every one. David Lynch would be on some of the musician's contracts; whether he was there or not is a whole other story. Meaning I am on every contract for *Twin Peaks*.

Kinny Landrum, Grady Tate, Al Regni, Vinnie Bell, and Angelo Badalamenti were crucial in recording the songs on this album. Let's take the tracks one by one.

"Twin Peaks Theme"

The album begins and ends with the same song, "Falling." It starts with the instrumental version that played with the opening credits. The theme song went on to win a Grammy for Best Pop Instrumental Performance. I asked David Slusser, who worked on the Pilot, if any changes were made to the instrumental version.

David Slusser: When the camera pans over the falls, I think they had Kinny Landrum play a cello patch there. We were listening to it, and I said, "Angelo, how about making that a French horn instead of a cello?" Angelo used to be a French horn player, so he said, "That's a great idea." I think it really makes the opening cue. When you hear that French horn and you see the waterfall, that is my stamp on the main theme. They were playing Kinny like a drum. All those walking bass notes in those songs sound like a bass player, but it's all Kinny on the keyboards. Back in those days, there weren't a lot of music libraries for keyboards. But Kinny had real-sounding French horns, and it was an authentic-sounding synth sound. The cello sample kind of sounds like an electronic keyboard. There might have been one session where they had a real bass player, but mostly it was just Grady Tate and Kinny. I think they had Grady playing sticks on a stool or phone book. It was a very improvised and unorthodox way of doing a score.

Kinny Landrum: I know that we added some French horn to play the melody for the TV theme version, but not sure if that was on Julee's version.

This instrumental version, which has the French horns taking the place of Julee's vocals, has been on every *Twin Peaks* release but the Season 2 album. It is a point of contention with me; do we need the same song on *Soundtrack from Twin Peaks, Fire Walk With Me, Floating into the Night, Twin Peaks Music from the Limited Event Series*, and *Twin Peaks Limited Event Series Soundtrack* soundtrack? I'm gonna say no.

On the original series, the opening-credits song plays a bit longer on the Pilot and the second-season opener because the song went from the credits directly into the episode, and both times the opening included a shot of the large log, which is actually located in the middle of Snoqualmie. That log is shown only those two times in the series. I love those little opening-credit differences along the way. The original series's opening credits song played for about ninety seconds, while for *The Return*, the song played for fifty-four seconds. The version of the song used for *The Return* starts with a sound called "Intro Cymbal Wind," created by Dean Hurley, but that isn't the version that was released on either of *The Return* soundtracks. The same version of "Falling", as always, was released. Rinse and repeat.

Lynch also uses this cue in *FWWM* when the story moves from the

Deer Meadow section of the film to Twin Peaks. Whenever you hear that bum . . . . bum, bum, you know you are back in town. And because you've read my chapter on "Falling," you know where that sound came from as well. See, reading this book has already made you smarter. The track is released on the film's soundtrack in a medley with "Girl Talk," "Birds in Hell," and "Laura Palmer's Theme."

"Laura Palmer's Theme"

If you ever heard Angelo Badalamenti being interviewed, you know the story of how he wrote this song. I am not going to repeat it, as it's been told a lot. Without a doubt, no piece of instrumental music is more associated with *Twin Peaks* than "Laura Palmer's Theme." It burrows into your DNA and becomes one with you. If it doesn't, you probably didn't finish watching the series and don't get what all the fuss is about. This song is so closely associated with Laura Palmer that when I talked to Sheryl Lee about how she crafted her character for *FWWM*, she cited two influences: Jen Lynch's *Diary* and this song.

Sheryl Lee: Fortunately, we had Angelo Badalamenti. So the second that music started to imprint on me as that character, to this day, no matter where I am in the world, if I hear that song there is something that happens to me. It was incredible to have Angelo's music. I always think music is a wonderful tool for actors.

It is always hard for anyone to follow Sheryl Lee. Her wisdom and kindness remind me of a Mexican chihuahua. But I think I have something to top it. Kinny Landrum was the person who actually played the keyboards on "Laura Palmer's Theme." When I interviewed him over the phone, he was sitting at his keyboard, and he went through the song measure by measure.

Kinny Landrum: We did the "Laura Palmer Theme" in 1989, probably February or March. The Julee Cruise album had long been done. Angelo called and wanted me to record for *Northwest Passage*. That was what *Twin Peaks* was called then. Angelo had a lead sheet written out in C minor.

[He starts playing the ominous beginning part of the "Laura Palmer Theme."]

Kinny Landrum: That's really one chord, and the upper note moves. We just recorded the analog string sound, and we may have combined it with the DX7. After we did that part, I suggested a low C should be played on the Steinway piano. In the 1990s, there weren't great piano sounds on a keyboard. It was half note, half note, rest, half note, half note. I said he should put a low piano note in that rest, where it holds out. He said, "Good idea, go do it." There are strings throughout. Then there is the piano part.

[He starts playing the beautiful, longing piano part that comes out of the ominous strings.]

Kinny Landrum: I played this part on the Steinway piano. Now that I think about it, there was a bit of hesitation in that part as it grows. It is possible we didn't play it to a click track. It sounds to me like there is a little bit of a *ritard* there, which you couldn't do if there was a click track. I think the first thing we did was the strings.

Scott Ryan: Did you know what this song was going to be used for?

Kinny Landrum: That was played "wild," which means without reference to the picture. It was just done as a standalone piece of music. We saw nothing in that session. I am not even sure David was in the room. He may have been shooting. I think I did the piano part as one take. I always liked that piece of music. I was never impressed with the Julee Cruise stuff, but I actually like this piece of music.

[He plays the dramatic piano section of "Laura Palmer's Theme" as he explains the music. I have inserted below the appropriate measure of the song to correspond with his explanations. If you are listening along on the CD, it starts at 1:04.]

Kinny Landrum: This first change [Measure 2] is unprepared; it is just because the melody keeps going up. Why did we go from C to E?

Kinny Landrum: Then, the next note is even more interesting. It is a Lydian, meaning a sharp fourth [Measure 4]. Then, all of a sudden, shotgun! With no preparation, F minor [Measure 5]

Kinny Landrum: Then, this is back to C [Measure 8]. The next part of this is predictable [Measure 9].

Kinny Landrum: One six minor. I like this [Measure 10], which is another Lydian thing.

Kinny Landrum: I played it just like that, with octaves and a third below the upper note [Measure 13]. Then it goes, with no setup because we are going from F major to A flat [Measure 15], back to C minor, but the first note is an A flat, technically dissonant, but because it is separated by octaves and it isn't fast, it doesn't sound dissonant, but it sounds different. That actually is a good piece of music.

Understatement? It is a beautiful and hauntingly human piece of music. I have always felt that this song captures the town's sadness. No one said that it describes who Laura was. It describes how the town feels about losing her. Angelo nailed this assignment. I love to play this song on the piano and have been able to play it at a few *Twin Peaks* events. It always feels like we are right back there with Sarah Palmer as she finds out her daughter is gone. The music expresses how she will be consumed by sadness for life.

Angelo Badalamenti: David said, "Don't change a note. You've captured 75 percent of *Twin Peaks*." I've never written such slow music in my life. [Laughs.] (YouTube interview)

"Audrey's Dance"

One of my favorite things about "Audrey's Dance" is that it is a song that actually exists in the imaginary world of Twin Peaks. Several times in the series it's heard not just by the home viewers but by the characters as well. Audrey dances to it in her father's office, and he comes in and turns the track down. Audrey also hears the song playing in the Double R diner and asks Donna, "Isn't this music too dreamy?" Donna has no answer, but I do. "Yes, it is." In Season 2, Bobby and Shelly hear it on the radio, and of course in Part 16, everyone watches Audrey dance to it at the Roadhouse. This is such a nice meta moment. Music really is always in the air.

The bass part of this song is the same as in "Dance of the Dream Man," "Freshly Squeezed," and *Wild at Heart*'s "Up in Flames." "Audrey's Dance" has a slower tempo and different melody from the other tracks. As far as a scoring connection goes, it works well for me that Audrey's main theme and Cooper's main theme, "Dance of the Dream Man," are connected by having the same bass part. It keeps these two major characters connected sonically.

Al Regni: There were three of us sitting together. There was Eddie Daniels on flute, André Badalamenti, Angelo's son, playing clarinet, and I played bass clarinet. We intermixed them and improvised. Angelo was standing in front of us giving us cues with his gestures. He was motioning us on what to do.

Kinny Landrum: It would have been hard for a drum machine to add a credible drum to that beat, and the brushes would have sounded corny. I know for a fact they used Grady Tate to play the drums on that song. He also played a little bit of brushes on the cymbal for "Falling," but that's all he played on that track. On the jazzy stuff for *Twin Peaks*, I was the one who recommended the finger snaps. I was looking at the screen and I saw Richard Beymer [Ben Horne] and Russ Tamblyn [Dr. Jacoby], who were in *West Side Story*. I said, "We should have some finger snaps." I started singing, "Boy, boy . . .

Scott and Kinny sing at the same time: "Crazy boy. Get cool, boy."

Scott Ryan: I love that Sondheim influenced the music of *Twin Peaks*. This is the best news ever for me.

Russ Tamblyn: David Lynch tried to ignore who Richard and I were. Richard was cast first, and then I was cast later. *West Side Story* was never mentioned. I think it was a coincidence.

"The Nightingale"

This track is taken directly from *Floating into the Night*. Julee Cruise performed this song in the Pilot episode as a fight breaks out with Bobby, Mike, and Big Ed. While it might seem funny that this was the music that inspired a bar fight at a biker bar, I have always felt "The Nightingale" is cousin to the Shangri-Las' song "The Leader of the Pack" from 1964.

They have the same drumbeat and are both slightly dramatic. The fact that Lynch used this song for the biker bar makes me think he might have felt that connection too.

"Freshly Squeezed"

What really is the difference between "Freshly Squeezed" and "Dance of the Dream Man?" The tempo of "Freshly Squeezed" is a little slower. "Freshly Squeezed" was famously used the first time Cooper laid eyes on Audrey Horne, just as he was ordering a glass of juice. "Freshly" starts with a much longer drum solo before the walking bass comes in. The overall melody is exactly the same. On "Freshly," the melody is played on a keyboard by Kinny Landrum. On "DOTDM," the melody is played on a saxophone by Al Regni. The melody of both songs is written in triplets. But when I compared and contrasted the sheet music between the two tracks, the main difference I could see is that Kinny Landrum seems to leave out one note from each triplet in "Freshly Squeezed." There are a lot more notes in "DOTDM." Take a look at the music here:

"Dance of the Dream Man":

"Freshly Squeezed":

While you might assume that the bass for this song is an upright acoustic bass, it isn't. It is all done on a keyboard by Kinny Landrum.

Kinny Landrum: That is a case where I sequenced the bass line. I put it into the Linn 9000 and quantized it to quarter notes.

[He starts playing that familiar bass line that runs through "DOTDM," "Freshly Squeezed," and "Audrey's Dance."]

Kinny Landrum: I always thought it was interesting that it starts chromatic and then goes off. Then, when it goes back up, it uses different notes. Then I added my suggestion of the finger snaps, and then after the sax played for a while, I played the vibes on the top part on a Roland piano module. [This is what echoes the main melody from "Audrey's Dance."] The lowest note on a real set of vibes is an F below middle C. On "Freshly Squeezed," that is me soloing on that same vibe sound, but it was all improvised. At some point, and I don't have it, they printed a *Twin Peaks* piano book.

Scott Ryan: I own it. I bought it in 1990

Kinny Landrum: You do? Then would you do me a big favor?

Scott Ryan: I will scan it and send it to you.

Kinny Landrum: Thanks. Because somebody, and I didn't do it, wrote out what I did note for note on "Freshly Squeezed." I improvised it on the spot, but I don't remember what I played. I think I also played E flats, which makes it kind of a joke for real vibe players. They would know it was on a keyboard because it is too low of a sound. Then we added some strings on the track for those thirteenth kinds of chords. [He plays the clanky sounds that come toward the end of the track, at 3:15.] Those are the same hand positions for "Purple Haze." Think like the upper third and fifth of a seventh chord and then put a flat third or a sharp nine on top of it. Every jazz player in the world playing the blues will play those notes.

Scott Ryan: I know. It is too hard for me to play. I can't play the right hand and the left hand at the same time.

Kinny Landrum: Oh. Well, I didn't play them at the same time.

Scott Ryan: I KNOW! I just learned that. For over thirty years, I've been trying to be you, and I just learned that even you aren't even you.

Kinny Landrum: Nope. I first put the bass line down and then played the other stuff.

Scott Ryan: You cheater.

"The Bookhouse Boys"

This is one of the tracks that was created in a mixing lab. It's not as if a bunch of musicians sat down and played this track or as if Angelo orchestrated it. It is a mixture of four prominent themes from Season 1. The track begins with a highly echoed version of "Dance of the Dream Man" with the solo sax that is often played when Cooper enters a scene. Then a track called "Solo Percussion 2 (Grady's Waltz)," which is just Grady Tate playing around on some drums to give that feeling of being in the sheriff's station, fades in. After a while the guitar refrain that usually plays for Bobby Briggs kicks in. This is actually what is known as "Bookhouse Boys." It is the guitar and bass, the guitar being Vinnie Bell and the bass being Kinny Landrum on keyboard. The original guitar track goes on for five minutes straight, but we get just a taste of it here. Then the track "Sneaky Audrey" fades in. "Sneaky Audrey" actually begins with the synth part of "Laura Palmer's Theme" before going into a woodwind that makes us think of Audrey Horne spying on Dr. Jacoby and Johnny Horne. This is one of my favorite tracks on the album because we get four themes in one song. I wish they would have done this with a few others. This is how we could have gotten my precious "The Norwegians" on the CD.

"Into the Night"

This song is also from *Floating into the Night* and is directly lifted from that album. The song plays in Jacques Renault's cabin when Cooper, Truman, Hawk, and Doc Hayward break in to investigate where Laura might have gone the night of the murder. (Who invited Doc Hayward? And did they get a warrant?) "Into the Night" is playing over and over again on a record player as a 45 single. (I am guessing that the singer in the biker bar got some copies printed and sold them after the show. Maybe Jacques traded some alcohol for a 45?) This is the song that leads directly to the quote "Always music in the air," since the song is playing on repeat in the cabin. Break the code, solve the crime.

Julee Cruise: I was really insecure about making this sound. Singing terrifies me. I am terrified about a lot of things. To sing so soft and vulnerable and almost naked, it's not really me (*New Visions*, VH-1).

Angelo Badalamenti: David loves to experiment. A song like "Into the Night" is very dark. It's going on very cool, slow, and dark. Then he suggests this one measure that sounds like a ninety-piece Wagnerian orchestra that blew us all away. I've learned to try things when David asks (*The Gavin Report*, 1990).

Kevin Laffey: I remember standing in the studio with Art, David, and Angelo. They were presenting what they had finished to me. We were listening to "Into the Night," and it was loud. Then that middle break comes around, where the music gets really loud, and it just blew my mind. I turned to David and I said, "You pulled a fast one on me." And he kind of giggled at that. It was at that moment I knew that we had done something great. [Studio picture of Julee Cruise on the next page.]

"Night Life in Twin Peaks"

Julee Cruise: Angelo writes the scariest music. Really scary, creepy (Warner Bros.).

Angelo Badalamenti: I've seen all the writing, and all the critics, and all the people are calling and saying the music is just setting up so many of these moods. The music makes you kind of wanna watch. I really don't take the credit for that. I think it's totally by accident (Warner Bros.).

Over time, this has become my favorite track on this album. I sort of wish they would do a bit more of this. Maybe when my vinyl box set becomes a reality, someone will get Lori Eschler to come in and mix a few of these together. This track, like "The Bookhouse Boys," isn't really an actual song. It's a mixture of stems put together to become a track that represents some of the score that went along with night scenes in the series. The first sound is very similar to what is played (along with "The Swan") when viewers first learn that Josie and Truman are a secret couple. It evokes the lonesome sound of a fog horn. There is a half-speed orchestra track playing throughout this song. It is hard to pinpoint which exact cue it is because it really sounds like the mixer has played with the pitch and speed, but the track then goes into "One Armed Man Theme (Solo Clarinet Improvisation)" backed by one of Grady Tate's solo percussion tracks. I listened to the percussion tracks that have been released and couldn't exactly match them up. Again, the cue could be several. That is how the sound mixers created the score for the show; they mixed many cues together into one. Then "Dance of the Dream Man (Solo Flute)" takes center stage to finish up the track.

It is interesting how much I enjoy this track even though I am not really a fan of listening to the individual stems on their own. The way that Eschler combined these pieces and made art out of it explains why the music of *Twin Peaks* is not just a score, but an actual character in the series. (To be clear, Lori Eschler did not mix this track, but on the series, she made similar mixes.) When you hear the strange and unworldly sounds of Al Regni's clarinet, you just know you are in the town of Twin Peaks. When you hear the improvised flute of Kinny Landrum's keyboard, you can just picture the sinister shots of late-night Twin Peaks. All that doesn't exactly mean I want to hear four minutes of just those stems, but combine them with a slowed-down and reversed orchestra piece along with Grady Tate's amazing drumming and I just might want to go hide behind a tree in an all-black ski mask.

"Dance of the Dream Man"

This was the track I listened to all the time when this CD came out. Whenever I hear of someone starting *Twin Peaks* today, I always want to talk to them immediately after they watch Episode 2, which ends with Cooper's Dream. (Which, you know, I am totally certain is not a dream at all, but everybody calls it a dream anyway. Yes, in Episode 3 Cooper tells Harry and Lucy he had a dream, but in Episode 8, in response to Cooper asking him where he comes from, the Giant responds, "The question is where have you gone." I believe Cooper is actually visiting the Red Room in Episode 2. This isn't a dream; it is the future. He is transported there, just like he is in Episode 8, but since the song isn't called "Dance of the Transported," we will stick with calling it a dream. That might have been my longest aside; I'll try to top it as the book goes on.) Anyway, back to Episode 2 and the prospect of people seeing it for the first time now: I don't think they can be as totally shaken as I was back in 1990, when

I first experienced Cooper's dream and this song. Nothing like this had been seen on television to that point. The music, the backward talking, the subtitles (which Gen Z watchers leave on all the time anyway, so they wouldn't find anything weird about subtitles on television, but in the nineties, no one was watching *L.A. Law* with subtitles.) The entire experience of seeing this on TV was all just so much.

I wanted to interview the man who played the saxophone solo on the song that defined the character of Agent Cooper. The only contact Kinny Landrum had for saxophonist Al Regni was his actual home address. So I sat down and penned Mr. Regni an actual letter on a piece of paper, put a stamp on it, and mailed it. I put my phone number in the letter, and two weeks later, he called me. Suck on that, internet. His story about recording "Dance" was incredible. I present it here in his exact words.

Al Regni: I've told this story to several other writers, but it never gets printed. I will tell you my version, and you can do with it as you like. I was called to play clarinet and saxophone. I got to the studio about a half an hour early. It was at Excalibur Sound studio, and Art Polhemus was the engineer. They were mixing the bass line to "Dance of the Dream Man." Since I was in the studio alone, I took out my sax, and started to blow along with it. All of sudden, David Lynch comes running into the studio. I thought he was going to scream at me for making noise while they were mixing. I said, "Oh, I'm sorry." He said, "No, I love what you are doing. Let's record that." So I was improvising that entire thing. Angelo, in his version of that story, said he wrote the first four bars, which is not true. He had to make some claim to doing the composition, so he said that. I don't even recall him being around when we did that. He came in later. They started recording, and I went on and on playing a minor blues and watching David Lynch through the window in the control room motioning to go on. It seemed like a long amount of time. I couldn't think of what he would use this for. I think what happened after was that Angelo probably wrote some background music, and they added drums. From my viewpoint, I didn't think the music was anything to rave about. David saw that scene right from the beginning. I didn't know anything about a dancing man talking backwards. I was just playing a minor blues that I didn't think was anything great. It is just a tribute to David's sense of being able to tell a story through music. It was one take, no overdubs, and that was it. Throughout the series, they used that theme as intermittent scenes with just the sax or with other instruments.

Amazing to learn that the person who truly wrote that melody was Al Regni. Kinny Landrum corroborated this story. There is no doubt that Angelo wrote the bass line for it. It is the same bass line used in "Up in Flames," "Audrey's Dance," and "Freshly Squeezed." But it sure seems like Regni should have gotten a cowriting credit, just like so many musicians gave David Lynch. I think everyone would admit that what makes this track stand out from the others is that minor blues improvisation, which became a sonic symbol of Agent Cooper. It was even used the first time his character shows up in *FWWM*. The music business is full of garmonbozia.

A version of "Dance of the Dream Man" that some fans may not be aware of is included on a 2016 release called *The Music of David Lynch–Benefiting the David Lynch Foundation*. This is a various-artists compilation on which Angelo Badalamenti performs a few *Twin Peaks* tracks. Duran Duran, Chrysta Bell, Moby, and Rebekah Del Rio are among the artists who perform songs from Lynch's filmography. It really is a great live album, and I am really bummed I didn't attend this night. It was one of the last public performances by Angelo. He performed "Dance of the Dream Man," and it is really fun because Angelo speaks a few lines from the show before getting into the tune. To hear that "Real Indication" voice saying "I've got good news. That gum you like is going to come back in style" really makes this a unique rendition. Kinny Landrum played keyboards in the band that night.

Kinny Landrum: Angelo called and asked me to come to the event. It was gonna be a union session, so it was all union scale, so there was no need to discuss money. I was a little surprised they put out the record, and I wondered if I would get paid, and sure enough I was like "Thank the Lord for the union." I got union payment for a record date. All I played on was Angelo's numbers: "Laura Palmer's Theme," "Dance of the Dream Man," and "Falling." Rob Mathes was the music director, and he didn't know I could play all that other stuff too. I actually brought with me the master keyboard sounds. Michael Thompson showed up with a baritone guitar to play the "Bum. Bum, bum" part. He said, "You played that?" I said, "Yes I did." But he loved that part, and I had to play the string pads on the keyboard, so I said, "You got it, baby. You play that part." The second time I came out was for the Festival of Disruption at the Ace Hotel. I played two keyboards at that event, and I did both parts on "Laura Palmer" and "Falling." I played on every single act because Rob Mathes knew me. We had Dean Parks on guitar, and he was great.

If you don't have this vinyl, I strongly suggest it. It is a really good mix of Lynch songs. Julee Cruise was supposed to perform there, but she backed out. I sure wish she would have. It would have been a nice moment for everyone.

"Love Theme from Twin Peaks"

This track always went down like burnt engine oil for me. If there were a limited number of songs going to be released on CD, why did we need two versions of "Laura Palmer's Theme?" This might be called the "Love Theme," but let's be honest: this is just the same song on a different instrument. Maybe it is called "Love Theme" because this version does play for Donna and James, but James's affections have a shelf life shorter than ABC's love affair with *On the Air*.

"Falling"

The final song on the *Twin Peaks* soundtrack goes back to *Floating into the Night* one last time. We get the theme song with lyrics. This is the only time "Falling" with lyrics has been released on a *Twin Peaks* soundtrack. All the other releases use the instrumental version. It makes sense that the lyric version is on this album, since Julee Cruise performed it with lyrics in the Pilot.

Julee Cruise: David wrote the lyrics to "Falling," and Angelo Badalamenti wrote the music. It was pulled from my album *Floating into the Night*. That was all our favorite. When we were recording the album was when *Twin Peaks* was being written. They ran out of time, and they just pulled a bunch of the music off of the album (Julee Cruise interview on CBC, 1992).

This became the lead single off this album. In fact, a music video was created with clips from the series and shots of Julee Cruise lip-synching.

Julee Cruise: "Falling," the video, is just a splicing of scenes from *Twin Peaks*. I did it while I was doing one of the television episodes. It was in LA. The song is about falling in love but being afraid that it is going to go away. Everybody is always insecure when you really fall in love with someone. You are slightly mentally ill anyway. You think it is just too good to be true, and that is what the song is about (CBC).

In rewatching the music video off of my Gold Box DVD set, I noticed that it contains almost exclusively clips from Season 1, and the clips are faded back and forth between the red curtains. I say *almost* exclusively because, strangely, there are two clips that are not from Season 1. The first is a shot of Bobby kissing Shelly in the hospital in Episode 8, directed by David Lynch, and the other is of James, Donna, and Maddy singing "Just You" from Episode 9, also directed by Lynch. I don't know for sure if this video was directed by David Lynch, but his love for "Just You" makes me think he did. I am positive they worked on this during the filming of Episode 14 because the shot of the red curtains is the same one in the end of Episode 14. Also, if you match Julee's hair style and outfit and the background in the video to her appearance in Episode 14, it is clear they shot her section of the video during this episode, when she was on set to sing "Rockin' Back" and "The World Spins." So Lynch directed her segment of "Falling" for the music video; whether he edited the video, I don't know. This scene was filmed on September 21,1990, just ten days after the album was released. At this point, numbers were probably coming back saying this album was a hit, so a new music video was needed. It seems so crazy to me that they were already filming the murder reveal scene before Season 2 even premiered. The video was a hit and was played in heavy rotation on VH-1 and MTV.

That brings us to the end of the first *Twin Peaks* soundtracks. Sacred Bones has released vinyl versions of this album a few times, and reprints have been issued through Warner Bros. Records. This is a great compilation, perfect for the casual fan. I don't listen to it very often, but like a first love, it occupies a sweet place in my heart. I still own the CD, which I bought the day it came out. I still have the long box, and I've purchased three versions of the vinyl, including an original from Europe. Yet I admit it's not really one of my favorites. Oh, crap, I really am one of those *Twin Peaks* fans who buy whatever they release. Heck with this idea of a vinyl box set, they might as well release the Pilot one more time on DVD; I'm sure I'd buy that for the sixth time too.

TRACK 5

"The Bookhouse Boys"

The Director's Trio:
Mark Frost, Duwayne Dunham, Tim Hunter

From the music editors, we learned how they suggested cues for scoring the episodes of the original *Twin Peaks* to the director of the episode. Here we get the memories from three directors of the series on how they took that advice and scored the episodes. Two of the directors I interviewed had pretty important side jobs on the series as well.

Verse 1: Mark Frost

I have to admit it was fun to send Mark Frost an email and tell him that I was looking to request an interview with the director of Episode 7. I like to think I was the first person to ever do that. I think he is a bit better known for having worn a few other hats on the series. He not only cocreated the series but also officially wrote or cowrote thirteen of the thirty hours of the original series and cowrote all eighteen parts of *The Return*. But his involvement with the series was so much more. Just about every aspect of production ran through his fingers. The press and the uninformed always want to call it David Lynch's *Twin Peaks*, but those of us in the know, know. Mark Frost has always been a gentleman to me personally through the years, always helping when I needed a quote for *The Blue Rose* or a kind word on an obituary for one of the passing actors from the series. He is a true professional, and if you've read David Bushman's *Conversations with Mark Frost*, you know he is also one hell of an educated writer and citizen. What more is there to say about him? Oh, I know. One time, I almost killed him.

Scott Ryan: Thanks for talking with me today. I often think about the last time we saw each other, which was when we were in LA doing events for *Conversations with Mark Frost* and COVID broke out that exact day. There I was, interviewing you at a bookstore, and one day later the airport shuts down and the world goes into lockdown. I was on one of the last planes out of LA. I'm glad we were all safe and none of us got sick because killing Mark Frost just would not be good for my brand.

Mark Frost: No, that wouldn't have been good at all. But I wouldn't have been around to criticize you for it.

Scott Ryan: There are many ways that *Twin Peaks* changed television, but one of them that rarely gets discussed is how advanced the score of the show was. What were other network TV shows doing with their scores before *Twin Peaks*?

Mark Frost: Music for most standard network shows was simply just slapping on a coat of paint that they probably already possessed, and the cue was already recorded. It was very pro forma, and it wasn't terribly original or creative. It was mostly done electronically. Shows weren't going to pay a lot of studio musicians to go in and record something new. I think that was what was different about us. We took the time to be careful and to make good choices. We thought about pretty much every cue we used.

Scott Ryan: You had previously worked on *Hill Street Blues*, which did have a famous theme song. How did they handle the score for that show?

Mark Frost: Mike Post was the composer, and he had a team of people. He'd obviously done the theme music, and he had a library of cues that he created. The show didn't use a lot of music, but when it did, it always went back to Mike, and he had a team of people who, if they didn't have the exact cue, could work with the guidelines Mike had left and create something. It was mostly a synth track. That's a lot of what Mike's work was during those years. So it was a fairly standard process. I directed one episode, and I can remember spotting cues for the finished cut. But I don't recall that I had much input. Usually it's just left to the producers, and they did it.

Scott Ryan: What was different about *Twin Peaks*?

Mark Frost: David came from a film background and had a preexisting relationship with Angelo, who created a very distinctive theme song and sound for the show. Our process from there wasn't all that dissimilar. Once we got the series, Angelo had a team of music editors that were working with him. We had the stems and all of the tracks that had been created at our disposal. They were all stored separately. So when it came time to direct my episode, I remember going through a spotting session with the music editor and saying, "I want this here, that here, this here." I asked her, in some instances, to give me maybe the same piece of music but played on a different instrument. It was mostly done on a synth, so it was easy for Angelo.

Scott Ryan: Would ABC have seen the Pilot before the score was added?

Mark Frost: No, we didn't show them any rough cuts. It was our belief to put our best foot forward. In fact, I remember screening it with David and feeling it was ready and superb from start to finish. We knew we could then send it off to them confident. They never would have seen the show without the score. It tested through the roof, even though the network couldn't make heads or tails of it, and it seemed to deeply disturb many of them. Then David and I wrote the first two episodes, and that was the extent of his involvement with the writing. Then he was completely gone doing *Wild at Heart*.

Scott Ryan: Obviously, you were the executive producer of the show, so you didn't have anyone to ask anyone to approve if you wanted new music written for a scene, but how did that work for guest directors?

Mark Frost: That was not something that we left to the episodic directors to decide. They were all accomplished filmmakers, and I invited their input, but at the end of the day, it was me sitting down with the music editor and doing the spotting sessions, pulling stuff from our pretty deep library and, in a few instances, creating some new tracks. That was the process. There wasn't a big line item in an episodic budget for new or original music for every scene. And that's pretty much standard throughout the industry. At least it used to be. I think it's different now. And I think we led the way toward moving episodic TV closer to film standards in a lot of ways, and that was probably one of the ways in which we did that as well.

Scott Ryan: Did the theme win any Emmy awards?

Mark Frost: I don't remember winning. I'm not even sure they had a category for that at the Emmys back then, honestly. It would be hilarious to see what actually won in our year if there was a category then. Most shows were associated with a single melody. If you really think about the history of the industry, usually it was an actual song with lyrics in the old days. But that's pretty much gone by the wayside, and certainly the big streaming shows now are well known for having their own original score.

[I looked it up: no theme won in 1990 because the rule at that time was that the winner had to get over fifty percent of the votes, and no show did that, so "Falling" was nominated and lost to no one. Is that better or worse than having lost to *The Simpsons*?]

Scott Ryan: What about the soundtrack coming out and it exploding? Was that something that you expected?

Mark Frost: We knew we had a distinctive sound for the show, and when it hit the way it did, I can remember saying to David, "You know, we really should release this as a separate CD."

Scott Ryan: And then it became a big deal, and Julee Cruise even performed on *Saturday Night Live*.

Mark Frost: It was a phenomenon across a pretty broad spectrum of pop culture, and music was certainly a big part of that.

Scott Ryan: Here's probably a question you won't remember the answer to, but I'm trying to get to the bottom of "Sycamore Trees," which plays in Episode 29 with Little Jimmy Scott coming in to sing and guest on the show. When you wrote the first draft of that episode, did you know he would be in it?

Mark Frost: I know there's a story there, and I can't for the life of me remember what it is. I can remember David telling me when he found Little Jimmy and how thrilled he was by the sound that he got.

Scott Ryan: I was talking to Dean about the lack of score, if you will, in *The Return*, and he traced it back to you and David watching Episode 29 and David just feeling he used too much music, and I wondered if you thought that too?

Mark Frost: It's funny, because he directed that episode, but I do remember him saying that. And also we both felt that because *The Return* was never intended to just be a stroll down Memory Lane and, at worst, an exercise in nostalgia, we wanted to stay as far away from that as possible and make it something new. And since the central themes had been so tied to that particular time and place—I don't mean just the fictional, but sort of it's time and place in people's memories—we didn't want to be sending signals, even at a subconscious level, that we're just gonna take you back to the good old days in Mayberry where you can have a cup of cozy tea with Aunt Bee. That wasn't what we had in mind with the whole notion of *The Return*. I remember him saying he'd met with Angelo, and talked to him about that, and said that we really were only going to use the familiar themes when they really counted. The obvious example of that is where we hear "Laura Palmer's Theme" for the first time when Bobby sees the photo of Laura just after we've learned he's working in the sheriff's department. Also, when Cooper kind of comes back to himself, we revive the theme. The idea was "Let's be very judicious about how we use the familiar cues and really make the most of them where they can really pay off emotionally," and I think that was successful.

Scott Ryan: Anything to say about Angelo's work on the new series?

Mark Frost: He always did maintain such an extraordinary level of craftsmanship and artistry that I expected nothing less from anything that he was going to give us. And of course, he delivered. Seeing him again was marvelous. I love the guy. He was just a beautiful human being.

Scott Ryan: Do you have anything else to add about the music of the series?

Mark Frost: No, I think I've probably talked more about it just now than in any single conversation I've ever had before.

Verse 2: Duwayne Dunham

There couldn't have been a better director picked to direct the first regular episode of *Twin Peaks* than Duwayne Dunham. No one had a better understanding of the characters and what had been done in the Pilot than the man who edited it. While Lynch and Frost were juggling a bunch of tasks to get the series off the ground, Dunham had been in the editing bay watching take after take, learning who these characters were and how the actors brought them to life. Dunham cultivated a strong relationship with George Lucas, having edited *The Empire Strikes Back* and *Return of the Jedi* before making his way over to working on *Blue Velvet* with David Lynch. I am an admirer of Duwayne's work and honored to call him a friend. He is a stand-up guy, always smiling, and is filled with stories like Laura is filled with secrets.

Duwayne Dunham: The way David went about doing the music for *Twin Peaks*— and we have to be clear the Pilot was one thing and then the first seven was a different thing, and then the second season and the reboot were all different.

Scott Ryan: Well, we are gonna cover all those topics. Let's start with Angelo. When did you meet him?

Duwayne Dunham: I first met Angelo on *Blue Velvet*, so I am trying to filter my mind for *Twin Peaks*. On both projects, Angelo wasn't around because he was in New York at Excalibur. Whenever music was recorded, it was done in New York.

Scott Ryan: Let's start with when you are editing the Pilot of *Twin Peaks* and you use "Laura Palmer's Theme" as Grace screams, and then the shot comes back to the phone. How did you edit that scene?

Duwayne Dunham: The music editor numbers cues so they can track it through to the recording, to editing the music takes. They are not editing in my room. Those cues come into the room as the completed music, and then I would lay it into the movie. I typically cut silent. Even if I had the music for *Twin Peaks*, I would not be editing with the music. I edit most times without any sound at all.

Scott Ryan: Even without the dialogue?

Duwayne Dunham: Yes, I know what they are saying. It gets annoying, and I know which performances I picked. It's a moving picture and I'm studying the images, and I'm getting the best images. When I put the music up, nine times out of ten it is spot-on. Now, they don't record that music out of thin air. Angelo is looking at my cut. He is writing the music, most of the time, to the picture. You mentioned that scene with Grace and the telephone; if I had to pick a scene to show somebody, that scene would be it: the whole beginning of the Pilot, from frame one all the way till when the police show up and Grace screaming like that, and tracking down the phone. All of the breaths, all of the pauses, all of the sobs, that is what I constructed in the editing room based on the performance of the actress. But that, as a moving piece, really is a symphony. It works with the music, really gangbusters.

Scott Ryan: It really does. It is fascinating that you weren't listening to the "Laura Palmer Theme" as you were cutting it, because it fits perfectly.

Duwayne Dunham: Keep in mind, the Pilot happened so fast. We started shooting in February, and we were done in May. So it goes pretty fast. I edit the movie; then we lock the picture. That means we turn it over to sound and music. Sound goes in, cleans up the dialogue, and preps it for Foley and sound effects, cuts the effects, and everyone is working from the same picture. That picture would have gone to Angelo, and he could sit down with the picture, and it's up to him to figure out what notes are playing.

Scott Ryan: What about when Julee Cruise sings a couple of songs in the Roadhouse? Are you editing that?

Duwayne Dunham: I would do that. The music editor edits the sound to have a perfect take. When it comes to the cutting room, I would cut it in.

Scott Ryan: Today is the thirty-fifth anniversary of when Lynch shot Cooper's Red Room backwards scene for the Pilot. It was July 3, 1989. So happy anniversary. But you finished editing by May, and then somewhere in there ABC asked for a closed ending?

Duwayne Dunham: No. That happened much earlier. So while we were shooting—I think the schedule was twenty-one or twenty-three days; it was hardly anything—David and I had breakfast one Sunday. He asked me, "What would you think of a guy who had a tattoo on his arm, and it was so revolting to him that he cut his arm off?" I said, "David, I think you've had too much syrup and caffeine!" He said, "I just found out from ABC that if they pick up the Pilot for episodes, the Pilot lives as shot. But it is their policy that they will not air a standalone movie if it has an open ending." Which really seemed silly to me, but *Twin Peaks* ends with somebody picking up the necklace, and you don't know who murdered Laura. David said, "ABC wants me to shoot an alternate ending." The very last day that I was up in Washington, I was in the cutting room alone and it was very late at night, and a delivery guy showed up with film boxes. He said, "Is this *Twin Peaks*?" And I said, "Yeah, what's that?" He said, "This is for you." I said, "What? We are done." I opened up the first box and loaded it up on the machine, and I am looking at this weird stuff of the set decorator, Frank Silva, as Bob. He is playing with candles on the floor, and there is a one-armed guy saying, "I mean it like it is." And I get up and lock the door because this is some weird stuff. I had no clue what it was because there was no script. There is nothing. It just showed up! That was the last thing that David shot up in Washington. Then we had editing rooms up at CFI in LA. We kind of got the Pilot edited, and then we had to start working on the alternate ending because we didn't know the determination of ABC. Trust me when I say that *nobody* thought we were gonna do additional episodes, because the cards that came back from ABC's testing were, let's just say, not positive. Though *Twin Peaks* is a brilliant piece of film. We screened it once at the Directors Guild one night, and it was like liquid gold. It was so beautiful. You could feel the people breathing.

Scott Ryan: But at this point, you didn't have Cooper's dream because that wasn't shot until July 3.

Duwayne Dunham: Right. Well, one day David had this vintage maroon Mercedes. My assistant and I walked outside with David to his car, and David leaned down onto his car to put his hands and arms on the hood of the car, and he immediately jumped back and shouted out, "Don't say anything." He jumped into his car and sped away. I was like "What the hell was that?" David would reveal that that is where the inspiration would come from for the closed ending with the Red Room. It came from there. He sped away to sit down and work it out.

Scott Ryan: So that makes sense that you wouldn't have gotten that stuff in Washington.

Duwayne Dunham: Right, because the Red Room was shot in LA. I remember it was summer, so that would make sense because we were almost finished in early May. David walked in with Monty Montgomery and said he was going to shoot *Wild at Heart* in a few weeks, and he didn't have a script yet. That was a real crazy period of time. Lots of stuff going on. The Red Room was shot, and he said, "Take the audio recording and record it backwards, and then turn it around and play it forward," and that is why it has that weird sound. It wasn't the actor talking backwards. It was recorded properly, rerecorded backwards. Then we reverse printed the picture as well, so everyone was moving backwards. David had Mike Anderson do everything in reverse. So people were walking in reverse, so it has a very strange look to it because it was all reverse. It is haunting and beautiful, and then you put Angelo's saxophone song ["Dance of the Dream Man"] in there and you just go, "Wow, what is this?" Somebody walks a silhouette of a bird across the red curtains. I mean David is one creative cucumber.

Scott Ryan: Then you get to direct the first episode of *Twin Peaks*. Did you also cut the opening credits of the instrumental of "Falling?"

Duwayne Dunham: Yes. In fact, when I did the saws in the very beginning, we had all kinds of footage of logs and logs in a river and saws. I cut something, and then when I got the music back, I did go through and ever so slightly adjust the cuts so the notes of that music hit on the sparks.

Scott Ryan: How different was the score of *Twin Peaks* from other shows at the time?

Duwayne Dunham: It was moody and dark, yet it was kind of jazzy. When you put the music to it, it's almost like people are moving in slow motion, like with Audrey. There is a sway to it. The music is instantly recognizable as "That is *Twin Peaks*; that is Angelo."

Scott Ryan: How was it to direct the first hour-long episode?

Duwayne Dunham: By the time we went back to film again, all the actors had been off doing other shows. I knew those characters and was a good choice because I had edited the Pilot. So I could remind the actors how they played the characters. The Pilot had been six or eight months ago. When we did the music, David had a great idea, and I just used it on my recent movie, *The Happy Worker*. I did the music exactly the way Angelo did the music on *Twin Peaks*. Angelo recorded certain themes in the same key. So then each director on the episode was given a cassette tape. You could play any music cue you wanted, wherever you wanted. David is the master of every aspect of his filmmaking process. Very few have that kind of talent. But he extended that to the directors on *Twin Peaks*. So you got this cassette tape, and you could listen to it in your spare time. But keep in mind that you had to shoot it in seven days and cut it in seven days. So the timeline was I was finishing cutting *Twin Peaks*, David went off and started shooting *Wild at Heart*, I set up a second cutting room right next to *Twin Peaks*. There wasn't much left to do on the Pilot, so I started cutting *Wild at Heart*. David finished shooting *Wild at Heart* on the same day that I finished shooting the first episode of *Twin Peaks*. We met back at the cutting room. He took some time off, and then he shot the second episode of *Twin Peaks*. We shot a little bit out of order. Episode 3 was shot after Episode 1, and then David shot Episode 2 later. But we were cutting the feature and the episodes at the same time.

Scott Ryan: You mentioned editing *Wild at Heart*. Do you remember seeing footage of Koko Taylor singing "Sycamore Trees" from *Wild at Heart*?

Duwayne Dunham: No. But *Wild at Heart* was four hours long, and we cut lots of things and moved that film all around. If you were to read the scene structure of the finished film to the script, it would read like a Bingo card. There was no rhyme or reason as to how it went together. It was "What is the film saying, and where does the scene want to be? Let's put it there, and how about we combine these two scenes?" and off we went. It is quite possible that she performed a number of songs, but it was just background.

Scott Ryan: Did you cut Episode 1 yourself, since you directed it?

Duwayne Dunham: I did. We brought Jonathan Shaw on, and he was the supervising editor on the first seven episodes. He knows my style. He worked on *Blue Velvet*. As if that was not enough to keep you busy, you were listening to these cassette tapes, and then the music editor, Lori Eschler, had these film boxes that had these 35MM loops on sound tapes. Then you would decide which tracks to put in. You could play the full theme as Angelo did it, or you could add instruments or take them away. Then it was Lori's job to edit those songs that way. So on *The Happy Worker*, I told my composer, Jan Kaczmarek, who was in Poland to record the themes, to give me all the isolated instruments. I wouldn't have had that idea if I hadn't done it in *Twin Peaks*.

Scott Ryan: I am surprised more people don't do that.

Duwayne Dunham: I don't have the talent that David Lynch or Johnny Williams has. Not everybody does. So this isn't the most efficient way to do it in the cutting room. We had such a tight crew that to this day, anybody who was on that Pilot or the first seven episodes, you call them up, and they are your best friends. That was a family. That was *Twin Peaks*. Not so much in the second season and not so much in *The Return*, but because those first episodes were so unusual, and because of how David gave everyone such freedom, as long as the freedom stayed within his vision, not many people will do that. That is why Season 2 struggled, when that vision started to drift.

Scott Ryan: As I have told you many times, that is why your Episode 25 is so important to me. You directed my favorite all-time *Twin Peaks* scene and really brought back the joy and wonder to the show. I love when Cooper tells the joke to Annie, and Gordon eats the pie and can hear Shelly. You really saved Season 2.

Duwayne Dunham: That is kind of you to say. The one photo I have that I like looking at is of me, Mädchen, and David as Gordon Cole in the diner, and we all look so young. [Laughs.] It was fun but intimidating. David and Kyle are such good friends, and I know them both. It was like kids in a clubhouse, and it was real easy. [Photo on next page.]

Scott Ryan: Let's move to *The Return*. There isn't a lot of score in *The Return*.

Duwayne Dunham: I don't know how David came to the decision, but it was his decision to not use much music from *Twin Peaks*. When I started cutting, I did go back to *Twin Peaks* music and tried laying in some of the music so that David would have some reference of what it would be like if *Twin Peaks* music played in the sheriff's department. And it was his decision, but we hardly used anything from *Twin Peaks*. I remember that I was in the cutting room, and he was in the mixing room with Dean Hurley. I could hear through the walls, and David was playing with mixing the theme of *Twin Peaks* and that weird, slow-down version of "American Woman" when Bad Cooper pulls up at the cabin at night. I wasn't in there, so I don't know for sure, but what it sounded like to me was that he was trying to crash *Twin Peaks* into that particular sound. Now, this was very early in the going, right after he finished shooting. He was just experimenting with what it sounds like when you take the beautiful sound of *Twin Peaks* and you crash it into that growling animal music. It was fun to listen to. I am not sure where he was going with that, but it is consistent with his creative process.

Scott Ryan: Most of the music in *The Return* comes from bands in the Roadhouse. How did you decide where to put each song? Did you move them around?

Duwayne Dunham: David shot all the Roadhouse bands in one long day. There was a lot of music. When it came to the cutting room, David had given me a list of this song that goes with this scene, and it did change a little bit, but at least it was a starting point. Then, pretty late in the shoot, we hired an additional editor who had experience with cutting music videos. I told him to cut each of these songs as a music video, and then David, when he was finished, would have edited musical videos, not necessarily for the movie but as an additional asset. As I was editing, it wasn't determined that every episode would have a Roadhouse song in it, but most times we ended an episode in the Roadhouse. The movie was so big; it was eighteen hours, which is nine two-hour movies that we did in one year. He started shooting at the beginning of September, and the next September he had to deliver a locked picture. I used index cards for every scene, and there were hundreds of cards. It surrounded the editing room. David and I could look on the left and move down the wall and see the entire movie on the walls. All of the Roadhouse music was on the same-color card, so you could look around the room and see where the live music was placed on the cards.

Scott Ryan: There were a lot of conversations in the booths. Were those conversations tied to particular songs?

Duwayne Dunham: What I recall was that most of those performances were not tied to a scene in the movie. A few were, but we did move some of them around. It was quite an undertaking, especially for David.

Verse 3: Tim Hunter

I reached out to several directors from the series whom I had never interviewed before, but if I'm being honest, there was one whom I really, really wanted to talk to. That person was Tim Hunter. For so many years I have said that Episode 16 is the best non-Lynch directed episode of the series. And while it might be seen as too controversial to say, I would say Episode 16 is the second-best hour of the entire series, which means it tops some of Lynch's episodes. (Go ahead and ban me; it's been done before.) The wrap-up to the Laura Palmer mystery is a marvel. But Hunter's other hours are also incredible. They also are quite musical. Episode 16 is a marvel in the layering of musical cues. There are over thirty cues in Episode 16, and he debuts "The Culmination" during

Leland's death. In Episode 4, "Hank's Theme" debuts for the first time, as well as two of the three *Invitation to Love* tracks. Episode 28 is his final episode for the series, and in it he debuts all the Miss Twin Peaks contest songs. So I figured that he must have had some really great relationship with Angelo for his episodes to debut so many new tracks. Hey, this wasn't the first time I've been wrong.

Scott Ryan: So what was your process in scoring an episode?

Tim Hunter: I would go to work with Lori, and we'd play the cues. There were quite a lot of them. I had them on cassette, but I sent them all to Andreas Halskov [author of *TV Peaks: Twin Peaks and Modern Television Drama*]. He has my cassettes of all the cues. Within those confines, we could do anything we damn well wanted to with those cues. Lori was brilliant in remixing them.

Scott Ryan: You directed Episode 4, which is the first appearance of David Lynch as Gordon Cole. He talks to Cooper over the phone. Did you have anything to do with that casting?

Tim Hunter: I had nothing to do with it. He must have just announced it and looped it in. I knew David from the American Film Institute, and working with David and Mark was a treat. But I didn't have anything to do with him showing up in that part.

Scott Ryan: Tell me about directing Episode 16 and directing Ray Wise in all that water?

Tim Hunter: It was very powerful. We built a trench around the set with a plastic lining. It was like we had a moat around the entire set to catch the runoff. Ray was wonderful. I was pretty good at letting him wail. It was very intense for all of us. I remember we shot a lot of it fairly late at night, and we went into overtime. That is something you could never do in television today. But back then, Mark and David had to put up some of their own money if the show went over; nonetheless, they were very supportive of directors who needed extra time. They gave us all the freedom to get the scene shot. I think that scene in the police station went very late. Today, it is a business of bean counters, and you can't go an hour over. [See photo on next page.]

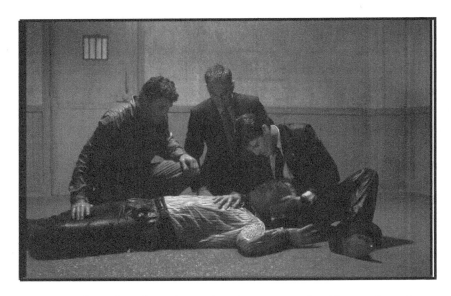

Scott Ryan: I have heard Lynch say that the mystery should never have been solved. But if it wasn't solved, your episode wouldn't exist. How do you feel about the idea that the mystery shouldn't have been solved?

Tim Hunter: I think we were all waiting for a solution. So when the script finally came out, it was a thrill to all of us. It was a thrill to land the episode. I always felt like David used me on *Twin Peaks* to direct an episode after one of his or before one of his. [Lynch directed Episode 14, Hunter Episode 16. Then, Hunter Episode 28, Lynch Episode 29.] He knew I was a clear storyteller, and if he went off into the flight of his wonderful imagination and it became a bit inscrutable, I could pull things back to Earth on the story threads. In the other direction, I could set up an episode for him, so he could come in after it with a fairly phantasmagorical season finale. I felt like I was a pretty good cleanup hitter or setup man for David on those episodes. That is just where I liked to be. We never knew what David was going to do. The other scripts came out in relative semblance of TV scheduling. I don't remember waiting for scripts to arrive. But nobody ever knew what David's episodes were. It was more in lines of "David is coming! What will it be? David is coming!"

Scott Ryan: How was it to work on the series as a director?

Tim Hunter: Mark and David did minimal stuff to my episodes. The episodes were released as the director's cut. They were very supportive of their directors.

They encouraged them to shoot it as they desired. I feel like in the second season they had some directors who were trying to use *Twin Peaks* as a springboard to show off various brands of directorial style that did not necessarily serve the show.

Scott Ryan: You had the Miss Twin Peaks contest in Episode 28. There is a lot of specific music in that episode. Did you request those tracks be written?

Tim Hunter: Maybe they came up with something for the beauty contest. I don't specifically remember. I never worked with Angelo. None of us ever worked with Angelo. Lori may have. He sent in the season's library of cues at the start of shooting. We just scored the show from the library. He never wrote any new cues for those specific episodes as they were being cut or finished off. Maybe he did for David Lynch, but basically he was completely resistant to writing anything new. Now we could do anything we wanted with the cues. That is where Lori was superb. She would reedit them; she would play them at different speeds and pitches. On occasion, we would play them backwards. It was a question of how creative we could get with the existing library. But Badalamenti never wrote any fresh cues for individual episodes as they were being shot and finished.

Scott Ryan: With the Miss Twin Peaks contest, how was it to direct the cast during that? I have heard stories that some of the cast weren't thrilled with that storyline.

Tim Hunter: I don't have any specific memories of the Miss Twin Peaks contest. You've made me curious to watch it again. This goes to your statement that people thought it was a mistake to solve the mystery. The reason people felt that way is because of the story in the second season. David didn't have much to do with those last ten episodes. It was all Harley Peyton and Bob Engels. The entire tenor of the show had changed. What was an enterprise that had been marked by an enormous amount of across-the-board enthusiasm for doing something so original, by the second season with the Windom Earle story, the cast and the other people there had grown quite disillusioned and had, by the time I did Episode 28, grown really cynical, Kyle MacLachlan especially. I went back to do that show because I loved them all so much and the spirit was so great. That spirit was just gone by the time I got back. Kyle was pacing around talking about "this piece of shit." They knew the show had gotten the ax from

ABC, and the quality had gone down.

When I waltzed back to do Episode 28, I was told by [producer] Gregg Fienberg that Frank Byers, the cameraman, had slowed down to the point where you could only get sixteen setups a day. That is just unheard of in television. It was not a two-camera shoot. To see if Frank had slowed down so precipitously, I went back to look at the production reports. There it was: he was only getting six to eight setups a morning, which is insane when you are shooting eight pages a day. I had to radically readapt the style of the whole thing to account for fewer camera setups. I decided to watch Yasujir Ozu's *Tokyo Story*, which I thought was as minimalist as one could get as far as camera setups. I have always thought of that episode as a Japanese-style *Falcon Crest*.

Scott Ryan: Wow, now I am excited to rewatch that episode with that in mind. When you were doing Episode 16, the reveal of Leland being the killer hadn't aired yet. So did the cast know that he did it? I have heard many of the cast say they never found out until it aired on television.

Tim Hunter: They would have known. They had the scripts. That is apocryphal. This was not a case where the script was being held from the cast to preserve the mystery. Once the script came out, everyone knew.

Scott Ryan: I always wondered how Lara Flynn Boyle wouldn't have known in your episode when she is dancing with Ray Wise and he pulls her in. Plus you have Bob in the mirror?

Tim Hunter: I remember that scene. I liked it. It was a creepy scene. I will tell you a reason why I am a good director, but David Lynch is a genius. When I had those scenes with Bob, I had him sneering or laughing in the mirror. You have Ray Wise looking in the mirror, but it's Bob. I pushed that nice Frank Silva way too hard to laugh evilly. When I looked at David's version of it, he would have him just have a little gesture or a small this or a small that, and it was so much more chilling than me pushing Frank to give a big fat leer on camera. I just thought, "That is why David's David." I am pretty good, but I am not David.

Scott Ryan: Well, your episodes are very strong and everybody loves them.

TRACK 6

"Sycamore Trees"

Fire Walk With Me, 1992

When *Twin Peaks* was canceled in May 1991, I was sure there would never be any more *Twin Peaks*, and I would never be happy again. Well, I was right about one of those things. If you have read my book *Fire Walk With Me: Your Laura Disappeared*, you know that the very day the show was canceled, the wheels started to turn for Lynch to create a film about the series. If you don't know who put that in motion, you better order a copy and find out. As for creating a score for the new project, it should all be so easy. With tons of music already created from the thirty hours of the series, there would be no need to record any new music to score the film. The production could save some money and just reuse the music from the Grammy-winning score that Angelo had already recorded. Good thing Lynch and Badalamenti are artists and not accountants.

The difference between the score for the series and the score for *FWWM* is the difference between high school and college. It's the difference between Chipotle and authentic Mexican food. It's the difference between Lara Flynn Boyle and Moira Kelly. (Hey, before you say that was uncalled for, in this case it is actually accurate, since Moira plays Donna in the movie, so settle down.) My point is, the film is a much more grown-up endeavor, and the music had to match. It

wasn't that the music from the series was less than; it's just that these newer compositions really just kicked the complexity up a notch. I mean there is a palpable difference between having a synth play a bass line and having Ron Carter or Buster Williams play the bass. This is an album that whenever it is over, I immediately want to hear it again. Of course, this record is missing almost thirty cues that are used in the film. While Lynch and Badalamenti did an admirable job of picking a fair representation of twelve cues from the film for the soundtrack, my main complaint is not having the mix of "The Pink Room" with "Blue Frank" or at least both complete tracks on the album back-to-back, but at least we finally did get "Blue Frank" released on the 2007 *Season Two* release. But that is just a small complaint. The truth is I could listen to this album every day, and if you ask my family, it probably seems like I do.

"Theme from Twin Peaks: Fire Walk With Me"

Badalamenti begins this new theme song with a throbbing synth sound that evokes fear, anxiety, and the pulse of a spinning ceiling fan. All this in only the first thirty seconds of music. A muted trumpet comes in, playing a hauntingly sexy melody. Later, at about 3:45 into the song, a wandering bass enters the orchestration to bring some jazz/rock feel to it. So we have sex from the trumpet, fear from the synth, and rock 'n' roll from the plucking bass. What do you get when you mix sex, fear, and rock 'n' roll? You get Laura Palmer, the star of the movie. The theme sets the tone for the entire film.

Scott Ryan: I think "Laura Palmer's Theme" is how the town sees Laura. The song that Angelo wrote that actually embodies who she was, in actuality, is "Theme from Fire Walk With Me." Do you remember that one?

Kinny Landrum: I don't remember that one. Can you play it for me? We did have a jazzish band for some of the *FWWM* stuff. We had trumpet player Jim Hynes and real upright bassist Buster Williams. Grady Tate played drums, and Vinnie Bell played guitar. Angelo had bought a certain kind of Korg that he liked at that point, and he did play some stuff on that session. But I don't remember what the difference was. We might have done that track live. There is some Rhodes underneath it. Probably Angelo is playing the Rhodes. It has some phasing on it as well. Let me see if I can figure out the chords.

Scott Ryan: Well, I have always suspected that it is derivative of the "Laura Palmer Theme," but I don't have the music, so I've never been sure.

Kinny Landrum: It is. Obviously.

[Kinny listens to the track from Spotify as he begins to simultaneously hit notes on his keyboard. He rewinds the song and tries again; in a few moments, he's got it, and he is playing along to the "Theme from FWWM." He is playing those beginning chords so effortlessly. These are chords that I have wanted to play my entire life.]

Kinny Landrum: It's just an augmented A flat chord. Maybe a C in the base. What's the next chord?

[He rewinds, and in less than thirty seconds he is playing the full "Theme from FWWM" on his keyboard, something I have never been able to do my entire life and never will because this sheet music has never been commercially released and I do not have the talent to play by ear. I am utterly in awe. The music he plays brings me back to the first moment of seeing *FWWM* on the big screen, August 28, 1992.]

Scott Ryan: So the Laura Palmer theme begins with an A flat and an E flat. This chord is ... ?

Kinny Landrum: This is an A flat and an E natural.

Scott Ryan: That is what I always hoped. That he would start with those notes. He just changed the E from a flat to a natural to represent life versus death, and then the trumpet comes in, which is an instrument that wakes you up and, boom, this track becomes all about being alive.

Kinny Landrum: Okay?!? [I can sense his skepticism.] If that's the way you hear it. [Laughs.]

[I take no offense in Kinny thinking my interpretation of the song is crazy. I get crazy looks all day, everyday.]

The theme in the film and on the album is an instrumental, but the song has lyrics, which Julee Cruise sings on her 1993 album, *The Voice of Love*. It is called "She Would Die for Love." It is impossible to hear the lyrics and not think about Laura Palmer when you hear words like

"She said she would go someday
She said she would go away
She told me she would die for love."

David Slusser: David and Angelo had written songs, not score, songs for *FWWM*. They would have Julee come in, and they'd take out the melody and have her sing the lyrics. David is very thrifty and smart. They would remove background parts and then have her sing after the song was recorded. David was very up on her. He said, "I found her. Nobody can believe how she sings." Julee was a bar singer and a belter, but he saw something in her. He asked her to sing like that.

"The Pine Float"

This is one of the tracks that I feel is solid proof of my claim that the songs used in the film are a tick more complex and original than those in the series. This instrumental sounds like no other song in the *Twin Peaks* canon. The melody is led by Al Regni on saxophone and moves along nicely with Buster Williams's acoustic bass. One of the reasons I love this song so much is that while it has the normal instrumentation of a *Twin Peaks* song, it is a completely new melody. This isn't a jazzed-up "Audrey's Prayer" or "Freshly Squeezed Version 34." It's a new song that belongs in the musical world that Badalamenti created, the usual band played it, and it swings like only this band can.

Kinny Landrum: The bass player I remember playing with on *FWWM* was Buster Williams. He was almost as famous as Ron Carter, who played bass on "Sycamore Trees." Buster was Ron's substitute in Miles Davis's band.

Al Regni: I never saw pictures from the film. The picture was added to the music. We never saw any filmstrips. I was probably called in about twenty times over the years to play for Angelo.

This cue scores the scene when Donna arrives at the Palmer house while Laura is getting ready to go out. Laura fixes herself a drink and makes Donna feel unwelcomed. That is how I feel every time I visit Mary Reber at the Palmer House. She puts this track on and gives me the stink eye until I leave. "Life is full of mysteries, Donna."

"Sycamore Trees"

And here we go. The song whose origin is surrounded by mystery. (Well, at least it always was a mystery to me.) There probably is nothing as classically *Twin Peaks* as the fact that "Sycamore Trees" is included on the *FWWM* soundtrack even though the song isn't in the movie. Nothing about *Twin Peaks* is ever logical. The song was in Episode 29. There are a few bars of the instrumental version of the song toward the end of the film, but this version is not in the film. As I said in the beginning of the book, this is the song I have been so curious about because how did they pull off getting this song on Episode 29 and having Little Jimmy Scott sing it when we have been told for so many years that David Lynch improvised the entire episode?

From the call sheets that Josh Eisenstadt owns, I have discovered that the scene in Episode 29 in which Jimmy sings was filmed on March 13, 1991. It was filmed on day six of an eight-day shoot. (For nerds like me, here is a fun fact I learned from studying these calls sheets: the final two scenes filmed for the original *Twin Peaks* were the Double R scene with Grace Zabriskie, Russ Tamblyn, Charlotte Stewart, and Don Davis and Cooper's bathroom scene with the "How's Annie?" moment. They were filmed on March 15, 1991.)

While it's nice to know that "Sycamore Trees" was filmed on March 13, we still don't know when Lynch and Badalamenti wrote it, or when they recorded it. And was it always written specifically for this scene? While we can't speak to the music, we can zero in on the lyrics. We do know that the lyrics are contained in a line of dialogue in an early draft of David Lynch's script *Ronnie Rocket*. Lynch was working on this draft right after completing *Eraserhead*, before he started work on *Elephant Man*. There's a scene in which a detective, frightened and lost on the street, overhears a girl say:

I got idea, man, you take me for a walk. [She moves closer to the guy.] Under the Sycamore trees. [Closer.] The dark trees that blow, baby. In the dark trees. I'll see you and you'll me. I'll see you in the branches that blow, in the breeze. I'll see you under the trees.

This line was cut from a later draft that he worked on in the eighties. But it must have stuck with him because it eventually became a song. As you may remember in his interview, David Slusser said Koko Taylor sang the song first, and it was supposed to be in *Wild at Heart*. I asked Kinny Landrum, who played keyboards on Koko's other track, "Up in Flames," what he remembered about "Sycamore Trees."

Kinny Landrum: Jimmy Scott came in with a three- or four-piece jazz band that was his own band that he had been playing with in New Jersey, including the vibes player Jay Hoggard. There is an organ on there; I may have played that. He brought his own band. I think it was a way to make him feel comfortable. It wouldn't have been part of another session.

Scott Ryan: David Slusser says Koko Taylor sang this song and she pronounced it "Sicky-Mo." Do you remember that?

Kinny Landrum: I don't remember "Sicky-Mo," but I remember hearing her sing the song. I take Slusser's word for that. I remember playing "Up in Flames." I probably did both songs, but I have also done "Sycamore Trees" with Jim James at one of David Lynch's Festival of Disruption events. I remember when we recorded with Jimmy Scott, he had a Japanese piano player named Ken-Ichi Shimazu. I did some synth over dubs, but I didn't play piano.

David Lynch confirms part of David Slusser's claim in the book *David Lynch Interviews* when he says, "Two songs were written, but only one, 'Up in Flames,' was used in the final cut. Koko Taylor, the blues singer from Chicago, is absolutely the one we needed. An entire story comes alive because of the sole fact that she sings a single word. It's terrific."

So Lynch claims two songs were considered, but he doesn't name the other one. We can't assume that it was "Trees" because it could have been any song that Badalamenti and Lynch wrote together, and Lynch also said they had forty to chose from. Also, how did Jimmy Scott even get involved? Think about it: Koko was such an interesting character that she would totally have fit in with the denizens of the Red Room. She has quite an otherworldly voice, so why not just get her to sing it for Episode 29—IF Lynch had her sing it six months earlier on *Wild at Heart?* When I was interviewing Julee Cruise's A&R man, Kevin Laffey, I figured there was no reason to ask him about "Sycamore Trees" because why would he know anything about it? Good thing I am obsessive and asked him anyway. He told me this story . . .

Kevin Laffey: I took David to the Cinegrill at the Hollywood Roosevelt Hotel on Hollywood Boulevard. There used to be a little jazz club on the first floor of the hotel. Jimmy Scott was there for a week, and David didn't know who he was. I played him a song from one of his albums. I just thought Jimmy Scott's otherworldly voice was right up David's alley. So, I was there the night that David went to the Cinegrill to see Jimmy Scott for the first time. The next thing you know, Jimmy Scott is in the studio recording "Sycamore Trees."

"Sycamore Trees" update: remember that Lori Eschler also went to see Jimmy Scott in the fall of 1990 at the same place. So Lynch discovered who Jimmy Scott was a few months before the filming on March 13. But when did they record the song? When did they first write the song? Was Lynch always going to use this in Episode 29 or did he and Angelo write it that week? How did the lyrics get from a line of dialogue in an unproduced script in the seventies to a scene in *Twin Peaks* in the nineties and then end up on a soundtrack to a movie in which the song isn't even played? Talk about keeping the mystery alive. More answers and questions to come as you read on. (Don't you dare skip ahead.)

"Don't Do Anything (I Wouldn't Do)"

As we know from Kinny Landrum, who said that he played the synth vibraphones on "Freshly Squeezed" and cheated by playing notes lower than the instrument is capable of, there is a difference between a synth and a real vibraphone. On this track from the film, Angelo brought in Jay Hoggard to play the actual vibraphones. This cue feels to me like an old-fashion detective theme song. When it plays, I feel like signposts should be flying over a driving car as Johnnie Farragut heads to New Orleans to bring Sailor and Lula home. This cue plays in Hap's diner. The song is so good it probably should have been used a few times; it is just that great a melody, and it has several movements that could have been broken out and used to score moments of the film. It also would be nice to have all the stems to this mix because everyone is playing an interesting part of the song. I would love to see how Lori would have broken this track apart and used sections to score scenes with other characters. I really love how sexual this tune is. I would submit this is hottest cue Badalamenti wrote for the world of *Twin Peaks*. It also doesn't connect to any other melody in the canon, and that is welcome. The piano by Bill Mays is so smooth, and the double bass by Rufus Reid makes the cue feel like it could be used to score a scene in the Black Lodge. This album is filled with songs that should be jazz standards but are relegated to a soundtrack that is all but forgotten outside of the fandom of Lynch.

"A Real Indication"

"A Real Indication" plays twice in *FWWM*, in back-to-back scenes. It plays when Laura charms Bobby outside the school and he walks away dancing and smiling, totally intoxicated by her. (Next time you watch this scene, notice how all the surrounding students start losing control of their bodies and wander around aimlessly. This is also what happens to me when I see Sheryl Lee smiling.) It plays again when Laura gets home and gets ready to make an entry in her secret diary only to discover that

Bob has ripped pages from her sanctum of inner thoughts. I love the idea that this song, with a vocal "rap" performance by Angelo Badalamenti, is the pop song that Laura and her high school friends are listening to. It makes those Madonna and Michael Jackson songs that my high school class of 1988 was listening to seem ordinary.

At first blush, it is easy to dismiss "Indication" as a bunch of nonsense lyrics, without meaning. It is the same dismissive attitude that filmgoers can bring to *Eraserhead*. "Eh, it doesn't mean anything. It is Lynch being weird for weird's sake." However, anyone willing to dig deeper into *Eraserhead* should be able to conclude that the film is about something more: the fear and horror that parenting can trigger. With "Indication," anyone who has ever had their heart broken should be able to recognize the narrator's pain. It is easy enough to hear Angelo's psychotic laugh, giggle at it, and leave it at that. In fact, as the mythology goes, when Lynch heard Angelo record his vocal in the studio, Lynch laughed so hard he gave himself a hernia. As someone who has had a hernia, I can tell you that operation is no laughing matter. Neither are the lyrics to this song. And I should know because just like Michael J. Anderson at the Cannes premiere of *FWWM*, I had the opportunity to perform this number at a *Twin Peaks* event.

I know this is going to come as a complete shock to you, but sometimes my mouth gets me in trouble. I know! Shocking! I was in Dallas as the Q&A host of a two-week-long David Lynch film fest. On one evening, the Lynch cover band Wisteria Lodge performed. I was talking with bandmates Dustin Carpenter and Lady K, and I asked if they would be performing "A Real Indication" that night. They said that they weren't because Lady K was the vocalist, and they didn't have anyone to perform the lyrics. I said, "You should have asked me. I would do it." Then they said, "Are you going to the Neon Dream event in Snoqualmie at Twede's Cafe in August 2023?" Actually, I was. Dugpa, who was so helpful to me in the research for this book, had interviewed me for a documentary that would play that weekend, and I was attending the event to see the finished project. The video was a tribute to *FWWM*, and he had asked me to provide context to Sheryl Lee's performance, since I had just completed my book *Your Laura Disappeared*. Before I knew it, Wisteria Lodge explained that they were going to be the house band for the event.

Twede's Cafe had recently raised enough money to buy a replica of the RR neon sign that was used in the series. [Photos above.] It was going to have an event where the light on the sign would be turned on. Then Wisteria Lodge would perform INSIDE the diner, and the band was asking me to perform "A Real Indication" at the event. What could I say besides yes?

I practiced the song everyday throughout the summer of 2023. This is a little secret I will let you in on: I know I look like I just wing my way through everything, but I actually work really hard to appear this careless. I knew I would be nervous to perform in front of people, but I also knew that if I practiced and got to the point where I could recite these lyrics anytime, with or without music, that I wouldn't be nervous. It was during that study of this song that I discovered how complex the story is. I knew I was not going to try to imitate how Angelo did it. I had to find my own way in. The key for me was when I stumbled on this lyric: like the night my girl went away gone off in a world filled with STUFF. He is in pain. His girl left him for a man with more wealth (his Dodge has rusted bullet holes). She found someone who could provide her with the "stuff" he couldn't. He is wondering if he will ever smile or laugh again. Will he ever feel happy? Girl has left me, not coming back again. He knows it. All the world is moving on. His shoes are there, as well as the street, the sewer, but he isn't sure he is gonna be happy again.

I changed him from an angry guy to a guy who was willing himself to look far enough into the future so that he would see himself smile and laugh again. But with this new idea, how would I perform the key part where Angelo laughs uncontrollably? People would expect that part, but I didn't want to do it the same way. I also knew that this sold-out crowd, filling every booth and barstool in Twede's Cafe, would be comprise of the most devout *Twin Peaks* fans. So I decided that during the uncontrollable laugh, I would start hooting like an owl and then say "That's a yes"—exactly as Ray Wise does during his confession as Leland Palmer in Episode 16. I wasn't sure if everyone would get that line, but I knew that Josh Eisenstadt was going to be in the crowd, and I knew he would get it. That was enough for me. This led me to the idea that at the end of the song, I would do a little coda where I would quote from the series or film. So I ended the performance with "I got a real indication, like a 'fish in the percolator,' of a laugh coming on. I got a real indication, 'I am the muffin,' of a laugh coming on." I did about five or six of these, and each one got a bigger reaction from the crowd. "I got a real indication, 'I'm Audrey Horne and I get what I want,' of a laugh coming on." I looked out at the crowd and saw George Griffith [To the side with Heidi the waitress] was in attendance. I said, "I got a real indication, of 'that fucker Ray,' of a laugh coming on." It was a great way to have an ending that tied the song to quotes from the series, and most importantly, it shifted the focus from me to favorite lines from the world of

Twin Peaks. Of all the things I thought I might do in life, performing a song written by David Lynch and Angelo Badalamenti in the actual RR diner, Twede's Cafe, in front of cast members and fans, in the town of Twin Peaks was never one of them. You can watch the performance on *The Blue Rose*'s YouTube channel. Just search for Neon Dream at Twede's/Real Indication. Angelo had already passed away by the time I performed this song, but I sure would have loved it if I could have emailed him the link. I am not so self-centered to think he would have enjoyed it, but I know I would have enjoyed knowing he saw it.

And while we are on the subject of those who left us too early, I dedicated my performance that night to Katie Edgin, and I wore her hat that said "Fight Like Katie." It was being broadcast over a live stream, and I asked people to donate to her medical bills. At that time, Katie was fighting her battle with breast cancer—a battle she has since lost, but she sure as hell didn't go down without a fight and without making so many people fall in love with her. I met Katie and her husband, Matt, in Dallas and became quick friends with them. She was getting chemo in the morning and then coming to the Lynch film fest at night. That is a true fan. She had a special bond with Sherilyn Fenn, who was at the event. [See photos below.] In fact, Sherilyn was part of Matt's proposal

of marriage to Katie. To watch Katie and Sherilyn talk and share during that weekend was a thing of beauty. Katie was a sweetheart, and she never once made anyone feel sorry for her, and we won't be sad when we think of her now. We will fight like Katie, we will attend events like Katie, and we will watch *Twin Peaks* like Katie. Matt is also a Golden Orb of a human being. He stood beside her, helped her always, made sure she had water and was rested, and traveled the country with her assisting in her goal of meeting everyone she could from the show. When you are a part of a fandom like *Twin Peaks*'s, you meet all kinds of people. Some are bullies, some are entitled, and some are Katie. I will always love her and miss her when I attend events, because I know she would have been there. Just a few days before she passed, I let her know that this book would be dedicated to her and that moving forward, all my books will have her name in them. Not sure if that is a curse or a blessing, but I guess after you dedicate singing "A Real Indication" to someone, it can't get much worse.

The experience of getting to perform one of my favorite tracks from my favorite *Twin Peaks* album is still one of my favorite things I got to do during my involvement with the series. I have been blurring the lines between a television show that I love and my career as a writer/performer, and I don't really know how any of this happened. I just know that when I am old and winding down life and I let my mind wander back to the gift that Wisteria Lodge, Dugpa, and Rachel and Max from Twede's gave me, I will always have a real indication of a laugh coming on.

"Questions in a World of Blue"

Julee Cruise: I did a song, a real tear-jerking song, in the Roadhouse, where I am wearing a blue formal. Why I would be wearing a blue formal in a biker roadhouse? I don't know why. I am in it and singing a beautiful song called "Questions in a World of Blue," which will be the next single off the next soundtrack (Julee Cruise interview on CBC, 1992).

Julee said that in an interview conducted between the Cannes premiere and the American release of *FWWM*. It is nice to hear that she had some hope that there would be a single from this album. If only we lived in a world where this film had been given a chance and MTV had played a video from this album. It was a short two years between "Falling" being in rotation and "Questions" not even being considered as a single. Unfortunately, the world had moved on from David Lynch; he was out of favor, and those feelings rolled over to the music.

The first time I heard this song, I felt like Lynch had just set words to "Audrey's Prayer." To me they have the same melody. I also feel there is a similar refrain in Angelo's original piece for *Wild at Heart* called "Dark Spanish Symphony." All three tracks certainly use the same series of notes, which became the lyrical section where Julee sings the words "Questions in a world of blue." I asked Lori Eschler what she thought about it.

Lori Eschler: Can you play both of them for me? I don't think they are the same. It is a variation. Angelo could just sit down and play something and that was it, and he would nail it. They have similar moods, but they are different melodies.

Whether they are the same melody or not, this is a pivotal moment in the film for Laura Palmer. She is just trying to go along with her life and not think about the consequences, but the Log Lady challenges her to try to extinguish the fire burning within her. Then she walks into the Roadhouse, and the singer is singing directly to her. "How can a heart that's filled with love start to cry?" Thanks to a combination of the music, the lighting, and Sheryl Lee's acting, "Questions" is an amazing moment in the film for Julee Cruise. This is certainly one of my all-time favorite Julee performances.

Julee Cruise: I was in a play, and I had to be flown out and record it. You don't miss Broadway, but it was David Lynch, so they let me. On that song, I did the harmonies as a French horn quartet. This one, I had to be real careful with my vowels. I used a European accent when I sang it.

"The Pink Room"
Doug Murray (sound engineer for *FWWM*): The music is so perfect for that scene. It is transportive. It makes you feel like you are really there in that amazing surreal, hypersexualized, transactional environment with all these weird people. It's very surreal, and with the tripping aspect, you kind of get into Donna's head (*A Sound Effect Podcast*, 2022).

Murray said that about the Pink Room music. This track plays at the second bar that Laura and Donna visit on their night out. This scene is a cacophony of noise and music. Only one of the songs that play during this scene was released on the soundtrack. "The Pink Room" was placed on this CD, and "Blue Frank" was released on the *Season Two Music and More* soundtrack. But it is the combination of these two tracks that is truly amazing. Neither track was written by Angelo. Both were written by David Lynch and the band Fox Bat Strategy. "The Pink Room" plays for the first 4:30 of the scene and then fades to "Blue Frank" just as you see the blue light on the wall of the bar. Several fans didn't even realize these were two different songs. That is all due to the wonderful fade Lori Eschler accomplished when editing the music for this scene.

Scott Ryan: Your editing and fade between the two songs are beautiful.

Lori Eschler: I remember lining those two pieces up, and they were recorded by the same people at the same session, so they had the same production value. I had to line up the songs at the segueway, and David Lynch did the segue way. He was mixing.

Scott Ryan: Were there other sounds in there that help go from A to B?

Lori Eschler: Yeah, there usually were. Kind of the easy-go-to effect was reverb. One of the things of music editing is that the tracks are produced, but then you are recreating them again. You are essentially adding more to them, and some composers just lose their mind when you mess with their music. David had so much fun. Every day was a lot of work, but there was a lot of joy and a lot of play. Dave Alvin was playing guitar. Lynch worked with Alvin on the songs, and Alvin wanted a piece of it as a writer. I remember a few phone calls about that.

"The Black Dog Runs at Night"

"The Black Dog Runs at Night" isn't just the title, but it is the entire lyric to the song. It is repeated over and over. I know the credits say that Angelo does the vocals, but I like to think they are voiced by Randy from *Dumbland*. This is a great song to put on during Halloween when the trick or treaters are coming. The cat growls and the screams come at random intervals and are jump inducing.

This track came from a project called *Thought Gang* that Lynch and Badalamenti created. They created a collection of songs during the early nineties, which were finally released to the world in 2018. The songs that were used in *Twin Peaks* were "A Real Indication," "The Black Dog Runs at Night," "One Dog Bark," "Frank 2000," "Summer Night Noise," and "Headless Chicken"(see *The Return* chapter for these final three placements). I preordered the vinyl as soon as I heard it was coming out. I was so excited to have more songs in the vein of the ones I knew. Honestly, the rest of the album isn't what I hoped for. They are mostly noise tracks at best. There really isn't any element of storytelling like in "Indication" and nothing as creepy as "Black Dog." This is most likely why it took over twenty years for it to come out. I feel like now is a great time to say that "Woodcutters from Fiery Ships" has been released on vinyl, but "Theme from Fire Walk With Me (Saxophone Version)" has not.

This track plays a few times in the film, but is most famous for scoring the scene in which Leland leaves the Blue Diamond motel after backing out of Teresa Banks's idea of partying with a few girls. That can happen when one of the girls turns out to be your daughter. As Leland leaves the area outside Teresa's room, Mrs. Tremond's grandson leaps out from behind a bush and starts jumping around while "The Black Dog" plays. Is this where I admit that I went to this exact filming location and leaped out of the same bush and jumped around the parking lot doing the same thing? I bet I'm not the only one who's done it. Although I may be the only one who filmed it and put it in a documentary.

"Best Friends"

Scott Ryan: Tell me about writing "Best Friends" with David Lynch for *FWWM*.

David Slusser: David was up in Northern California doing postproduction on *FWWM*, and as usual, he didn't have enough music because he and Angelo only wrote a couple of songs, and that doesn't score a whole movie. So he was following his normal modus operandi, which is "I finally got the picture done, and I need some music here." Like he had in *Wild at Heart*, he contacted me. I was his music editor on *Wild at Heart*. He called me up and said, "Slusser, can you get a band together ... TOMORROW?" [Laughs.] I said, "You bet. I'll be there.

Studio C, Fantasy Records." I got there, and David didn't show us footage, but he would just describe what he wanted, and I would interpret that to the band. So that's what is called the "cocomposer" [Laughs.]—David waving his hands while I am playing, while *I'm* improvising. That's the cocomposing. With "Best Friends," he just described how these two girls are talking, and they are best friends. He wanted something to capture that relationship—it was very intimate. So everything I played was too big. He kept saying "smaller, and simpler." So I was just playing minimal chord movement and as quiet as I could. I tried to play very relaxed. The entire time I'm playing, he is making gestures saying "quiet." I've got the band behind me, but they are playing one or two notes. That is the collaboration. I like the tune. It is very touching. It came right out of David Lynch trying to telepath to me right into my head—him being with me as I played while he moved his shoulders and arms, conducting in his own way.

Slusser nailed composing this track. The piano part he plays is beautiful, but it is actually Myles Boisen's guitar that I love in this song. It sounds so much like the music of *FWWM*. And I know that you could be saying, "Scott, it *is* from *FWWM*." But once you learn the story of how Lynch didn't have any music for this scene and Slusser just made it up in the studio, you realize it is so perfect not just for the scene, but for the rest of the movie as well. At first blush, it really feels like an Angelo piece. The song plays twice in scenes focusing on Donna and Laura's relationship. It plays first when Laura asks Donna if she is her best friend and again after their Pink Room escapade. It truly is a beautiful piece of music that represents their friendship. They had a complicated relationship, as teenagers often do. That is what makes those relationships so important. The peaceful, soothing piano represents the calming influence that Donna and the Hayward house have provided for Laura.

"Moving through Time"

This song has a repeated refrain performed on the vibes by Jay Hoggard that goes up and down, over and over for the entire 6:41 runtime. We feel like we're stuck in a time loop. While that spins obsessively, an acoustic bass played with a bow moves back and forth, hypnotizing the listener. On top of the arrangement a piano plays in the upper range, improvising a path anywhere it wants to go, like a dreamer walking aimlessly through the clouds. "Moving Through Time" scores the scene in which Laura visits Bobby and goes through the motions of kissing him. She doesn't want his love or affection; she wants his drugs, to accelerate her death. She perfunctorily says goodnight to her mother for the last time and dresses in lingerie for her meeting with Leo. She plans to meet up with James, but she is just going through the motions, simply moving through time. The repetitive song stops when Laura stands and sees the angel from the photo on the wall disappear before her eyes. Her destiny is set. As she wrote in her diary, according to Episode 16, "Tonight is the night that I die."

"Montage from Twin Peaks: Girl Talk / Birds in Hell / Laura Palmer's Theme / Falling"

This medley starts with a song called "Girl Talk," used during the scene in which Donna and Laura talk about whether Mike could write a poem (answer: no). Then the track fades to a portion of "Birds in Hell" for 1:18 before melding into a piano-only version of "Laura Palmer's Theme" and finally "Falling." (Thank goodness. What if we actually had a release that didn't have these same songs on it?) See the chapter on the *Twin Peaks Archive* for more on the complete versions of "Girl Talk" and "Birds in Hell."

"The Voice of Love"

"The Voice of Love" ends the film. Laura has died. She sits in the Red Room with Agent Cooper standing by her side, his hand on her shoulder. She finally sees her angel, and Laura weeps with joy. Badalamenti was tasked with the assignment of writing a piece of music that would wash away all the pain that Laura and the audience had experienced. Only three minutes elapse between the end of the brutal train car death scene and the first notes of "The Voice of Love." Badalamenti had to transport the audience from the deep despair of graphic violence to the highest peaks of sweet forgiveness, love, and peace. Laura, and the viewer, have suffered for over ninety minutes. I can't imagine sitting down and writing a piece of music that could wash away that amount of pain. Lucky for all of you, Lynch tasked Badalamenti with it and not me. He came back with a gorgeous piece of music. Badalamenti says on the Criterion Blu-ray bonus feature, "David says, 'Angelo, there is gonna be an angel and

tears coming out of [Laura's] eyes. As she is crying, I want everyone who sees it to cry and feel for her because everyone loves her.'"

"The Voice of Love" has no lyrics in the film, but a year later, Julee Cruise sang the song with lyrics written by Lynch to end her second album, of the same name. Lynch wrote, "Listen. Listen. I hear the voice of love." Julee sings it so sweetly. Laura gets her angel; we get our voice of love. The song and her second album didn't have the splash that Cruise's *Floating into the Night* had. Cruise was still sore about it when I interviewed her in 2018. She told me, "I think a lot of people forgot about that entire song. Warner Bros. acted like they didn't know us. I am glad it is out there because it didn't get any attention before. People got sick of *Twin Peaks* real fast, and they didn't support it."

Some may still not have heard Cruise's interpretation of the song because it has never been released on an official *Twin Peaks* soundtrack. I implore you to seek it out. It caps Laura's journey so powerfully. I believe the music for this track is the pinnacle of melodies Badalamenti created. The combination of his keyboards, Sheryl Lee's acting, the journey of Laura Palmer, and Julee Cruise's performance combine to become the true voices of love.

TRACK 7

"Just You"

Twin Peaks: Season Two Music and More, 2007

Once I had settled into the belief that I would never own the music from *Twin Peaks* that I truly loved, the announcement of this CD found its way to me via the internet. It was 2007, and there was nothing doing in the world of *Twin Peaks*. And in the middle of this vast emptiness we got my all-time favorite *Twin Peaks* soundtrack. The tracks on this release, from both the series and *FWWM*, are beyond iconic. This collection is filled with themes that should have been released earlier. Hands down, this is the vinyl I listen to the most. In the next chapter, you will read my full interview with Dean Hurley, in which he talks more about this album, but here is a snippet from that discussion explaining how this 2007 CD came to be at all.

Dean Hurley: David put together the *More* music thing, and my head was a little crooked on that. It's like the age-old thing where you are trying to cram all kinds of different themes into a CD, and it doesn't really feel like the Season 2 compilation that it is supposed to be. It is a weird format to try to put into an album.

Scott Ryan: Sure, because it has some *FWWM* cues on it.

Dean Hurley: It had like the barbershop quartet song on it. Like who really needed that?

Scott Ryan: Hey, I needed that.

Dean Hurley: You did?

Scott Ryan: And "Hook Rug Dance."

Dean Hurley: It had some good stuff, but when you have the website format, then this stuff doesn't have to be sequenced well, and it could be more fragmented. You could group songs together, like I did when we finally did the *Twin Peaks Archive*, where it was more than one track. You had an alternative format that could slowly drip out and create traffic to come back to the website and create a small monetary stream. That was the evolution of how all the music started to get released. Once I started work on this CD, I was just going through the archives to find stuff.

So, for all intents and purposes, *Season Two Music and More* is the birth of the *Twin Peaks Archive* releases. The songs on this CD are basically the greatest hits of the series that had never been released, although it sure didn't have my "Norwegians" on it, did it? (Don't talk to me about codes; we will get there.) The album was released on CD in 2007 [CD Cover below] because the vinyl rebirth hadn't started up yet. But on an April Record Store Day in 2019, it was finally released on vinyl. The cover of the vinyl album is horrific. Anytime you try to do the Red Room floor with white and black, instead of brownish red and tan, you lose me, but the book inside has some wonderful pictures. There are full-page photos of Audrey, Cooper, Catherine Martell, the Log Lady, Laura, Harry, Donna, James, and others. The

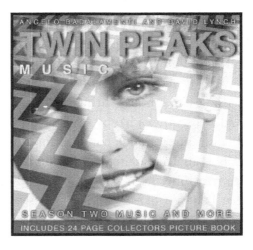

book is worth the price of admission right there. The vinyls are colored blue and green, which is a nice touch.

As with all items in the modern *Twin Peaks* era, the name of this release is just awful. It begins a craze of no one really knowing what to call anything. The official name of this is (I think) *Twin Peaks: Season Two Music and More*. That sure rolls off the tongue, doesn't it? I am just going to refer to this album as *Season Two* from here on out. And good luck comparing the name on the CD to the one on the vinyl. Crappy name and cover aside, I am so happy with the song selection on this release. If you have never purchased this album, I strongly suggest you do. If you can still find one.

"Love Theme Intro"

This is a medley of themes to bring us into the musical world of *Twin Peaks*. It is like a minitribute to Lori Eschler, showing how seamlessly the cues from the series can blend from one track to the other. The songs that are part of this intro are "Solo Percussion 1," "DOTM Solo Sax," and "Laura Palmer's Theme" (strings and synth mixing to just solo piano). This track is just a teaser and doesn't offer a lot of substance, but it gets you in the mood. It is a short piece, at just over two minutes.

"Shelly"

This song captures the sexuality and charm of Shelly Johnson. It is the rare song in which the melody is carried by an acoustic bass. This song's bass melody is highly connected to "Audrey's Prayer" and "Questions in a World of Blue." Just like Season 1 had connections to "Freshly Squeezed" and "DOTDM," Season 2 is all about musical connections to "Audrey's Prayer." Exactly halfway through the cue, the countermelody comes in using vibraphones, bringing a nice fifties feel to it. One can picture Mädchen Amick's happy smile as Shelly talks with Norma in the diner. This is a rare carefree composition among the songs from the series; it really is an accurate representation of Shelly. It is light and fresh despite a hint at inner sadness. The main feeling the listener is left with is love. That is how I like to think of Shelly Johnson. She had a lot to be sad about, but she still found her way forward with love.

"New Shoes"

With this track, we get to see why Grady Tate is so important to the music created for Season 2. His drumbeat here is completely different from those he uses in the first season. Tate creates all the feelings of a mystery as his brushes dance across his drum set. This song is strongly associated with the scene in which Bobby is trying to figure out why Leo is so worried about his shoes. This musical cue was sort of used in the early section of Season 2, similar to how "Sneaky Audrey" was used in Season 1. It was played when characters besides Audrey were up to no good. I'm looking at you, Bobby. You were gonna blackmail Ben Horne? Great idea.

"High School Swing"

One idea I have always had when it comes to the music in Season 2 is the worse the storyline, the better the music. (I will continue to point out examples in the *TPA* chapter.) Nadine thinking she is in high school isn't the best plot of the second season, but this cue has all the feelings of classic Angelo mixed with Lynch's beloved fifties feel. Vinnie Bell gets to take the lead on this one when the melody is plucked out on an electric guitar. It also has triplets played on piano by Kinny Landrum. Landrum mentioned that he didn't want to add them to "Falling," but it looks like he found a place for them here. This cue scores much of Nadine's belief that she is a high schooler once again. Love the cue, hate the storyline.

"Hayward Boogie"

This is an uptempo piano boogie performed by a teenage Alicia Witt in Episode 8 as well as on the album. Alicia Witt was introduced as the third Hayward sister, Gersten, as the Palmers attend a dinner party at the Hayward house. While the song is not played during dinner, it does play during the end credits for Episode 8. It is credited to Angelo Badalamenti, but as I have learned in working on this project, not all the credits are accurate. So when I interviewed Alicia Witt for Issue #14 of *The Blue Rose*, I asked her about it.

Scott Ryan: During the end credits, you play what's called "The Hayward Boogie." And I was curious if you're playing an Angelo Badalamenti piece?

Alicia Witt: That is not by Angelo. That is a piece that's actually called "Pinetop's Boogie Woogie." That was recorded in the 1930s by an artist that went by Pinetop Smith. He recorded it on the piano. And then there was also a big band version that Tommy Dorsey recorded.

Scott Ryan: And you just knew it?

Alicia Witt: I just knew it. I had been playing piano in restaurants from the time I was ten. In addition to the classical pieces I was competing with, I knew some jazz and swing that I would play as background music while people were eating. So I had quite a big repertoire of unusual things for a fourteen-year-old.

Scott Ryan: On the Season Two vinyl it is called "The Hayward Boogie." So it's interesting that that is not even the correct title. We're rewriting *Twin Peaks* history.

Alicia Witt: I have known before that it was called "The Hayward Boogie" on the *Twin Peaks* release. I wonder if David just didn't realize that it was an existing song. I don't know. I know for a fact that my family and I were as surprised as everyone else to see me play during the end credits. We watched it live in Worcester, Massachusetts. We were back home by that point. David had heard me playing it in between setups. I was just playing around with a few different things on the piano in between takes, and he asked me to keep on playing it and rolled the cameras. I did not have any idea that he was planning to use it.

Scott Ryan: It's one of only three times that the original end credits doesn't have the "Laura Palmer Theme," so it stands out for that as well.

Alicia Witt: Yeah, that's really special, isn't it? It means a lot to me.

"Blue Frank"

When I was a little kid, I heard a story on the radio that said someone was imprisoned in a basement and their torturer played Kate Smith's recording of "God Bless America" over and over. The person, of course, went insane. Ever since I heard that tale, I have always wondered what song I would want to hear on repeat. I mean, no matter what it would be, you'd go nuts. That being said, I am pretty sure I would pick "Blue Frank." I feel like I could listen to this forever. I do know that every time it is over, I wanna hear it again. So if Melanie Mullen is thinking of locking me up in her basement to torture me for eternity, I hope she picks this song to play.

I have said many times that I don't want a box set release with songs we already own, and this song has been released on CD and vinyl, still, I would really love if we could get a release on vinyl that has the actual mix from *FWWM* that contains the medley of "The Pink Room" and "Blue Frank" as it plays in the film. Even though each song has been released separately, it would be great to have them as one long piece of music. I think the way Lori Eschler put these two songs together is pure genius and should be preserved.

The main difference between "The Pink Room" and "Blue Frank" is the difference between *getting* drunk and *being* drunk. The songs switch when Donna and Laura are no longer trying to consume alcohol and drugs; those drugs are now settling in. "The Pink Room" is brash; "Blue Frank" is so much more of a sway, a meditation. Donna is under the spell of outside influences while "Blue Frank" plays. This song is written and performed by Fox Bat Strategy and is listed as being cowritten with Lynch in the same way that David Slusser and Lynch cowrote "Best Friends." The band is also cast as itself in the film.

"Audrey's Prayer"

This cue is the most critical building block of the score in Season 2 of *Twin Peaks*. If "Laura Palmer's Theme" is the main theme of Season 1, this is the main one of the second season. The tune made its debut in the premiere of Season 2, and while the track does play during Audrey's prayer to Agent Cooper, the track actually plays for the first time in one of the most famous scenes in all of *Twin Peaks*. When Major Briggs finds his son at the Double R diner, he takes a moment to share a vision with Bobby. This wonderfully written scene by Mark Frost and acted to perfection by Don Davis and Dana Ashbrook is scored by the new track for the season. One might conjecture a world where this song could have been called "Garland's Vision," but the song was used again in the same episode when Audrey tries to send Cooper a psychic message to save her at One Eyed Jacks, and that is the scene from which the cue received its name. [See photo below.]

Throughout the season this track is used as the new love theme for the series. There are shades of this melody in "Questions in a World of Blue" and "Shelly." There must have been something contained within this melody that Angelo liked so much that he kept coming back to it. I have never heard of anyone asking him about the composition of this

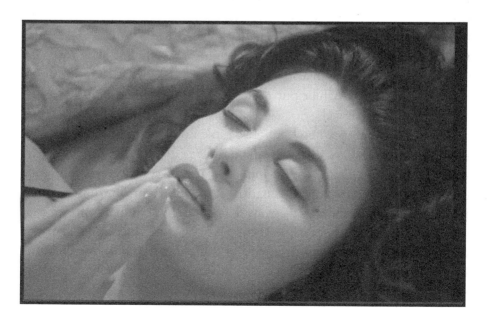

song; it was on the list of tracks I wanted to speak with him about when I was trying to track him down for an interview, but that interview never happened. We will never know for sure when and why this became the theme for Season 2, but it sure is one of the most beautiful tracks written for the series. We were lucky that it was finally released on this amazing collection of songs.

"I'm Hurt Bad"

This is such an interesting track to end up on a Season 2 release because this song played most famously in the Pilot episode. This is the track that Bobby plays on the jukebox when he leaves the diner, subtly offering to give Shelly a ride home. (Why is she getting off work at like 7:00 a.m.? I have no idea either.) The track actually made its debut in the Lynch world in *Industrial Symphony No. 1*. But there are no lyrics, so it wasn't like Julee Cruise sang it. It played during that live stage show when a six-foot deer ran around on stage, you know, like that happens. The track begins with all kinds of wailing saxophone sounds and a lot of noise. Then it settles into a more pulsating sound. The differences between the two movements of this track are as different as the White and Black Lodges. It really is a strange composition. But just like "Audrey's Dance," this is a song that exists in the town of Twin Peaks and the surrounding area. In Episode 18, James plays this same track on a jukebox at Wallies Hide-Out.

Maybe this is like playing "Stand By Your Man" by Tammy Wynette on a jukebox in the Pacific Northwest? I'd pay fifty cents to hear this song at a truck stop. I know I'd flip if I ever heard it playing at Twede's Cafe. This version actually has a bit of "James and Evelyn" and a *TPA* track called "Trail Mix," which basically is just a work session for the band that became the bass line for "James and Evelyn." I have no idea why these tracks moved together, but they were used during these episodes, so maybe this was the mix that they used last, so it ended up on the soundtrack.

"Cop Beat"

It is hard to complain about getting to hear anything new, but it is strange that while there were hundreds of tracks to release, "Cop Beat" was placed on this *Season Two* release, because the track never plays in the series or film. It is an uptempo drum-based song that certainly could have been used to score a scene in the sheriff's station but never was. I would rather it be released than for us to never hear it. I am assuming it was written for the series and just never made it in. Too bad it wasn't slipped into *The Return*, but there was so much woosh to get in, there probably wasn't room. So we get one new track among all the greatest hits.

"Harold's Theme"

Harold Smith is one of my favorite characters introduced in Season 2. On second thought, he IS my favorite character introduced in Season 2. Harold holds so many secrets for so many townsfolk. We learn only that he holds Laura's and Donna's, but I am more than certain others have made their way to Harold's door, only to find a trusting albeit lonely soul. Angelo wrote songs for *Twin Peaks*, and then the themes were doled out depending on where the directors felt they should go. Because of this, Harold's theme is often played for Josie's story as well. This has never bothered me because both of these characters speak, breathe, and eat in the secrets of others. I think they are mirror images of each other. Josie preys on secrets, and Harold survives on them.

Musically, this song's climbing bass notes evoke "Falling"; they're not exactly the same, but close. I have always felt this cue has a similar left hand, but the melody is nothing like that of "Falling." There is a longing in this track that immediately makes me think of the tender actor who brought Harold Smith to life. Lenny Von Dolen, who passed away in 2022, was also such a kind and thoughtful person. He took the role of Harold seriously and loved his time on the series. He told me, "I made a pretty extensive backstory for Harold. Harley Peyton, one of the writers, was really helpful. We talked for a very long time about Harold. It was really one of the first times I've ever felt, certainly in television, where I really got to be a part of the fleshing out of a character." Lenny also played the sheriff in the *Psych* episode that spoofs *Twin Peaks*, and he did a great job in it. I love that he got such a major part and got to reunite with Sheryl Lee.

"Barbershop"

What kind of peaceful music would you want to hear after being visited by a giant the night before? I think a harmonizing barbershop quartet might be just the tonic. That is exactly what scores Cooper and Albert's breakfast in Episode 9. The episode begins with Albert and Cooper recapping Jacques Renault's stomach contents and Albert even making a joke. The quiet tones of the quartet are never mentioned by Coop and Albert, nor anyone else. This begins a season-long running gag of groups of compatriots staying at the Great Northern. Maybe this quartet was just in town to perform for a night at the Roadhouse. We will never know, but I sure loved this scene the first time I saw it and am delighted the cue was included on this release. It was strange musical moments like this that made *Twin Peaks* what it was.

For fun, I sent Harley Peyton a Facebook message to ask him if he wrote the quartet into the scene or if Lynch added it. This is what he said, "Funny. I have no idea. It sounds like something Diane Keaton would have added to her episode, but this is apparently the second episode in Season 2. In which case, it was likely Mark or David, or both."

Lori Eschler: David would have put the barbershop in there, and there was no prerecorded music. They were just posed there in the background, and I think Angelo just recorded some a cappella singers, sort of harmonizing. And that scene is so funny, the way that they are blocked. [See photo below.] It's just the composition of that shot that cracks me up. The colors are such a contrast to the dialogue. It obviously was only used the one time, although that's a missed opportunity. I dropped the ball. I could have woven that in somewhere.

"Night Bells"

This is one of the very few instrumental tracks recorded in LA, on the same day as "Just You." It is interesting that the first time it is used is in Episode 8, yet the cue was recorded while Episode 9 was being filmed, so it is fresh off the press. This guitar sound is something that Lynch obviously has affection for, because Lynch recorded a different song with Dean Hurley and himself on guitars called "The Night Bell with Lightning" on Lynch's solo album *Crazy Clown Time*. The solo song has a similar feel to "Night Bells," as well as a similar name. It is that fifties guitar sound that Lynch obviously associates with the words "Night Bells" even though he didn't feel that way in July 1990, when this was recorded.

Dean Hurley: When we released the *Season Two Music and More* compilation, there was that "Night Bells" song that was used in the series. It was titled "Abstract Mood." When it came time to release that CD, David's like, "Let's call this one 'Night Bells.'"

That explains why in the *TPA* there are versions of this guitar sound called "Abstract Mood." I have always felt like this guitar sound is the sonic representation of a question mark. It really sounds like the guitar has no idea what is going on, and neither do some of the characters in *Twin Peaks*.

"Just You"

On July 31, 1990, the "Just You" scene was shot. [See photo on the next page.] Episode 9 is such a classic episode, and I think one of Lynch's most proficient directing jobs on the series. Every scene in Episode 9 has a "Lynchian" tidbit. The idea that three kids would sing a song together is so perfectly juvenile. It is innocent, but like all things in the series, it turns dark. I love this song, and I find nothing silly about it at all. If you love the work of Angelo and David, then you love this song. It has all the ingredients of a classic Lynch-Badalamenti composition.

Scott Ryan: What can you tell me about "Just You," the song that James Marshall and Sheryl Lee and Lara Flynn Boyle sing?

Lori Eschler: They did a prerecord of the song, and I'm not sure where they did it. I don't remember who the picture editor was, but when it needed to be edited in the picture department, they would bring me in for the edits and I would say, "Cut from here to here and you'll be fine." I would just look over their shoulder and make sure they were making the right musical edits. Some of the editors were musical and others weren't.

In Episode 16, Donna was almost killed when she brought a tape of this song to Leland for him to give to Maddy. The song is cause for a murder to some and kitschy to others, but to me, it is just as critical as "The World Spins." I asked Sheryl Lee once about recording this track, and for the life of me I couldn't find her answer in any of my notes. I guess I'll have to just ask her another time. I have heard Fuck You, Tammy! sing this song, and it is a delight.

Devery Doleman: So way back in the day, we had our former guitar player David Andreana sing "Just You," and Julie Rozansky and I would harmonize, and people loved it, especially because David has a great voice, but is pretty shy as a singer. Then we ended up actually singing it WITH James Marshall at Eraserhood. I really love Sheryl Lee's and Lara Flynn Boyle's backups, and I think it works with James's vocal. They don't sound like professionally trained singers, but then I like that quality in a lot of actors who sing. It can be so much more moving than a performance that is pitch-perfect and glossy.

"Drug Deal Blues"

In Episode 9, Shelly and Bobby are sitting in Bobby's car, and "Audrey's Dance" is playing on the radio. Bobby tells Shelly to change the station, and she tunes the dial around to find "Drug Deal Blues" playing on a different station. They listen and jam to the music before going on to hatch some hare-brained idea to nurse Leo Johnson back to health for insurance money. Like Leo would have had an insurance plan. I guess life in the eighties really was different. I do like this callback to the scene in Episode 1 in which Audrey is dancing in Ben Horne's office to "Audrey's Dance" on the radio. The idea that the music we are hearing is also playing on the radio in the town of Twin Peaks is fun. But "Drug Deal Blues" wasn't around in Season 1. It was recorded the same day as "Just You," in Los Angeles. When Dean Hurley was searching through the archive he found that the original title of this track was "Just You: Blues Version." I suspect the final title wasn't bestowed on the cue until *FWWM*. This is the musical cue used when Laura and Bobby meet Deputy Cliff in the woods. In the series, it usually is associated with Bobby and Shelly. I think this song really rocks and is a perfect cue for when Laura is high and obnoxious with Bobby in the woods.

"Audrey"

Grady Tate is key to this song. He gets your nerves going immediately with a relentless drumbeat. Then we get a sample of "Sneaky Audrey" on this version. I will write more about this cue in the *TPA* chapter, but I will say this particular mix was never used in the series. One of the things I like about "Audrey" versus "Sneaky Audrey" is that "Audrey" is used to score the scene where Audrey goes to Cooper to tell him about her father; there is nothing sneaky left in her behavior. She is turning her own father in to the police for the murder of Laura Palmer. This music cue never lets up on the beating drums. The end of the song has a dramatic flair, and we have one of the most energetic cues of Season 2. Amazingly, it was used only this one time. I guess it was because Audrey was never placed in danger again for the rest of the season.

"Josie and Truman"

This beautiful saxophone melody conveys the sadness intertwined with Truman's love for Josie. This cue just screams out Season 2 to me. When you hear this tune, you can see the opening of Episode 25, when Truman is devastated at losing Josie. The vibraphones also exude such sadness. This is a song that makes you want to pour another shot of whiskey as you wonder what the point of love is if it doesn't work out? Well, Harry, maybe don't fall for a sex worker from another country who was sent over to sleep with half the town and shoot your best friend. But what do I know?

This track swells and builds on the circular melody that is a precursor to the more evolved music of *FWWM*. This seems like a growth in Angelo's skills as a songwriter and is connective tissue between the music of the series and songs like "Don't Do Anything I Wouldn't Do" from *FWWM*. This really feels like a jazz or blues number. It is truly one of the most emotional cues in the entire series, one that listeners shouldn't sleep on.

"Hook Rug Dance"

This was a song that I wanted to own so badly. When this finally came out, I made it my ringtone for years. This scene is such a perfect moment in *Twin Peaks*. In Episode 15, Jerry is visiting Ben in jail, where the bunk beds remind him of Louise Dombrowski and the flashlight dance she performed for them as teenagers. The music kicks in, and we get a classic *Twin Peaks* scene of music, images, and character development. This is by far one of my favorite cues and moments in the series. The fifties feel works to perfection because it is the kind of music that was popular when Ben and Jerry were teens. I was curious if Caleb Deschenel, who directed this episode, requested a new piece of music or if this was a track that came in with the new Season 2 music.

Lori Eschler: That was all Angelo. I think Caleb was one of the directors who thought Angelo needed to do more scoring to picture and more new cues. So he asked for it. I loved working with Caleb, but he was tempestuous about that. He was so passionate.

I have more to say about this track, but strangely I am waiting for the chapters on *The Return* to really dig into this one. I bet that should keep you guessing why I am waiting, but if you want to read more, you will have to wait till my discussion about "Green Onions."

This cue was used again in Duwayne Dunham's Episode 25 in what I have dubbed "The Happy Scene." The scene contains this cue along with the Milford wedding song. "Hook Rug Dance" evokes pure happiness for me. I love when music does that. I hope that as I grow older, and my memories of real life become more confused with scenes from television, I believe Louise danced this flashlight dance for Steven Miller and me. I am certain we too would wonder what we have become.

"Packards' Vibration"

This is another critical song from Season 2, especially the final five or so episodes. The pulsating beat always seemed to me to be Josie's beating heart. Josie knew her time was coming, so much so she could hear the final beats of her heart as the walls started to close in around her. This is another track whose lack of a release always seemed criminal to me. It was used so much during the Andrew Packard/Josie/Thomas Eckhardt scenes. It also is kind of the "Sneaky Audrey" of the later half of Season 2. It plays whenever mischief is in the air. Kinny Landrum did play on this track. When I played it for him, he said, "I like this. Yes, it's me. I love the French horns from my Emulator II."

"Half Heart"

The half-heart necklace was found in the Pilot episode and is so associated with Laura Palmer that Lynch put her inside of one for the poster image of *FWWM*. It was James who gave Laura the necklace, and in a really nice continuity touch, Lynch uses "Half Heart" twice, both times when James and Laura are together in the film. The first time is when Laura meets James in what looks like a locker room at school. The song scores the classic line of dialogue: "Gone like a turkey in the corn." (What would a Ryan Thanksgiving be without this line?) The second time is when Laura and James meet in the woods on the night she dies. Here, Laura whispers, "Let's get lost together," before she slaps him and says his Laura disappeared. This second version has more of an echoed saxophone, which plays the beautiful melody expressing the pain of this song.

The song itself has the typical *Twin Peaks* bass, but it does not bounce along. It's played slowly, exuding more sensuality. The saxophone says longing; you can feel it calling out for something. The cue is very lonely for a love theme. We know that James and Laura's love affair is doomed, so it fits perfectly. The song's title, plus the fact that it scores all of the James/Laura kissing scenes while being heartbreakingly sad, makes it perfect for the two of them. Problem is this song was not used specifically for just the two of them.

"Half Heart" was also used for a blip in the short-lived ABC series *On the Air*, which was hardly on the air at all. Seven episodes were produced; only three aired. Created by Frost/Lynch, it ran from June 20 to July 4, 1992. When the *Twin Peaks Archive* came out is when I discovered this song is the love theme from *On the Air*. It is used in the Pilot episode for a very short time. Lynch released three other versions of the song, which are not as full of longing as the one used in *FWWM*, but they are most certainly the same song. Since *FWWM* was released the same year that *On the Air* was broadcast, it made sense to use this track, since no one really saw the short-lived series. This song was too good for just one use.

Lori Eschler: That was definitely written for *FWWM*, and then I apparently used it for *On the Air*. It happened so fast, and it was during a very busy time. I just don't remember using it again.

"Laura's Dark Boogie"
Lori Eschler: There are a lot of things going on in this song. I'm hearing the ponticello violins. I'm hearing that the track with the strings is Angelo's *Twin Peaks* music, and it sounds to me like Al Regni was improvising based on direction from Angelo and David. As I recall, it was a solo track that we used to sort of weave in and out.

Scott Ryan: So was "Laura's Dark Boogie" created by David and you, or was it something someone gave you?

Lori Eschler: Oh, no! It was created on the final mixing stage. I mean David worked in conjunction with Angelo in designing all of this. So Angelo provided these tracks, and then we affected some of them. We would take things from

Angelo and sometimes reverse them and half speed them. We changed things a lot on the fly as we were working.

Al Regni: It all runs together because I did a lot of dates with Angelo. You got to give credit to Lori Eschler. She edited a lot of that stuff together. I would do something and I wouldn't remember what it was the next day, and she would put it together, and it would really sound nice. In the eighties and nineties I was really busy. You do these things, and then you forget about them. It was a job.

Angelo Badalamenti: I think the scoring is more darkness than horror. We imply power through the darkness of the music. At least that is what the intention was (Cannes press conference).

All these comments sum up "Laura's Dark Boogie." It is the kind of track that just couldn't be created live in a studio. It is mixed and remixed with music going frontward and backward. There are many dream sequences in the canon of *Twin Peaks*—hell, for all we know the entire thing is a dream—but Laura's dream in *FWWM* will always be my favorite, and this piece is a perfect score to accompany it. Laura is totally unsettled as she enters the piece of art given to her by Mrs. Tremond and her grandson. As Laura slowly enters doorway after doorway, going deeper and deeper into the Black Lodge, the bass moves around illogically. Compare this bass line to that in "The Dance of the Dream Man," which logically moves down the scale and then back up (albeit, as Kinny Landrum pointed out, using different notes for its ascent compared with its descent.) But in "Laura's Dark Boogie," there are no patterns. There is no fun melody to hum. The cello, which is a reverse playback, moves around unsettlingly. There is no part of this song that Laura can grab a hold of. Al Regni's saxophone isn't playing a fun, finger-snapping tune. It hits notes from all over the scale. This is a nightmare for Laura, and the song matches it perfectly. This is truly an avant-garde musical moment in the film and on the soundtrack. Again, why is it on a Season 2 release? Who can say? But I sure am thankful it was at least released.

"Dark Mood Woods / The Red Room"

These tracks are a medley of two of the major themes from the final

episode of the original series. "Dark Mood Woods" debuted in Episode 29 if you go by what is released on DVD or streaming. But if you are an original fan, you should know that "Dark Mood Woods" was actually first heard on the extended recap that played before Episode 24 when the series originally played on ABC. The back half of Season 2 was aired so haphazardly by ABC that episodes played in a row only during a single three-week period. Following the continuing story was not an easy task for casual TV viewers. *Twin Peaks* was pulled for six weeks before it returned to the air. ABC decided to have Agent Cooper do an extended recap to remind viewers what was going on. [See photo above that is from my VHS tape from 1991.] Lynch used "Dark Mood Woods" to score this recap. I remember loving the track immediately. It just *is* the sound of *Twin Peaks*. There is no better description of this track. This was one of the few songs Lynch used again in *FWWM* and *The Return*, which means it was used in every iteration of *Twin Peaks*. It is because "Dark Mood Woods" is possibly the best piece of music in the entire series at capturing the feeling of "these old woods."

The version released here was mixed together with the cue "The Red Room" from Episode 29 when Cooper is walking from room to room in the Black Lodge. It is similar to "Laura's Dark Boogie" in that the bass isn't logical and the song is more a collection of sounds than a melody. It has a bit more "Abstract Mood" guitar in it than "Laura's Dark Boogie," which has very little of the Vinnie Bell guitar sound. This cue is over eight minutes long, and it can immediately make a listener feel that they have left this world and entered another. "The Red Room" section of this song has repeating ponticello violins, which is created by moving the bow on the strings close to the bridge to make a sawing noise that feels just right for the Red Room. "The sounds of sawing wood." Then Lori put the ponticello violins in reverse and slowed the speed down. It has that abstract mood with echo on the guitar, and again, there is no melody to hum. Cooper's first trip to the Red Room has a snappy tune, but this trip isn't fun, and the arrangement lets us know that he is deeper in the Black Lodge than when we first saw him there. (I know what we saw first was twenty-five years later, but remember: time doesn't exist in the Black Lodge, so don't bust my chops on that. I am talking about the order in which viewers see it.)

The song returns to a bit of "Dark Mood Woods" at the end, just as it does in Episode 29. In the *Twin Peaks Archive* releases, a few versions of "Dark Mood Woods" are released, as well as a separate version of "The Red Room." Look for Dean Hurley to explain how "Dark Mood Woods" was recorded in that chapter.

"Love Theme Farewell"

When you listen to this vinyl in order, you seamlessly go from the creepiness of "Dark Mood Woods" to the sound of wind blowing, and then the synth of "Laura Palmer's Theme" comes in while the wind is still blowing. The album ends with one more reprise of the famous theme. The crescendo section played on a super synthy sound that isn't all that pleasant to listen to. If you leave the vinyl to play to the end, it eventually goes to a hidden track. This is where one can hear "It was Laura." While that is where it is placed now, it was different on the CD. But maybe nobody today even knows about hidden tracks on CDs or vinyls?

Hi, kids, I am an old guy, here to explain hidden tracks, which were a big thing for CDs back in the nineties. Hell, I probably need to explain CDs as well, but I don't have that kind of time. There was a stretch of time when artists thought it would be fun to include hidden tracks at the end of a CD to see if you would let the CD play through to the end. Many bands did this, and it was a fun little thing. Lynch did something even sneakier. He had the CD open with the hidden track. The only way you could get to it is by putting the CD in your player and holding down reverse and letting go of the button once you get there to let the track play. It was really kind of annoying. When this album was released on Record Store Day, the hidden stuff was at the end, but the vinyl had a bunch of grooves in it, so it takes a really long time for the needle to reach the track. So what was this treat that we waited for?

Well, first you get some good old-fashioned ominous whooshes, and then Lynch gives you a code that back in the CD days would unlock my beloved "The Norwegians" on DavidLynch.com, enabling you to download the song. (Really, we couldn't just release the minute-and-a-half song for old Scott? Nope, I would have to wait till the *Archives*, and I'm still waiting for the vinyl release.)

But the main hidden track was the piano part that Alicia Witt played while Harriet Hayward recited the poem she wrote for the Hayward/Palmer dinner party. (Man, would I hate to have dinner at their house. Just what every adult wants to do when they visit their friends' house: hear their kid read a poem while another of their kids plays the piano in a pink tutu and a crown. "Sorry Doc, can't make it tonight; I need to go to the Nelsons' house and look at the Shrinky Dinks Mike made. I hear he made one look like the Steeplejacks's mascot.")

When I interviewed Alicia Witt, she didn't even know about this track, so I played it for her. Here is the interaction:

Scott Ryan: Did you write the song that you're playing when Harriet Hayward reads her poem about Laura Palmer? It's very airy, and it seems like it's live on the set. Do you remember?

Alicia Witt: Yes, I do remember now that you've asked me. I forgot about that tune. That was a Mendelssohn piece that I knew. David had asked me to just play something. I think I offered him a couple of options that I thought might work out of my classical repertoire. And he chose that one.

Scott Ryan: You do play "Opus 14" while they eat dinner. I am talking about when Harriet reads her poem. And the reason I'm asking is it seems like something you would have just written right on the spot. It has recently been released as a hidden track on the vinyl of Season Two.

Alicia Witt: REALLY?

Scott Ryan: I don't know if you wrote it or not? Do you want to hear it?

Alicia Witt: Yes.

[I quickly play her Harriet's poem "It Was Laura," scored by Alicia's ethereal piano.]

Alicia Witt: I forgot about that until just now. You know, I believe that you're right. I think I made that up.

Scott Ryan: It seems to me like you did, but I just want to give you the credit for that. Let's get it out there: that is your first composition, and you played it on television.

Alicia Witt: It technically would be. If it's true that I wrote it, then Lynch is *not only* responsible for my first acting job that qualified me for SAG [Screen Actors Guild], but this means he's also responsible for the first music credit I've ever had, although I wasn't a member of ASCAP [American Society of Composers, Authors and Publishers] yet and though it was uncredited. That is cool. If you wouldn't mind, can you send me that recording? I'd love to listen more closely. I truly do believe it was something I just made up.

Always happy to help spread the music of *Twin Peaks*, even when it's to the people who actually created it. Alicia Witt is a wonderful piano player, and I like that her first song is in Episode 8 for the world to hear forever.

TRACK 8

"I'm Hurt Bad"

Dean Hurley

"So it is best to start at the beginning." - The Archivist.

This is how Mark Frost began his 2016 book, *Secret History of Twin Peaks*. The book contains all that Major Briggs, aka the Archivist, compiled about the history of the town. With all due respect to the major, and I hope he doesn't slap the cigarette out of my mouth for saying this, there was an archivist of much great importance who rose to internet prominence five years before. The true archivist of *Twin Peaks* is Dean Hurley. He was the one who opened the music vault nearly ten years after it was sealed when *FWWM* was completed. It was Dean who climbed down the twenty-nine flights of stairs to the underground lair that Lynch had built under the *Lost Highway* house. Here is where Lynch stores the music tracks from *Twin Peaks*; the deleted torture scene of Grace Zabriskie from *Wild at Heart*; the fourth season of *Twin Peaks*, shot during *The Return*; the six episodes filmed in 1991 that followed Episode 29 but ABC refused to air; the musical version of *FWWM* with Sheryl Lee and Lara Flynn Boyle singing Julee Cruise numbers; and, of course, the plot to *Inland Empire*.

Okay, maybe that was too much. Possibly, all he really had to do was search through some DAT tapes or hard drives and listen to some cassette tapes, but in 2011, it was hard to find a cassette player and DATs were long out of style. But still, Dean Hurley took it upon himself, as you will learn in this interview, to do more than just find one or two tracks and shlep them up on the internet. He curated all 212 music cues that were created for the television series and the feature film. None of these tracks were released on the three soundtrack versions that had come out up to that point in time. NONE. Do you have any idea how rare it is for any *Twin Peaks* release to be all new? It pretty much doesn't exist. All of these tracks will be covered in the next chapter.

In this chapter, you will learn how Dean went about curating these cues, how he bundled them into themes, wrote wonderful prose about where each track was found, and discovered moments that were long forgotten. I set up a phone call with Dean, who has worked with Lynch on music and recording projects since 2005. The first major Lynch project that he worked on was *Inland Empire*. I realized immediately that we weren't going to be able to cover everything in one talk. What follows in this chapter is our discussion about the *Twin Peaks Archive* releases. Annie Blackburn once said, "I know just enough of the words to realize how little I understand." I could relate with her in talking with Dean. He has a ton of recording knowledge, and like Albert, he doesn't suffer fools gladly, and fools with badges never. Dean and I had never met before, and I love that at the beginning of our interview, he was less than thrilled with my idea for this book.

Scott Ryan: I want to do a book where I cover every *Twin Peaks* cue that there is. All the stuff that you released through the *Twin Peaks Archive*.

Dean Hurley: Okay. Um. Just a quick reaction to that. "Cover every cue?" It sounds like a grandiose statement, but is that really gonna be an interesting read?

Scott Ryan: Well, I haven't been interested in if anyone's been interested in what I write about in a long time. [Laughs.] I think people will be interested.

Dean Hurley: If I saw a book on the shelf and it was called *Always Music in the Air: The Music of Twin Peaks*, I would want to read a lot of the story and nuances to how everything evolved. It is such a magical element. Like a great magic trick, you see it and you are desperate to know how the illusion was manufactured and how it came into existence. To me it's more interesting to be taken through the history of how this stuff happened, as opposed to reading a dissertation on reading about every single cue. You know what I mean?

Scott Ryan: I do understand, and I'm a personable writer. My books are not academic. I'll send you my *FWWM* and *Lost Highway* books and you'll see.

Dean Hurley: This is a good starting point because the reason I have such an adverse reaction to "every single cue" is because there are a shitload of them.

Scott Ryan: There are 212 in the *Twin Peaks Archive* alone plus the other albums. It comes in at around 290 total.

Dean Hurley: The one thing that was illuminating for me when I was doing the *Archive* releases—obviously there was a lot of fervor and thirst for those releases—but what I saw happening was a lot of mindset that was birthed out of a completist attitude. "What about this? What about that?" It's like "Guys, that is not a cue." There is a lot of sound in *Twin Peaks*. I'll give one example. In *FWWM*, Laura is outside of the Roadhouse. There is a distant train horn sound. Did I release that?

Scott Ryan: Yes.

Dean Hurley: See, I was on the fence because it's not a fucking cue. Yes, it's a magical sound. But it's not a cue. It's not music from *Twin Peaks*. It is almost like a ravishing of the carcass. I just couldn't get into that mentality. In a weird way, it was like this overarching force riding what was the architecture of the show. I was more interested in learning. *Oh, this isn't a music cue.* It made me feel something, but it's a train sound effect from a library and has been used before in other shows and it's not unique to Twin Peaks. It made it more magical to me, but other people kind of seemed to fixate on a different dimension that I couldn't understand outside of obsession.

Scott Ryan: Well, this entire project started because I pitched to Sabrina the idea that she and I should work on a vinyl box set of some of the best of the *Twin Peaks* music that has never been released on vinyl.

Dean Hurley: It's a complicated scenario. I get the passion because I have wanted things to be released before. It is kind of difficult. There are more powers involved, and decisions get made that are beyond your control, and you lose it.

Scott Ryan: But there are some beautiful cues that have been passed over on the releases, and Lord knows every *Twin Peaks* release has the same version of "Falling," and I don't need another version of "Falling."

Dean Hurley: For sure. I am a hundred percent with you.

Scott Ryan: That is why what you did from behind the scenes to get the *Twin Peaks Archive* released really mattered to me. You didn't know it, but you did all of that, every part of it . . . for Scott Ryan.

Dean Hurley: I was doing it for you, Scott. I had a little photo of you on my desktop. That is a good place to start. When I was doing it, it was a weird side angle of my job's responsibilities that I invented. It was one of the most rewarding, and whenever I see someone out in the wild, like at an event, that is usually what they bring up—those *Twin Peaks Archives*. It is something that I knew if I was a fan and I heard about it, I would be all over it.

Scott Ryan: So how did these archive releases come to be?

Dean Hurley: It started with David saying in 2006 or 2007, "We've got the soundtrack to *Inland Empire*." David was working with Eric Bassett in Irvine. Eric had been doing the *Eraserhead* 2000 and *Dumbland* DVD releases. David was very headstrong about releasing these DVDs himself. David had this idea that he wanted to have a record label. I knew it would fall on me. My main job was recording stuff and making new stuff with David. Now he wants to throw all this new stuff on me, and it sounded like a ton of work. So we were releasing the *Inland Empire* CD and then the *More Music from Twin Peaks* CD, which was the first attempt at that. He wanted to do more. So I said, "Let's build a destination website." We put up a few things, but it became obvious to me that in order for the website to become a destination, you'd have to always have new content being put up at the website. Knowing we needed a stream of stuff to keep it populated, I was like, *Well, there is a lot of Twin Peaks stuff that hasn't been released*. This was the perfect format.

Scott Ryan: What is the archive? Where is it? Is it all a hard drive?

Dean Hurley: A lot of this stuff lived, primarily, on DAT tapes. There were also some things on cassette, some on quarter-inch reel-to-reel masters. There was some stuff on twenty-four-tracks. In the way the show was scored, and for this book, you have to interview Lori Eschler. The thing to get into your head about the music was that the

show was unique in the fact that music was not written to picture in a classic composure way. There were incidents of that, but it was more like spackling to connect things. "Oh, we don't have anything for this. Angelo has to write this cue." But by and large, the show was music edited to create its soundtrack. That is very interesting because it doesn't happen a lot. This always fascinated me about *Twin Peaks*. It was the evolution of David Lynch working with music for his projects. I feel like it was a little bit of a return to *Eraserhead*. There is no composer on *Eraserhead*. It is scored with ambient noises and Fats Waller stock music. It is an editorial soundtrack. The score is created by editing. But when you move to *Elephant Man, Dune, Blue Velvet*, those were traditionally scored, where a composer was hired and they wrote to picture. Some of that was slightly frustrating for David. I think that is very important to understand the success of the music in *Twin Peaks*. A lot of those songs were David and Angelo writing stuff before the show was even shot, going in and recording stuff at Art's Excalibur studio and basically making songs like "Fast Cool Jazz," then breaking down that song into stems and components to make cues. They built a DAT library. I forget how many DATs there were. You had hundreds upon hundreds of musical configurations. You had solo clarinet, clarinet, and sax, just percussion, bass, and drums. So many combinations that it developed a library of material to piece together episodes in the editing room. Angelo was not sitting in the studio compositing music for every episode.

Scott Ryan: And you had access to these songs that Angelo wrote. Were there just a ton of tapes of him writing?

Dean Hurley: A lot of the info that was interesting to me which illuminates how something came to be was that David and Angelo had these work tapes. Much like Agent Cooper walking around with his dictaphone recording his every thought, they had a dictaphone, and they recorded their work. You can hear them talking out certain ideas. It wasn't just music from *Twin Peaks*. They were always making music. It could be a song idea where David would bring in lyrics and Angelo would put music to it. They did that even though *Mulholland Drive*.

Scott Ryan: Was it hard to convert these files to a WAV or MP3? What formats did you release?

Dean Hurley: We were using Top Spin to power the David Lynch website. I would upload a WAV file, and then the site would generate either an MP3 or whatever version the end user wanted. Just like on iTunes, where you can select the output. I only uploaded WAV files.

Scott Ryan: Were there any tracks that never came out?

Dean Hurley: I think there were a few executive decisions I made to not release stuff, like maybe the Civil War stuff. Did I release that? I would be depressed if someone put those on vinyl.

Scott Ryan: Many of the Civil War cues are released on MP3, but not vinyl. But there are so many great tracks that are not on vinyl, like the Great Northern piano tracks or the Double R music tracks.

Dean Hurley: If a record company owned all these tunes and wanted to beat a dead horse and get profits, they could just rearrange the songs and release them. They could do a *Night at the Roadhouse* version with rearranged tracks. And a *Quirky Cup of Coffee* vinyl on Record Store Day. You could play musical chairs with these tracks forever.

Scott Ryan: But here is what I think is funny. Every five years Twin Peaks Productions releases the Pilot of *Twin Peaks* again on a new format with one new bonus feature and charges double the price, but they don't do releases with the music that has never come out, and at least this would be a release that has something no one owned before. It's like saying the *Missing Pieces* was a waste of a release for *FWWM*. I'd much rather buy something I don't already own and give them money for that instead of buying the same thing again. I have bought the Pilot of *Twin Peaks* at least five more times than it ever played on network television, and that is beating a dead horse. I mean how many times does the original soundtrack from Season 1 need to come out?

Dean Hurley: That's because it is easy to do. They don't have to get David's permission. Warner Bros. owns it. You could license that and do a printing of that just like Sacred Bones did with *Floating into the Night*. It gets into the messiness of that stuff with the contracts with Worldvision.

Scott Ryan: Well, there is no record executive in the world that is worried about "Attack of the Pine Weasel" coming out. No one remembers that cue.

Dean Hurley: Well, it will only be on their radar if someone is making money on it.

Scott Ryan: Doesn't that say it all. To me, "Attack of the Pine Weasel" matters just as much as "Laura Palmer's Theme." The music really matters to me. I can tell it matters to you. You can say whatever you want, but you searched for these tracks, wrote about them, then searched for the best MP3 cover for each track release. You cared about it, and that means a lot to me. [Four examples below.]

Dean Hurley: Some of those pictures came from slide scans that were found in David's storage unit. Occasionally, I would find some. I did try to do my best because I hate when people botch up opportunities, and my memory of releasing those things is that I tried to get them out once a week. I remember writing some of the paragraphs for the releases at night, after work, because I wanted them to be good, but it was satisfying, and I did feel like I was putting myself in the fan seat and wanted to do it justice. It was a huge reverie, and it is the holy grail of David's output in terms of music. A couple years back, I got a call about doing that with *Blue Velvet* because they did record a bunch of pick-ups, and that came out somewhere. It was a multidisk set of the bonuses. I knew where some of it was because I had gone through the library looking for *Twin Peaks* stuff. I tried to find a theme, pick an image, and write some stuff, so it seemed like a magical nugget. If you just presented it all, it is so overwhelming because it's the same thing again and again, and you run the risk of it ruining the magic.

Scott Ryan: I don't want to ruin any of the magic. I want to support the art and be sure we get the stories correct of what actually happened.

Dean Hurley: I remember when I first started working for David, I heard people say—and it seemed like the general consensus online, which was wrong—people said, "The second season of *Twin Peaks* went a little south because David was focusing on *Wild at Heart.*" That timeline makes no sense. But that's how people rationalized it.

Scott Ryan: That comes from Martha Nochimson. I did ask her about it on my podcast, but she won't back down from it. Even though a director does not edit his film six months after it debuts.

Dean Hurley: It's really funny. And that's what I'm trying to avoid here because that stuff enters canon, and then it takes so much effort, beyond somebody like yourself, who's doing their own research, to change the narrative.

TRACK 9

"Black Lodge Rumble"

Twin Peaks Archive, 2011-2012

On March 10, 2011, Dean Hurley uploaded two tracks to DavidLynch.com and started the sixteen-month odyssey of sharing 212 unreleased *Twin Peaks* musical cues with fans who never thought this would happen. I was one of those fans. I wish I could remember how I discovered these releases. I really didn't have any friends who were into the series at that time of my life. It was before I was hosting *The Red Room Podcast*, before I ever attended an event, before I had written a word about the series. It was back when my love for the show was not something that was widely known in my circle. Now there isn't a day that goes by that I don't interact with someone who loves the series as much as I do, and some days that person is actually *from* the show. (By the way, you owe me a call, George.) The Scott of 2011 wouldn't have believed any of what was about to happen to him over the next decade. He didn't believe the show would ever come back, he didn't ever conceptualize meeting Sheryl Lee, and he certainly never thought he would own the "Great Northern Piano Tune #2."

Despite the fact that I was living a Courtenay-free life, I do know that I bought the first release, "Deer Meadow Shuffle," before the second track was released. I guess I always think I am not really one of those crazy *Twin Peaks* fans, but who are we kidding? I was probably going to the Dugpa forum every week and checking out DavidLynch.com all the time to see if they were finally going to release *The Missing Pieces* or who knows what else. Either way, I was there from the beginning, and I bought all 212 tracks. Most of the tracks were only ninety-nine cents, and the bundles were either $2.99 or $3.99. They were honestly priced fairly for how rare they were.

Each week, I would refresh DavidLynch.com to see when the next track would be released like I was Nadine waiting for a Dr. Amp episode to drop. Each was an amazing revelation. For years, I had hoped to get a few songs, but the idea of getting ALL the songs was as unthinkable as Lucy cheating on Andy with a men's clothing salesman at Horne's department store. But both happened. It was as crazy an idea as bringing *Twin Peaks* back to television and actually having it be about *Twin Peaks*. (One more just to be obnoxious). It would be as crazy as releasing the first season of *Twin Peaks* five different times, but not officially releasing *On the Air* or *Hotel Room* even once. While those things would never happen, the music releases actually did. It took from March 10, 2011, to July 12, 2012, to release over nine and a half hours of music. The original run of *Twin Peaks* lasted from April 8, 1990, to June 10, 1991 (fourteen months). *The Return* aired from May 23 to September 4, 2017 (five months). That means the longest active release of content from the world of *Twin Peaks* is the sixteen months of the *Twin Peaks Archive* (*TPA*). I love the fact that it is the music that had the longest release period, because Angelo's music has always been my favorite part of the *Twin Peaks* world.

Listed below are all the songs officially released through the *TPA*. Every time a new track or bundle was released, Dean Hurley wrote a post explaining the release. I have transcribed Hurley's posts and placed them with the date of the release. Then I give my two cents for each track. I use different fonts for Dean and for me so you will know who said what. These cues have remained on my hard drive, with the original MP3 picture icons, some of which, as Dean Hurley explained in the previous chapter, were of slides that had never been released. I have included some of them as thumbnails. The icon helps point listeners in the right direction as to where the track played on screen. A picture of Laura and James in the woods on a version of the "Laura Palmer Theme" or a slide of Lana sitting in the sheriff's station with Hawk on "Lana's Theme" makes it easier to remember where the cue was used. I have also included some of the ones that Ross Dudle created. He added the title to the picture so you will be able to know which are his. (Wow. I just realized that there is a chance young people don't know what MP3s are. "Is this thing on?" Am I really that old? I was just getting used to explaining what CDs were. Now I have to explain downloading MP3s to your desktop and loading them onto your iPod?) These songs did not stream on DavidLynch.com. They were available for download. You purchased them and then you owned the MP3 that was actually downloaded to your computer. They didn't disappear like *Invitation to Love* in the second season of *Twin Peaks*. You truly possessed them forever. Streaming is more like Bob: you just borrow their souls for a moment and then move on. The website also gave you the choice of downloading the higher-quality Apple Lossless version or a compressed MP3 version. (I downloaded both versions of course.)

If these tracks would have been available to stream in 2011, they would all be gone today because DavidLynch.com just redirects you to his YouTube channel. Luckily, in 2011 streaming wasn't as widespread, because if it had been, all of this music would be gone like a turkey in the corn because none of the *TPA* tracks are available on any legitimate streaming platform, and they were never released on hard copy on any official release—CD or vinyl. I am sure it is mind-blowing to music streamers today, all you Spotify and Apple Music people, why anyone would buy music on the internet. I can tell you that if I hadn't done that, I wouldn't have each track in the high-res form of the Apple Loss versions, and this book wouldn't be possible. This is why I so badly want a vinyl box set release of the important tracks. So as we go through the tracks, I will single out those that I believe should be placed on an official release. (They will be marked as **Scott Pick**.) I end this chapter suggesting what I believe should be released as the *Twin Peaks Archive Box Set*. I am not suggesting that all the tracks be released, because as you will discover while you read along, many of these tracks are just the same version of the same song with different instruments. While I am thankful they were released on MP3, I am not sure that anyone needs to listen to nineteen versions of the "Laura Palmer Theme" in a row. So I have whittled the songs down to what could be a manageable four-disc vinyl. (Are you listening, Warner Bros. Records? I am doing your work for you.) Also, we all know they wouldn't name it something that made sense or was short. So they would call it something like *Limited Edition of the Collection of Tracks That Are Collected Here as One and More*, or something convoluted. Just release them.

When these tracks were available for download, all were credited as written by David Lynch and Angelo Badalamenti. I have tried to credit the actual writer. No doubt Lynch influenced some of these tracks, but as Lynch admitted himself in *David Lynch Interviews*, "Angelo Badalamenti is the one who introduced me to the world of music. He writes the music and I do the words." Since all of the tracks released are instrumentals, Angelo gets the writing credit. On the few songs that were written by either David Slusser or David Lynch, I have notated that fact. The music business is renowned for dubious copyright claims, and in many cases, it has been impossible to figure out who actually wrote each of these songs. When in doubt, I'm gonna go with the classically trained maestro, Angelo Badalamenti. So if I don't mention it specifically, Angelo Badalamenti wrote the cue.

March 10, 2011

Hurley wrote: "Deer Meadow Shuffle" is the first installment in the *Twin Peaks Archive*, an 'open album' intended for unveiling rare and unreleased music from both the television series as well as the feature film prequel, *Twin Peaks: Fire Walk With Me.*

"Deer Meadow Shuffle" should be instantly recognized as the sparse jazz instrumental that stitches together several early *FWWM* scenes. This particular version of the cue comes off the original DAT mix and features the full 5 min 20 sec of the track (:40 sec longer than what is featured in the film). When downloading "Deer Meadow Shuffle," you will also receive the 'film version' of the track, taken directly from the mag mix of the film's music stem. The 'film version' is an interesting blend of several other layered cues (a common occurrence for most of the musical sequence in the film and series), woven throughout the track almost like sound design to push/pull onscreen moments. Side-by-side, these two tracks allow for unique insight into the evolution of music from studio to screen.

1. "Deer Meadow Shuffle"

This is the straight studio version of this track. So this is exactly what they recorded in the studio and doesn't include the sounds that Lynch

and Lori Eschler added to match the picture. This lets you hear the David Slusser tune just as written. This was a great first release because no one had ever heard this version before. Plus this track plays for much of the front part of *FWWM*, so it sent up quite a flare for those of us who had been wanting this track since
1992. Also remember that when this was released, this cue hadn't yet been officially released, so it was extremely rare.

2. "Deer Meadow Shuffle (film version)"

"Deer Meadow Shuffle" could have served as the theme song for a television show that Sheriff Cable and Deputy Cliff starred in. It would have been canceled quicker than ABC pulled the plug on *On the Air*, but it would have had a hip theme song. There is a sense of danger at the outset that lets you know this is not the studio version. This track plays for most of Chet Desmond's first scenes in *FWWM*. It has a samba beat and makes you want to move your head back and forth and snap your fingers like Big Ed does in Episode 29, in the final moments of his belief that he and Norma are going to finally be together. (Don't worry, Big Ed, you only have to wait twenty-five *more* years.) How this track was left off the original *FWWM* soundtrack is a mind scratcher. This version finally got an official release on *The Return* soundtrack, which is good because it's the superior version. "Deer Meadow Shuffle" is synonymous with the first twenty minutes of *FWWM* and is something I had longed for for years. Dean Hurley set the tone for future online releases by giving us two versions of the exact same song. This let us know we weren't getting sanitized releases vetted by a marketing department. No, this was going to be for die-hard fans. He was releasing everything.

So what is the difference between the two versions? Track 1 is the studio version recorded by David Slusser's band. Track 2 is what happened after Lori Eschler and David Lynch got their hands on it and matched the cue to what was happening on screen. This second version is what plays in the film. You can hear the difference between the two at around 2:34 into the second track, when one of the slow-speed orchestra cues kick in. This could have been added when Desmond mentions the blue rose to Sam Stanley or when something "Red Roomy" happens.

One of the things that I never knew before working on this book is that "Deer Meadow Shuffle (film version)" is a perfect collaboration between the only two people to ever serve as music editors on the original *Twin Peaks*. Slusser, who was the music editor on the Pilot, wrote and performed the song; Eschler, who was the music editor on the series and *FWWM*, mixed other cues into this version. Because of that, I suggest you put the film version on your playlist. In the chapter about *FWWM*, Slusser already explained how Lynch was short on cues for the score, so Slussser was asked to put a band together and contribute a few tracks to help fill in the blanks. Slusser didn't know that he was going to basically score all of the Deer Meadow section of the film because he thought this track was going to be used for Phillip Jeffries's appearance in the FBI office. Here is what David Slusser remembers about writing "Deer Meadow Shuffle":

David Slusser: I was asked to write a song for the scene about going through doors. It was for when David Bowie was going through all these security footage monitors. It was a mysterious walk. I got the bass player to do this walking thing, and I had one of the greatest drummers of all time, Donald Bailey. He is playing the brushes. It is like this detective walk you would hear on *Peter Gunn*. We weren't doing this to picture. I am the piano player doing my best job at imitating Angelo, which is just Angelo imitating Charlie Rich, a country piano player.

Scott Ryan: The [sings] "No one knows what goes on behind closed doors" guy?

David Slusser: Yep. That's the guy. He's a great piano player, and Angelo could play piano exactly like that guy. Julee sings this song that has a piano track like it. It's a vocal about a mouse and a blouse.

Scott Ryan: "Kool Kat Walk?" Julee sings it on *The Voice of Love* and an instrumental version is in *Wild at Heart*.

David Slusser: That's the one. Angelo took a piano lick from Charlie Rich for that song. It is something you do. You take these moods, and it is something familiar. He didn't steal it; he took a very common rift by a very popular piano player. So when you hear it, it sounds familiar, and it gives you a shot of dopamine because you hear it in a familiar way. Angelo and David would use idioms in a good way to paint the scenes, so it's less about the score hitting the Mickey Mouse things and door closings. It's more about the mood. Their collaboration is more about mixing up these idioms and giving you something that holds the sonic space together. Idioms help us understand moods and become shorthand. Movie music is a big shorthand.

Lori Eschler: I had known David Slusser since I started *Twin Peaks*. He was friends with a bunch of my friends in that Bay Area crew. I had no idea how talented he was. When they brought him in to record with just direction from David Lynch about mood, Slusser started playing, and then people start jamming, and it was beautiful. It was exciting to witness it.

March 14

Hurley wrote: Without a doubt, one of the more memorable musical moment of *Twin Peaks*' second season was the teenage living room rendition of "Just You." Here we have one of the only alternate versions of "Just You" in the form of an outtake, arranged for guitar and synth. Albeit brief, this stirring instrumental version utilizes Vinnie Bell's spotlighted baritone guitar (a signature of the main titles) as an instant reminder of all that is essential to the *Twin Peaks* sound.

3. "Just You (Instrumental Baritone Guitar)"

In this version, a lonely guitar sound hits just enough of the melody to remind us what song it is, but honestly it's a much lonelier sound than the actual song's. An added synth sound in the style of "Audrey's Prayer" gives the ear some treble to focus on with all that bass. This is a short track, but is so connected to James and Donna. This cue was never used in the series, but should have been. It fits the James of Season 2 much more than "Americana" ever could.

March 17

Hurley wrote: The instrumental of "Falling" must have seemed like an atypical choice for the main titles of a prime-time television show back in 1990. However, it is certainly difficult to fathom *Twin Peaks* without it today. This is a partially strong testament to how connected this unique combination of chords and melody are to the show's essence. This alternate version of the *Twin Peaks* theme highlights the elegant simplicity of the composition, choosing to spotlight only a handful of elements from the original arrangement. Save for the opening spring pad, the first half of the track is simply electric piano and baritone guitar. The pair together are so evocative that it is easy to forget the additional instrumentation that decorates the original version.

4. "Twin Peaks Theme (Alternate Version)"

This track doesn't really stand out that much from the original, superior version of the instrumental theme. This is one of the examples David Slusser talked about where he took all of the mixes so that he could drop out different instruments to make the song sound distinct. This track was used a few times, but you probably always thought it was the main theme due to the similarities.

March 25

Hurley wrote: This sultry jazz rendition of "Audrey's Prayer (a.k.a. "Questions in a World of Blue") appears in Episode 27 of the series and in the archive under the faded label "Sleazy Audrey." A wonderful theme prevalent throughout most of the second season, "Audrey's Prayer" weaves its way through scene after scene as a kind of secondary love theme. Although "Laura Palmer's Theme" receives the premiere spotlight in terms of a flagship love anthem, "Audrey's Prayer" hangs humbly in the shadows as an equally stirring love theme complete with alternate versions such as this one.

5. "Annie and Cooper" **Scott Pick**

I find it interesting that Dean Hurley connects the dots of "Annie and Cooper" to "Audrey's Prayer" to "Questions in a World of Blue." I really think the fact that the main theme from Season 2 was chosen to add lyrics to in *FWWM* is an amazing connection. "Annie and Cooper" certainly has the same melody, just a new arrangement and new instrumentation. The arrangement is so incredible I had to ask Kinny Landrum about it.

Kinny Landrum: This track is obviously a live band. Yes, I'm playing piano, but I don't remember doing it.

It is amazing how so much of the music in *Twin Peaks* can be filtered into just a few themes. It is why the score fits together so well. So many of the tracks are built off the same backbone of the same melody. The walking bass in "Freshly Squeezed," "Audrey's Dance," "DOTDM," and "Up in Flames" is another example. But "Annie and Cooper" is such a beautiful arrangement and the saxophone is so intertwined with Agent Cooper that it fits perfectly in this cue.

This is what happens when a striking melody is rearranged with different instrumentation. There is little doubt that these three tracks have the same melody and chord progression. This is just easier to hide because it doesn't have the recognizable bass notes that "DOTDM" has.

Whether this song is another version of the prevalent Season 2 theme or not, it is critical to the love story of Annie and Cooper. The scene in which they dance at the Roadhouse and the Giant appears is the beginning of the end for these two characters' interaction. I can't hear this track without thinking of Cooper making the same mistake he made with Caroline. I love that someone named this track "Annie and Cooper" because the sadness of the saxophone is starkly different from the swinging sax that introduced Agent Cooper to us in the Pilot. Coming to the town of Twin Peaks was really rough on Dale Cooper.

This is one of the most crucial tracks that has never been commercially released. This track will fade away like Marietta Fortune's picture in *Wild at Heart* if we don't do something about it now. In fact, when I was rereading this chapter, I doubted myself that this isn't on the *Season Two* vinyl, but it isn't. I don't get it. So this begins an ongoing selection for this chapter. I will be selecting important cues never officially released on hard copy. This is the first of the thirty-nine "Scott Picks." This is one of the tracks I would pick for the proposed vinyl box set I want David Lynch's estate to release.

March 29

Hurley wrote: "Nightsea Wind" makes a brief appearance in *Twin Peaks: FWWM* during Laura's Bedroom epiphany about instances of "the same ring." In some ways, "Nightsea" bears a kinship to the previously released *FWWM* cut: "The Voice of Love," almost foreshadowing the film's emotionally-charged finale. Both feature tonal fabrics that are very similar. While "Voice of Love" showcases pastoral beauty with lush chordal movement, "Nightsea" plots simple synth lines that meander aimlessly (think "Dark Mood Woods"). "Nightsea Wind" is indeed a rare cut and presented here in its entirety at 5 minutes and 25 seconds.

6. "Nightsea Wind" **Scott Pick**

This is when I started to realize that the *TPA* might go for actual deep cuts, sometimes so deep I didn't even know I needed them. It would be easy to think this track is just a bunch of wind noises, but it also has an original synth melody that plays among the wind. This cue is played when Laura sees Teresa Bank's ring and electricity sparks on her bedroom ceiling. It has a ton of ominous tension and gives you that unique *FWWM* feeling. This is a must-have for the vinyl box set.

One of the things that sets this track apart from "Dark Mood Woods" or the "Mulholland Drive Theme" is how fast it is. Most of the synth-only tracks Angelo wrote for David are murky and slow. But this track almost sounds sped up. It also has a glimmer of hope, or maybe it's inquisitive. (I may have made that word up, but I like it.) Laura is trying to figure things out. She is thinking. She is still trying to defeat Bob, and I really think Angelo captured that sliver of hope, even as the wind blows and Laura is lost in the woods.

April 4

Hurley wrote: "Freshly Squeezed," as it was titled on the original 1990 *Twin Peaks Soundtrack* release, actually began with the working title "Slow Cool Jazz." Additionally, many variations of what became "Audrey's Dance" also appear in the archive under the same label of "Slow Cool Jazz." A critical ingredient in the *Twin Peaks* sonic equation, the element of slow-paced hip jazz infused the show's bitter-sweet with a finger popping chaser of chrome-plated cool. There are many versions of this song that float throughout the series. Most are isolated stems (solo vibraphone) or combinations of two or three tracks. This particular version swaps out the signature lead vibraphone (and often heard sax lead from "Dance of the Dream Man") for the concert bass clarinet.

7. "Freshly Squeezed (Bass Clarinet)"

When you see a track labeled bass clarinet, you know it is Al Regni improvising. Later on, there is a bundle release of a bunch of versions of this cue. It is difficult to pick which version is the best. It is basically whatever instrument you prefer the most. This track is one of the stems that David Slusser made for the original library when he mixed down each song recorded to the individual instruments. That is how you get a "Freshly Squeezed" with just the bass or just the clarinet. Here is Dean explaining what a stem is. There are several tracks in the *TPA* that are basically stems from a recording.

Dean Hurley: A stem comes from when a song is recorded in the studio. Take "Fast Cool Jazz"; when it's recorded in the studio, it has the components that make up that song. So you'll have Grady Tate on drums, Al Regni's sax. There's Angelo and Kinny playing keys. You can break that song down into stems. Each component is a stem.

April 11

Hurley wrote: The "Nostalgia Version" of the "Twin Peaks Theme" receives its namesake after a brief appearance in the second season spotlighting Benjamin Horne, disheveled and alone, reminiscing against projected 8mm home movies. It's a poignant scene that, in a way, appropriately relates to the connection many fans have with the show today. Media sometimes has a way of crystallizing subjective memories and emotions that parallel with its creation and *Twin Peaks* certainly is no exception. Just as Ben Horne looked so fondly upon a lost era with wistful remembrance, so too do many viewers revisit the series with a certain distinct sentimentality, tapping into thoughts and emotions connected with their first experiences viewing the show.

Included with the download of this track are two additional track components from the cue in their original form: the unpitched versions of the brief "harp and guitar" portion of the cue, plus a 5 minute 34 second version of the "Twin Peaks Theme" for solo electric piano.

8. "Twin Peaks Theme (Nostalgia Version)"

The MP3 icon for this track is a picture of Ben Horne. While some of Ben's stories in Season 2 might be a little uncivil, his mental breakdown after being accused of the murder is a touching moment for an unsympathetic character. This is a nice nostalgic version of the theme. About halfway through, the track changes to a solo Rhodes. This is the cue as Lori Eschler mixed it. Tracks 9 and 10 are the stems.

9. "Twin Peaks Theme (Harp and Guitar)"

This cue mixes into Track 8 about thirty seconds in. This is a short one but a nice stem to have and a wonderful reminder of Ben Horne's best scene. This cue was first used in Episode 7 when Nadine attempts suicide. The Nadine scene was directed by Mark Frost.

Mark Frost: I remember for Nadine's suicide scene, I said I'd like the main theme, but I'd like it played on a harp. So Angelo gave me that.

Lori Eschler: The scene where Nadine attempts suicide, we had Patsy Cline's "Crazy" in there as a temp track. Mark Frost was very passionate about licensing the Cline tune. He just felt like it was the only thing that could work and that it was perfect. He was really attached to it in a very passionate way, and nobody was batting it down. It just cost big money to get it.

10. "Twin Peaks Theme (Solo Rhodes)"

This is a full version of "Falling" on Rhodes only. Most likely this is Kinny Landrum. A bit of this cue plays toward the end of Track 8, but most fans would connect this cue with food critic/Norma's undercover mom M.T. Wentz.

April 18

Hurley wrote: Close minimal cousins to "Deer Meadow Shuffle," "Mysterioso #1 & 2" aid in connecting many of the events in the opening few reels of *Twin Peaks: FWWM*. Along with "Deer Meadow Shuffle," these two tracks represent the sound of the Deer Meadow locale with a type of sophisticated improvisational jazz that meanders amidst a fairly pendulum-esque tempo. Their sparse voicings lend support to *FWWM*'s establishment of a distinctly different tone right off the bat. The jazz elements at work here are not necessarily as composed and playful as some of the series' music, yet it still maintains key elements of the *Twin Peaks* musical DNA. When coupled with some of the slow-speed orchestral music relied so heavily upon in *FWWM*, these tracks effectively convert the Deer Meadow and Fat Trout locales into far more mysteriously sinister places.

Included within this bundle are the original versions of both "Mysterioso #1 & #2," as well as two film examples of the same tracks.

11. "Mysterioso #1"
12. "Mysterioso #1 (film version)"
13. "Mysterioso #2"
14. "Mysterioso #2 (film version)" **Scott Pick**

David Slusser: "Mysterioso #2" is definitely me cocomposing with Lynch. Famed drummer Donald Bailey is barely heard keeping a pulse on cymbal. The late Bill Fairbanks provided the backbone on acoustic bass. Sparse chords were provided by me on piano, followed by David Cooper on vibes, followed by Myles Boisen on electric guitar. This was done as "another take" of the going-through-doors security camera footage that produced "Deer Meadow Shuffle." I think David used the situation as a prompt for some general moody music that he obviously repurposed when he did the final postproduction.

This cue is used during the Deer Meadow section, and the sparseness fits so well with the sounds of the backward world of the Red Room realm. The MP3 cover photo that Dean Hurley chose to represent these tracks is a picture of the morgue in Deer Meadow. Anyone who has ever taken a film location tour with the great Josh Eisenstadt knows this was actually filmed at Olallie State Park. The morgue filming location was the garage for the park ranger. The morgue building is gone, but the sheriff's station, which is the ranger's house, is still there.

I usually don't like to listen to interviews that others have conducted with people I've personally never talked to AFTER I finish a book, but Dugpa told me I had to listen to the *Sound Effect Podcast* interview with Doug Murray. It really is a fascinating look at the sound design of *FWWM*. Doug worked closely with Lori Eschler. He discussed how they put together the sound effects with a few of the music cues. Here is what he had to say about the use of the "Mysterioso" tracks:

Doug Murray: The music in the film is so amazing because there are so many layers of music going on. He would find cues he liked for a certain mood, and he could imagine them being even better and weirder and more dreamlike if they were played backward. So he would say to Lori Eschler, the music editor, "Can you play the music from reel four in that scene? Play it here, only backward and on top of the music that is already there."

This is why there is a difference in these four tracks. The versions that do not have (film version) in the titles are what David Slusser and his band recorded. The tracks with (film version) are the actual tracks as you hear them in the film, after Lori added more sounds—some at normal speed, some backwards, and some slowed down.

Dean Hurley: When we talk about the stem of the mix of the show, they deliver a final mix of the show that has a dialogue stem, an effects stem, and a music stem. Sometimes when a cue was created on the spot, like something from *FWWM*, where it was more rampant, something like "Mysterioso," where David would just try combining two unrelated things on the dub stage, when you look at it from the fan perspective of "Hey, I want to hear this piece of music that was playing during this scene," it's like "Okay, well, in the library we have all the components, but that version only exists in the music stem of the *FWWM* mix."

Angelo doesn't write the score to the Deer Meadow section; Slusser does. This is just another way in which the Deer Meadow section stands in contrast to the *Twin Peaks* we know—down to the fact that each town has its own composer. Many writers who have covered the film, including me in my *Your Laura Disappeared* book, have mentioned that Deer Meadow is the reverse of Twin Peaks, but I don't think anyone ever knew that Deer Meadow was also scored by someone else. Slusser says he was called in was because Lynch was short on music. I am sure that is true. But I'd like to think that once he got the extra music, he situated it all in the front reel of the film so that even the music wouldn't be the same. I love learning new things about a film I've watched more than any normal human ever should.

April 25
Hurley wrote: Similar to the previously released alt. version of the "Twin Peaks Theme," this alternate version of the "Love Theme From Twin Peaks" provides just enough variation to spotlight a fresh listen to the actual composition itself. The flute and Rhodes are still the main focus here, with new additions being the baritone guitar punctuation and piano doubling flute on the B sections.

Unlike the more optimistic baritone guitar in the "Twin Peaks Theme," the dark intro to the love theme transposes the instrument into a much more ominous sound, supporting the "bitter" section of the "bitter/sweet" composition with an added sense of dread. The story Angelo Badalamenti tells about the creation of this composition is worth re-telling, as the song (in all its various forms) truly represents the epitome of the *Twin Peaks* equation: equal parts darkness mixed with "tear-your-heart-out" melodramatic beauty:

David would say that the music should begin very dark and slow. He said, "imagine you are alone in the woods at night and you hear only the sound of wind in the forest . . . now keep playing . . . but get ready for a change because now you see a beautiful girl. She's coming out of the darkness, through the trees . . . she's all alone, coming toward us . . . so now go into a beautiful melody that climbs ever so slowly until it reaches a climax. Let it tear your heart out."

Additionally presented with the download of this alternate version of the "Love Theme From Twin Peaks" is a version for solo Rhodes electric piano. It is worth noting that this is the instrument that the song was originally composed on.

15. "Love Theme (Alternate Version)"

It is interesting to try to decide what makes something the "Love Theme" and what makes it "Laura Palmer's Theme." There isn't much of a difference. The main difference I can come up with is that the melodramatic part of the song is played on another instrument besides a piano when it's the love theme. I prefer the soundtrack version over this one. Dean's icon is James and Donna getting pulled over by Harry and Cooper in the Pilot episode, but this track mostly evokes the scene in which Donna tells Harold Smith about Laura and her escapade with some random boys in the river. This same story can be heard from Laura's perspective in Jennifer Lynch's *The Secret Diary of Laura Palmer*.

16. "Love Theme (Solo Rhodes)"

This is the same song without the orchestrations and is only on solo Rhodes. Similar to Track 10, which is "Falling" on Rhodes, but this is "Love Theme" on Rhodes. The sound just doesn't work for me. The echo at the end of the melodramatic climb is just not pleasing to my ears. I prefer this song on piano. This track is used only in the Pilot when Cooper talks to Donna for the first time. The "Love Theme" is used quite a bit for Donna and is a de facto theme for the character.

May 2

Hurley wrote: It's staggering just how brief and nondescript "Americana" appears amidst the archive. Labeled "Bell's 50's Guitar," the well-known theme lasts a mere :34 seconds and stops suddenly without any musical resolution. It's impressive that such a short, seemingly impromptu fragment of music became such a mainstay through the course of the show's thirty episodes. "Americana" weaves its way throughout a majority of the series, fusing Vinnie Bell's signature roots guitar with the show in a way that is no less iconic than that of the instances of "Laura Palmer's Theme" or the "Twin Peaks Theme." Unlike many of the other various themes utilized in the show, however, "Americana" does not share its usage with numerous arrangements or multiple versions. Virtually all of its instances are derived from the same :34 second take either looped or superimposed with an additional element.

Included with the download of "Americana" is a rare full ensemble "variation" of sorts originally labeled as "James Hurley Full."

17. "Americana" **Scott Pick**

"Americana" is such a gem of a short song. We will never know how it came to be and from what session, because guitar great Vinnie Bell is no longer with us. Knowing these legends passed away before having their memories captured is always rough for me. The capturing of the artist's memories is just as important as making sure the art they created is preserved.

This little track is first heard in Episode 1, so it must have been on some tape from the beginning. Most likely Vinnie Bell was just fooling around between takes, and by doing that he created a bit of fifties rock 'n' roll for the town of Twin Peaks. Despite its short length, this would be a critical track for my box set release. I love that Dean Hurley acknowledged back in 2011 that "Americana" is just as important as the other themes. Here we are almost a decade and a half later and I'm still shouting it.

18. "James Hurley (Outtake)"

This track was never used in the series, but it sure should have been used in *The Return*. It has enough of a sonic connection to "Americana" that it would have been really cool and hence would have proved Shelly's contention in the Roadhouse. If this track had been played when James entered the bar, it sure would have lit up fans like me. I don't know if Shelly is correct about James Hurley, but Vinnie Bell was always cool, and his guitar playing on this unused cue should have seen the light of day. I am not picking any unused cues for my box set, but maybe we need a side release of all the unused cues?

May 9

Hurley wrote: Included in the 7-track bundle is a sampling of jukebox tracks that were included as the sonic backdrop of the RR diner. Part jazz, part truck-stop country and part miscellany, this assortment of music is what one would hear at the friendly Northwest diner while enjoying the archetypal cherry pie and black coffee. A perfect "break-time" EP collection to enjoy with your very own "present to yourself" everyday, each day.

Note: An extended version of "I'm Hurt Bad" is featured in this collection as it appeared in the stage performance of *Industrial Symphony No. 1*. The version included here makes due with a composite version lifted from one of the two program's DATs used specifically for the Brooklyn Academy of Music performance. It is the only locatable record of the composition in its entirety.

19. "Mister Snooty" **Scott Pick**

Kinny Landrum: Sounds even more old-fashioned, and this piano is definitely too ornate for Angelo to have played it. Sounds also like an upright. This could be from another source. I wonder if this is even library music that they purchased. It doesn't sound like it was recorded by us in New York.

Who am I to argue with Kinny? Well, I'm Scott Ryan, and I *say* what I want. I think his memory is incorrect on this one. I think this is Angelo. He is actually doing his own version of an old Italian song from 1933 called "Tornerai," composed by Dino Olivieri. Angelo's version includes enough changes that I am sure he could have called it a tribute or a pastiche. Pastiche is basically when a songwriter pays "tribute" to another song, but claims it as their own. Is pastiche what Vanilla Ice did with "Ice Ice Baby" from David Bowie's "Under Pressure"? Sure, let's call that trash pastiche. There are many times within the series where Angelo was tasked to write a music track instead of licensing an existing song. It's cheaper and easier that way to release the show on home video. We all know there were never any issues releasing *Twin Peaks* on video.

"Tornerai" translates to "You'll be back." The first time this song is used is when Dick Treymane takes Lucy to lunch. No one wants him to be back with Lucy, especially Andy. Probably the more famous use of this track is in Episode 16 when Leland puts this song on to dance with Donna. So this makes it another cue that actually exists in the world of Twin Peaks.

20. "Freshly Squeezed (Fast Cool Jazz Version)"

This is an uptempo version of "Freshly Squeezed" and has Kinny Landrum on the vibraphones playing the melody of "DOTDM." This is one of the best versions of "Freshly Squeezed" because it swings.

21. "Picking on Country (RR Tune No. 3)"

Can someone get Toad a plate special? This is a fun little country song that could have easily been performed by Jerry Reed on the *Smokey and the Bandit* soundtrack. This was used quite a few times during Double R scenes. It really shows how versatile Angelo was at writing assignment cues.

22. "I'm Hurt Bad (Industrial Symphony No. 1 Version)"

Dean Hurley: There were a couple of white whale tracks that I couldn't find while we were working on it. Then I did find them when we stopped working on the Archive. One of them was "I'm Hurt Bad," which plays in the Pilot when Bobby hits the jukebox. You know where that came from?

Scott Ryan: *Industrial Symphony.*

Dean Hurley: Right. In the DAT library they only put on a chunk of that song, maybe the first thirty seconds of it. I couldn't find the full version that was in *Industrial Symphony*. There were show assemblies of the *Industrial Symphony* DATs, but they had all the sound effects littered over the entire thing. So there was just this blaring electricity over everything. Where is the master tape? Then one day I found it and got it transferred. Angelo had such crazy handwriting that there was this scribble that said it, but I couldn't find it. But I found it. The other one was "The Swan." Without having access to Julee Cruise's original *Floating into the Night* mixes, which now I do know where those are, but at the time they were just tucked away in David's personal archives, and that is delicate to deal with because you have to bake the tapes in order to preserve the emulsion when you rethread and not have everything flake and fall off. I wanted to limit my engagement in that stuff, especially when I am just releasing stuff on the internet. I always wondered about the instrumental version of "The Swan." Some fans had pointed that out that it was used in the Pilot. I came across it on a cassette after we were done. So I emailed both of them to Brian at Dugpa and let him get them out there.

Julee Cruise: One of David's famous things that he told the sax player, Al Regni, this is a guy from the symphony, "You know Al, big chunks of plastic, can't you play that?" And Al knew what he was talking about.

While this song does play in *Industrial Symphony*, it also plays in the jukebox of the Double R in the Pilot when Bobby leaves and tells Norma he will see her in his dreams. This was a track that saxophonist Al Regni thought should have been used more times.

Al Regni: There was something that was used in a jukebox in the diner that had a swing sound on a tenor sax that I really liked. It wasn't very prevalent in the show, but I always liked it. It was an obscure thing. I thought they would use it more than they did.

This isn't the version that played in the series, but it is awfully close. Dean didn't want to release the version that had the *Industrial Symphony* sound effects on it. They never bothered me. This certainly is a track I associate with the jukebox and *Twin Peaks*, much more than I do with Julee Cruise, since she doesn't sing on it. This track was used again in another jukebox at Wallies. This time James selects it.

23. "Western Ballad (RR Tune No. 5)" **Scott Pick**
I suppose it is dealer's choice as to which of the Double R tracks you prefer. For some reason, this one sounds more like the Double R than any of the rest of the cues. It has the flavor of good old-fashioned country

cooking. Having access to this track is so fun because you can put it on your phone, take it to Twede's Cafe, and play it on your headphones while you eat and pretend that you are actually eating in Twin Peaks. Wait. Am I the only one who has done that?

24. "Preparing for M.T. Wentz"

This track has a French flavor to it. It is a good representation of how Norma wanted to impress the food critic that was coming to town and was longing for that French cuisine. Now why she thought anyone who walked into the Double R would want that kind of food, or this kind of music, is a question for another time, but Angelo created the feeling they needed for the scene. But it does show that Angelo would create some music for specific scenes, because this isn't the kind of music that would play in a normal Double R scene. Lynch used this cue again in his 2012 short "Memory Film."

25. "Secret Country (RR Tune No. 2)"

Here we have another country-sounding track from the Double R. This one has a lot more movement and is a little busier than the other country-sounding song. For some reason, this is my least favorite of the RR tracks, but I can't really pinpoint why.

May 16

Hurley wrote: The words "dark," "mood," and "woods" are very important to the architecture of *Twin Peaks*, as is undoubtedly this very unique-sounding piece of music. Badalamenti and Lynch had a particular way of working on the music for *Twin Peaks*. Sitting at either the Fender Rhodes or synthesizer to write, it wasn't uncommon for Badalamenti to use a dictaphone to record the proceedings in order to catch the evolution of ideas. In fact, it is because of this practice that this recording even exists. The version of "Dark Mood Woods" used in the series is this very dictaphone recording . . . made by the recorder placed near one of the studio's loudspeakers. The track retains a uniquely mysterious sonic quality that is due largely to this factor. Although not audible in this download, Lynch's voice can be heard earlier on the tape enthusiastically reacting to the first few initial notes of "Dark Mood Woods." His words are emphatic, underlining this particular track's importance among the larger body of music created for the show . . . he states: "Everything, everything [that] I ever want to do is right there . . . right there in that music. . . "

Although "Dark Mood Woods" does additionally appear in excerpted form on Track 21 of the *Season Two* CD release, it appears here in its previously unreleased full stunning length of 4 minutes, 30 seconds.

26. "Dark Mood Woods (Full Version)"

But doesn't it sound almost exactly like "Dark Mood Woods" (Studio Version)?

Dean Hurley: At the time, years ago, I overlaid each track on top of each other and realized they were the same thing. The reason the lengths are different is I had to trim off the head of the one from the dictaphone because Angelo was playing, and they're talking over it and the phone rings. So you hear the ambient sound effects of what's going on.

Thanks, Dean, for explaining one of the greatest mysteries of the *TPA* to me. I could never understand how the (Full Version) was shorter than the (Studio Version.) Naming things that deal with *Twin Peaks* will always be confusing.

May 22

Hurley wrote: Yet another track to add to you own RR Diner-themed jukebox, "RR Swing" would be the only *FWWM* diner track on rotation. Recorded specifically for *Twin Peaks: FWWM*, "RR Swing" had the original working title "Tex Desmond." Undoubtedly the perfect tune to cue up next time you find yourself "preparing a great abundance of food."

27. "RR Swing" **Scott Pick**

If you zone out (or worse, check your phone) while watching *FWWM*, you could totally miss this cue. It plays for a few seconds while Laura pushes through the swinging door in the Double R with a tray of food for Meals on Wheels. But this would be in my top five of the *TPA* releases. This track really swings and just evokes that finger snapping feeling that *Twin Peaks* music creates. For years, I had read the end credits of *FWWM* looking for song titles that were never released. This was not an easy thing to do on the VHS release, since the font and text were like a vindictive eye chart set up to make you fail. I loved this little guitar cue, and I assumed it was the "RR Swing" that was listed in the end credits because no song with that name was ever released before and neither was this song. The other thing I was certain of was that it was written by David Slusser and David Lynch, because that's what it says in **ITC Franklin Gothic** in the credits. That always surprised me because this track seemed so much like an Angelo piece and has the flavor of Vinnie Bell's guitar on "Drug Deal Blues." Well, we all know what happens when you are sure of anything in the *Twin Peaks* world . . .

Scott Ryan: Your third song in *FWWM* is "RR Swing." Do you remember writing that?

David Slusser: Nope.

Scott Ryan: That is sad because it is one of my top songs. Here, I will play it for you. [I play him the track.]

David Slusser: That might be miscredited to me. I am not getting any royalties from that song. As the music editor, I have to turn in how many feet and frames a song is played in a movie because you are paid royalties by how many feet or minutes you have in a film, whether the cue is part of the score or a song. I think Lynch had a country rock band in a couple of scenes. Maybe they wrote this song.

Scott Ryan: Yes, Fox Bat Strategy wrote "The Pink Room" and "Blue Frank." But they didn't do "RR Swing." This song sounds nothing like their sound. Plus, I have read about how they recorded those two tracks.

David Slusser: When David hired me at the last minute, he said, "We might have to do a bar band thing." I did bring Donald Bailey along because he is a killer harmonica player, and I brought him along to do a blues/roadhouse type of song, but we didn't do it.

Scott Ryan: Maybe he didn't need it anymore because he worked with Fox Bat Strategy on the Canadian bar scene music. If "RR Swing" is not you and your band, it sounds to me like Vinnie Bell's guitar playing.

David Slusser: He very well could have had Vinnie Bell record something.

Scott Ryan: In the end credits, the song is listed as you and David Lynch.

[Slusser pulls the song up on YouTube and listens.]

David Slusser: Not me. There is a pedal steel underneath the guitar picker. My guess is someone is doing an imitation under a very good guitar player. It could be Vinnie Bell and Kinny Landrum, or Angelo. That is not my drummer either. But the guitar player I had on my session is good enough to play that. He can do that. But we didn't have anything to get that lap steel or pedal steel underneath. I wouldn't have had that keyboard at the session. Your instinct may be correct. I would side with you on Vinnie Bell. My bass player is a little different too. Interesting. I never followed these things after the original release.

Lori Eschler: I thought that was something David Slusser recorded with his band when David Lynch brought him in. When we were mixing the film, David Lynch realized he needed some other music, but this could have been Vinnie Bell. It doesn't really sound like Vinnie's guitar style. I'm gonna have to pass and say I don't recall. If Slusser says it is not him, I am baffled.

Kinny Landrum: I don't remember this cue either, although I do remember doing some rock 'n' roll things with Vinnie. Probably it is Vinnie, but I am not on this track. Vinnie was a great guy. He helped me get a Broadway show in the pit when I really needed a job. It does sound like Vinnie, and it could be.

Well, some mysteries are solved and some aren't. It could be Slusser or it could be Badalamenti who wrote this track. As fas I can tell, it's a fifty-fifty proposition. Depending on who actually wrote the track would determine who is the mystery guitarist on the track. I suspect it is Brad Dukes.

June 1

Hurley wrote: Included within this bundle are three piano tracks heard during the second season of *Twin Peaks* as incidental background music for the Great Northern Hotel. Guests staying at the Great Northern would have most likely heard these songs emanating from the bar and dining area, unless of course the occasional wedding or Miss Twin Peaks Pageant was in progress. As an added bonus and proper contextualization for these piano pieces, a solo piano version of the "Twin Peaks Theme" is additionally included.

Sometimes there just isn't an exclamation that sums up your excitement. Let's try "I'm a whole damn town!" No, that doesn't apply. "My socks are on fire!" That isn't right either. I'll have to think on it, but whatever your phrase of excitement is, it applies to this bundle release, which is hands down my favorite of all the bundles. While watching the series back in 1990-91, I always loved the piano that was playing in the background of the Great Northern scenes. Many series have a piano player serenading patrons in a restaurant scene. It isn't that original a scoring idea. But they are usually playing standards. If you are a fan of the American songbook like I am, you might say out loud while watching one of these other series's scenes "Some Enchanted Evening" or "Night and Day." This is just one of the many ways I annoy my family when we watch a movie or television show. And while it is true that Leland Palmer serenaded patrons of the Great Northern with a song from *The King and I*, all the instrumentals playing at the hotel are original compositions that *feel* like typical songs played live by a piano man but have shades of actual songs from *Twin Peaks*.

It is hard to explain how much the Great Northern or Double R tracks mean to hard-core fans of the series. Listening to these tracks makes the world of Twin Peaks feel so real. I have listened to these piano tunes while having breakfast at the Salish hotel. It almost literally transports you into Twin Peaks. All four of these tracks (another one is released later on in the *TPA*) are crucial and should be released on vinyl, not because I am nuts, but because it is impressive that Angelo could have Kinny Landrum interpret songs from the score like "Josie and Truman" and play them as a lounge lizard performance. Angelo could have easily phoned in these tracks, but he didn't. They are beautiful, and I love them.

They first appeared in Episode 13 and continued to be used during most of the Great Northern dining scenes from then on.

28. "Great Northern Piano Tune #1" **Scott Pick**

This short piece of music, lasting just over a minute, feels like a grandiose version of a pop song, thanks to the trilling of the piano keys. The melody could easily be set to lyrics and recorded by Barbra Streisand, Frank Sinatra, or James Hurley. This track is used, among other times, when Ben meets with Tojamura in Episode 13 and during the wine tasting scene in Episode 26 when Lucy tells Dick that they should just "skip the wine and have a banana split."

The first time any of these types of tracks are used in the Great Northern is in Episode 13, which was directed by Lesli Linka Glatter. I asked Lori Eschler what she remembered about these tracks coming in.

Lori Eschler: Yes, they came in Season 2, but not at the beginning of the season. I don't remember if they were requested by Lesli Glatter specifically, but it's likely, as she had a close rapport with Angelo.

29. "Great Northern Piano Tune #2 (Truman and Josie)"

"You're not from around here, are you?" Pete asks Tojamura in Episode 13. Here again major kudos go to Angelo. Both of these tunes debut in Episode 13; he could have just used the same one twice, but he gave us two new tracks for two different scenes. The care and attention to detail on the score of *Twin Peaks* is a marvel. I am literally writing about every track, and I still don't think that is enough of a tribute to what Angelo did. This is a piano track where Angelo had Kinny Landrum basically "piano-fy" the track called "Josie and Truman." This song is titled "Great Northern Piano Tune #2 (Truman and Josie)" because of that. I'm not sure why the names got turned around, but it could be because every title is designed to be confusing and difficult. That being said, it really should be subtitled "Pete and Tojamura," as that is when the track debuted, and it is reused in Episode 14 when Catherine reveals herself to Pete as Tojamura. Oh, crap, should I have given you a spoiler alert for that? By the way, Ray Wise told a hilarious story at one of the Mike McGraner *FWWM* screenings I was lucky enough to help out with. Ray said he

was told to pretend to not know who Tojamura actually was. He said, "Oh, you mean, Piper Laurie, who is over there dressed as an Asian man?" They shushed him and said, "She wants no one to know, so pretend you don't know." According to Ray, everyone knew it was Piper and played along so she would feel better about it. I have no idea if this story is true or if it is just Ray being hilarious in front of a crowd, but I don't really care; it makes me laugh.

Anyway, I think the subtitle should be "Pete and Tojamura" because the only time any of these piano tracks was used outside of the Great Northern was when Catherine tells Pete she is Tojamura. In that scene, the track is slowed down and feels completely different. This is another prime example of the magic that Lori Eschler summoned as music editor, remembering that she had used this track at normal speed when Pete and Tojamura first interacted. This is also mixed in with slow-speed orchestra tracks 53 and 129. So that means there are three different music cues just for the moment when Catherine reveals to Pete that she is Tojamura. That is how complex the score of *Twin Peaks* is. And we aren't even talking about some major storyline. The Tojamura plot is one people want to forget. I was a guest speaker at Em Marinelli's college course that included a class about the series; several of the younger students called this story out for being offensive and asked me if people were offended by it in 1990. I told them that no one was offended by anything in 1990, and what these students should actually be offended about today is the fact that it is so unbelievable that Catherine would be able to slip into that makeup and costume in the time between the insurance agent telling her there is a life insurance policy on her and the fire later that day.

Getting back to the actual track, this release is a shortened version of "Tune #2," and later in the *TPA* releases, Dean Hurley found an extended version that is a minute longer, so I selected track 188 for the vinyl.

30. "Great Northern Piano Tune #3" **Scott Pick**

This track has the exact same beginning as the Great Northern Piano Tune #4, which wasn't released until Track 150. Maybe Dean couldn't find it at the time or didn't notice they were different. I was curious to find out if Angelo or Kinny Landrum played these piano tracks, so I sent this MP3 to Kinny. We listened to it over the phone, and he even noticed that he had made a mistake while performing it.

Kinny Landrum: It sounds like me. Angelo probably gave me a lead sheet. Wow, there is even a mistake there. [He backs up the cue and listens again.] Right there! [He stops between :28 and :29 into the track.] That high note I played two notes, and they didn't fix that. That's a nice chord [:40]. Did I make that up? It actually is nice. Oh, that's good. That's me. Angelo was a French horn player; it might be a little beyond his canon.

This track plays in Episode 15 when Ernie and Hank have dinner with their wives. Thank goodness this music is playing so I don't have to listen to these characters talk. I always focus on the music during this scene.

31. "Twin Peaks Theme (Solo Piano)"

Here is another piano track version of the theme. It plays during Big Ed and Norma's afternoon delight in Episode 20. This is a shortened version of "Falling." I like how often "Falling" plays for Big Ed and Norma because this connects back to the Pilot when they are undercover listening to Julee Cruise sing "Falling" live onstage. I like to think they made it their song after that night. But maybe Big Ed doesn't even remember that night, since an invisible Jacques Renault slipped some drugs in his drink, and Bobby clocked him.

June 8

Hurley wrote: Previously unreleased in its full version, this *FWWM* track is a great extension to the feature film's growing body of released music. "Girl Talk" presents us with an excellent example of the late 50s/early 60s component to the *Twin Peaks* musical equation. It wouldn't be a far stretch to imagine a teenage guy/girl group such as The Teddy Bears or The Fleetwoods providing vocal harmonies over such a track. Previously released in truncated montage form, this new full-length version of "Girl Talk" reveals a beautiful C# minor chord change variation beginning around 1 min 5 sec . . . a nice variation audible in the film, yet absent from the montaged composite included on the original soundtrack album.

When you download "Girl Talk," you will additionally receive the full version of "Birds of Hell."

32. "Girl Talk" **Scott Pick**

Only forty seconds of this track played on the *FWWM* CD release in 1992. It is the same first forty seconds of this track, but now we get to hear the rest of the song for another minute and a half. The final minute of this track has some different guitar flourishes and a few improvisations. The song ends abruptly, presumably where Angelo felt that he got what he needed for this scene. In the film, the cue starts the moment Donna says "James is the one." I like that this cue is played on the guitar. It connects to "Americana" and "Bookhouse Boys." The cue stops as soon as Donna says "faster and faster." It plays for a minute and ten seconds in the film, which is about double the length of the version on the *FWWM* soundtrack. Even though some of this is on the original release, I think the full version is a must-have for fans of the film. Laura and Donna on the couch talking is one of the best filmed scenes two characters ever share. In my *Your Laura Disappeared* book, I talked to Ron Garcia about how he set up the cameras for this shot. Ron Garcia is a *Twin Peaks* legend.

33. "Birds In Hell" **Scott Pick**

On the soundtrack, this song plays right after "Girl Talk," it does not play during the couch scene in the film, which goes from "Girl Talk" to the sound of wind to just a touch of "Voice of Love," which audibly foreshadows the arrival of the angel waiting for Laura. "Birds in Hell" plays later in the film, when Laura is suffering through her final day on Earth and the clock spins on the wall  at school. But it plays for just a few seconds. The version on the original release of the *FWWM* soundtrack plays for just over a minute. This complete recording of "Birds in Hell" plays for a glorious 4:18. I believe this is in the top three of the most beautiful songs Angelo wrote for the entire saga of *Twin Peaks*. It is just as moving and amazing as "Voice of Love" or "Laura Palmer's Theme." I never really realized how beautiful it was until I heard it in all its glory, and it has become one of my favorites. It so powerfully captures the utter pain Laura is experiencing in that moment. Obviously, this is one of my vinyl picks, as it is truly one of Angelo's best works.

Remember that the bird is a significant image in *Twin Peaks*, whether it is Waldo, the bird from the opening credits, the owl, or the statement "Where we're from the birds sing a pretty song." The fact that this piece of music coincides with Laura's final day means she is the bird stuck in hell. Bird is also a slang term for a female in England. Laura is in hell, but Angelo's music is pure heaven. This song should not be relegated to a montage. The end of the song has trilling piano keys in the upper register of the piano. I asked Kinny if that was him on the piano. The CD credits list Angelo and Kinny on keyboards, so once again, it's a fifty-fifty proposition.

Kinny Landrum: I don't remember this song, and the piano sounds more like an upright piano than a grand, but it's possible it's me. It is fairly good piano playing, so it's possible Angelo is not playing. Weird that the strings and piano are not in the same keys. It is almost like they came from different precordings. It also has a weird cut off.

June 15

Hurley wrote: Guiding musical motifs are an important part to much of the music, associating characters and story lines throughout *Twin Peaks*. This musical concept is an old one, yet it's most commonly associated with operatic work by composers such as Richard Wagner. Typically a brief melody, chord progression or even rhythm-based phrases, these recurring motifs are usually transformable and recur in different guises in order to assist with relating stories without the use of words . . . or to add subtext levels to an already present story. "Audrey's Prayer" is a great example of a musical idea in the series that has both specific attachments to a character, yet also journeys onward to bring thematic overtones (the idea of a hopeful prayer, or a sense of questioning) to a considerable number of other scenes during the show's second season.

Included with this synth-only version of "Audrey's Prayer" is an additional version for clarinet and synthesizer. Even more variations of "Audrey's Prayer" as well as other Audrey-related cues will follow in the coming weeks.

34. "Audrey's Prayer (Clarinet & Synth)" **Scott Pick**

Both of these versions of "Audrey's Prayer" made their debut in Episode 17, which is directly after the Laura Palmer case has been solved. Lori Eschler told me that Lynch asked that "Laura Palmer's Theme" be retired from that point on, and while the love theme does play in the opening scene as Sarah Palmer prepares for Leland's funeral, "Audrey's Prayer" becomes the de facto theme of the later half of the season. This version on clarinet and synth is my favorite alternate version of the track. It is used in the scene in which Audrey says goodbye to Agent Cooper in his hotel room. This melody first was used when Audrey prayed to Cooper that he would find her at One Eyed Jacks. So to call it back when they have to say goodbye is perfect. The sad, longing clarinet just breaks your heart. Audrey thinks she will never see Cooper again because he is supposed to leave town. He ends up not leaving, but the two characters are not together in any scenes of matter for the rest of the series until *The Return*, where we see a grownup Audrey reunited with her first real crush twenty-five years later and they interact in scene after scene after Audrey saves Cooper from the Red Room. Oh, wait, no, that's not what happened. Instead, Audrey was stuck in a Pinter play, and Cooper was in a reboot of *Being There*.

35. "Audrey's Prayer (Synth Version)"

"Two people in love couldn't have caused all this, could they?" [See photo on next page.] That is the question Donna asks Big Ed in Episode 17. Well, Donna, I'm not sure that statement applies to your relationship. James is basically the musician Hozier. He falls in love with someone new every day. This version of "Audrey's Prayer" fits the scene well, but it's never been a favorite for me to listen to. I prefer the orchestrated or clarinet version. This version was recorded by Kinny Landrum.

Kinny Landrum: Yes, that is me. I remember the chords. I like this one.

June 22

Hurley wrote: All previously "released" in some fashion or another, these three tracks are necessary additions to further the Audrey arc of the *TPA*. Unveiled as a bonus track from the 2007 *Season Two Music and More* soundtrack, "The Norwegians" was streamable through the subscription-based www.DavidLynch.com until last year. For those who owned the Season 2 CD, the access information was hidden before the CD's track one index (accessible by rewinding the disc behind track one on a standalone CD player), where one could hear the Alicia Witt piano-accompanied poem from Season 2 followed by a code to unlock "The Norwegians" track online. The track is now finally available for download as a permanent addition to the *TPA*. Similarly, "Sneaky Audrey" can be found amidst the previously released montage track "The Bookhouse Boys," and "Freshly Squeezed (Solo Vibraphone)" has only been available in bootleg form until now.

36. "The Norwegians" **Scott Pick**

As I mentioned in the prelude to this book, this track was the great white whale for me. It was the first instrumental track from the series that I coveted, and I waited from August 5, 1990, until June 22, 2011, to have it. That was a long wait. But it was worth it. I didn't know about the hidden track on the CD back in 2007, so I never got the code for this download. This eighty-second song captures the chaos that Audrey creates by letting out a little secret. The Norwegians didn't last very long in the town of Twin Peaks, but "The Norwegians" lasted over a decade in my memory and helped shape how I wanted my comedy to be scored.

People in the industry call a score that is directly on point in a comedy a "Mickey Mouse." David Slusser mentioned this term earlier in the book, and Kinny brought it up when I played him this delightful track.

Kinny Landrum: Absolutely, I remember this well. I think Angelo is playing the real Fender Rhodes. Angelo at least started playing it, and it got kind of difficult, and I overdubbed some things. I can tell by that opening thing, where it has the sound of the tyme coming back up. It has this kind of noise that is sort of undesirable, but Angelo took advantage of it. I remember that cue well. One of the things I learned long ago about scoring comic scenes in film is "Don't score the comedy." Score it like it is serious. Otherwise it becomes a cartoon. They have a term for that: don't Mickey Mouse it.

37. "Sneaky Audrey"

This track has moments of "Laura Palmer's Theme" punctuated by a guitar before it slips into the mysterious melody known as "Sneaky Audrey." The title comes from the fact that it was first used when Audrey spies on Dr. Jacoby and Johnny getting ready for Laura Palmer's funeral. This is one of the components that became part of the official soundtrack release of Season 1 on "The Bookhouse Boys." Here we get the full minute and a half of that composition. I like that these two tracks came out together because they both show how innocent Audrey was in Season 1. She was a lot of fun, and the music that scored her scenes matched that.

38. "Freshly Squeezed (Mid-Tempo Solo Vibraphone)"

Here is one of the tracks from David Slusser's mix down. This is a cue in which only the vibraphone plays "Freshly Squeezed," or "DOTDM," whichever you want to call it. I don't find this particularly pleasant to listen to.

June 29

Hurley wrote: Presented in this bundle is the music of the twentieth annual Miss Twin Peaks Contest. I think we can all presently relate to the idea of acknowledging the history behind twenty years of something. After all, it's the same length of time ago that *Twin Peaks* the television show took its final, albeit premature bow. Showcasing the ensemble effort at work in the show, the Miss Twin Peaks

Pageant was one of the few town-wide events that brought many of the actors participating in disparate story lines throughout the series into the same scene. With the "Miss Twin Peaks Theme," Badalamenti does his part by wrapping the sequence in an appropriate musical bow ... giving a nod to the golden-era *That's Entertainment*.

Included within this bundle are five tracks that guide us through rehearsal, opening, talent section, and final winning announcement of Miss Twin Peaks.

39. "Miss Twin Peaks (Piano Rehearsal)"

This short piano track was never used in the series. It is a hurried piano take of the actual Miss Twin Peaks theme. I don't know if it was labeled as "Piano Rehearsal" because it *was* Angelo's rehearsal for the theme or if there was a scene intended to be a rehearsal for the Miss Twin Peaks contestants. Whatever it was, we know Sherilyn Fenn wasn't going to show up for filming that scene, no matter what.

40. "Miss Twin Peaks Theme"

This sure sounds like it could be an opening number for the Oscars. This is actually a little too good of a theme for Miss Twin Peaks. It would be nice if it had some errors in it. I actually rewatched *On the Air* listening for cues from *Twin Peaks*. I was so sure I would find this one, but I didn't.

41. "Lucy's Dance"

This has such a kick line feel to it that you just want to get up and let your inner *Chorus Line* dancer out. Lucy crushed her talent section, and I think if the judges knew she was pregnant while she did that split, she would have beaten out Annie.

42. "Lana's Dance" **Scott Pick**

This is another fun track that shouldn't be forgotten. It could certainly be used as a theme song for a late-night detective series on Skinamax. Lana's dance is a fun moment for a character who doesn't have a lot of great scenes. The amount of new music Angelo had to write for one of the most maligned plots in all of the series is pretty hilarious. I actually think Angelo really flourishes when he is writing pastiche numbers. Cues like this are more in his wheelhouse than the music Lynch wants for most of his films.

43. "Miss Twin Peaks (Finale)"

The dramatic slowdown of the tempo at thirty seconds in always makes me laugh. It really feels like winning this beauty contest is considered the best thing any female can do in this small town. I love the mayor's reaction when Annie wins. "This is an outrage. She's been living in this town about fifteen minutes."

July 7

Hurley wrote: "Sycamore Trees" was recorded, along with a majority of the music from the series, at Art Polhemus's Excalibur Sound in New York. The small studio at 46th and 8th Avenue, which has been described by Lynch in interviews as vaguely "Eastern European" in mood, was a crucial component in capturing many of the Lynch/Badalamenti musical collaborations throughout the late 1980s and well into the 90s. Although Excalibur had a vocal booth, it did not have a control room in the classical sense, meaning everyone (including the engineer and console) was in the same room as the material is being recorded to tape. This is evident specifically in the instrumental of "Sycamore Trees," where Little Jimmy Scott's vocal bleed is audible through several of the other instruments' microphones (this can even be heard in it's onscreen instrumental usage in *FWWM*). Interesting, although the track is primarily a live performance, Ron Carter's characteristic double bass work was overbudded after the basic vocal/piano/organ/sax/drums were initially recorded. The song on its own harnesses such a palpable mood, but to see it spotlighted in the final episode of the series is a great example of the alchemy that can happen when image and sound forge a very special reciprocal relationship.

44. "Sycamore Trees (Instrumental)" **Scott Pick**

I love that an instrumental version of this track was released. And yes, I have recorded myself singing this song to this exact track so that I could have my own Scott Ryan version of "Sycamore Trees." This truly is the take that Jimmy Scott sang to, because you can hear his vocal bleeding through the instrument mics as the musicians play. This instrumental track plays in *FWWM*, but only for a few seconds, as Leland enters the Black Lodge after killing Laura.

Dean mentions in his blurb that Ron Carter's bass was overdubbed for the "Sycamore" track. This jives with Lori Eschler saying that Ron Carter's bass was mixed in at different parts of *FWWM*, reversed and slowed down. This was because he recorded his part separately.

An instrumental is one thing, but what about a cover? Fuck You, Tammy! does an amazing job with this song, and lead singer Devery Doleman has an interesting way of interpreting it from the female perspective.

Devery Doleman: Every time I sing "Sycamore Trees" live it is different. I always have to take a beat at the beginning and figure out where she [the singer] is at and who she is singing to. The "I got idea man" is always an invitation. "I got idea man / you take me for a walk / under the sycamore trees." Sometimes it's to a lover; it's an invitation to make love under the sycamore trees. Sometimes it's to a lover who is gone, and they come back for one last time under the sycamore trees. Sometimes it's a lover turned enemy-an invitation to face off, to fight to the death under the sycamore trees.

So the first part of the song is always delivered with this intention: it's like pulling back an arrow, and aiming it at a target, and then the first half is letting the arrow fly. And when the saxophone comes in—that is the presence she has summoned, meeting her there, speaking to her. So when she comes back in with "and I'll see you, and you'll see me," if it's the lost lover, the second half is full of the emotion of being reunited one last time and having to say goodbye again. If it's the enemy, that half is full of the feeling of having been in combat with that person—"I'll see you, and you'll see me" is "Now we have said what we have to say." If it's to the crowd, it's acknowledging that we all just experienced the saxophone interlude together.

One thing I realized in thinking about and writing about our recording of "Sycamore Trees" is that the original is sung by a man, and we see it in the Red Room, full of men. It feels to me like they are all hearing a story about what happened to a woman, what happened in the past. But when I sing it—I have to find some emotional throughline or reason to sing it. I feel like we are REENACTING the story in real time. Me/she is the voice that goes into the woods, and we are with her in the actual woods when she meets the sometimes supernatural presence that is the saxophone solo.

I have their *Sycamore Trees* EP [See above], but I also have a 45 of the track that the band recorded and put on vinyl just for me. Devery even says, "This is for you, Scott" on it. There are perks to writing a book about *Twin Peaks* music.

July 14
Hurley wrote: Included within this bundle are three Dr. Jacoby-related tracks: Two Hawaiian tunes used within the series ("South Sea Dreams" and "Hula Hoppin'") and a unique version of "Laura Palmer's Theme" for piano and Rhodes.

45. "South Sea Dreams"
46. "Hula Hoppin'"

Both of these songs are super short and play for under ten seconds each as Donna and James search Dr. Jacoby's office for the heart-shaped necklace. I love that Angelo had to create these throwaway tracks instead of the show paying to license the songs as "needle drops." More shows should create their own music cues, but I guess you need a composer as versatile as Angelo to do that. Tracks like these are so much fun to listen to because we are immediately transported back to Lara Flynn Boyle in that sexy blue ball cap she is wearing. Or is that just me? Dean Hurley also wrote out Dr. Jacoby's complete hypnosis monologue that Cooper reads to him in Episode 10, but I didn't transcribe that because I figure this book is already putting you to sleep, so I was afraid I would hypnotize you and then you would be a stalker of mine for life. Lori and Lynch must have liked "South Sea Dreams" more than "Hula Hoppin'" because they never used "Hula" again, but "South" was used in Episode 10 when Jacoby is hypnotized and again in his *Missing Pieces*'s scene.

"South Sea Dreams" was also used in the second episode of Frost/Lynch's *On the Air*, during a scene in which the cast is prepping for an episode and in the background a Hawaiian dance is going on. It was smart to use this track again, since it really wasn't used for more than a few seconds on *Twin Peaks* and probably only a few people in the world know the song well enough to recognize that it is in both series.

47. "Laura Palmer's Theme (Piano and Rhodes)" **Scott Pick**
This song plays in Episode 1 when we discover that it is Jacoby who has the necklace, but I have to say that of all the versions of "Laura Palmer's Theme" released through the *TPA*, this is by far my favorite. The piano that plays during the spooky part at the beginning is really different. The rest of the song is pretty much the same, but I love hearing the piano run up the octaves during the synth part of the song. It really adds something to the track. I wish that just once, instead of putting the original version on every major release, Lynch would have used this version, because it has enough of the original but mixed with enough differences to make it unique. I think this is so special that it is the only alternate version I picked for my vinyl box set.

July 21
Hurley wrote: Although probably a track that would have never appeared among a sequenced CD soundtrack release, "Owl Cave" is a nice repeating mini-motif that surfaces somewhat significantly in the final chapter of the series. Labeled "The Giant Appears" in the archive, it is a good example of the synthesized portion of the *Twin Peaks* sound. Although many cues from the series were recorded with an ensemble of musicians in a studio, just as many additional cues and even sound "effects" from the show were created exclusively by Badalamenti on synths such as the Roland JX-10.

48. "Owl Cave" **Scott Pick**
This cue is such an important track from Season 2. When the synth high notes hit random sounds it is like stars popping out in the sky. When I hear this track, I always picture Andy staring at the map to the Black Lodge or Windom Earle entering Owl Cave,

which is also the Bat Cave from the 1960s *Batman* series. Dean Hurley mentions that this track would never be released on a sequenced CD, but why not? This is a critical track for me and would be on my release because it is an often used cue in the latter half of Season 2 and it occurs when Jupiter and Saturn are in conjunction.

July 28

Hurley wrote: Much of the sonic glue to the series is due in part to the heavy use of "slow speed orchestra" music. The concept is a basic one. When looking to alter a piece of pre-recorded music, what is the easiest way to radically change the sonics of something? Thread the tape backwards and/or lower the playback speed. The interesting thing that happens when reducing the playback speed of music is that the slower it is reproduced, the closer it gets to a non-musical sound. This is probably what attracted Lynch so much to the technique. With the rotation of a tape machine's vari-speed knob, one could actually "blur" the line between music and sound design. And that is exactly what is at work here with these selections of "slow speed" and "half speed" orchestra pieces. Badalamenti would occasionally record "E" tracks (short for "Extra" tracks) while at work on other jobs as "firewood" material for Lynch. Working on the series, Lynch had at his disposal a number of these "E" tracks, of which some would be reduced to playback speeds as slow as 25 percent (two complete octaves down in pitch and 4x as slow as the original recorded material). Most of the resulting slow speed versions would be utilized in a fashion similar to sound design, yet some actually became very recognizable sonic motifs throughout the series. Several of these tracks, when returned to their original recording speeds, reveal entirely different compositions with a beauty and merit in their own right. Other compositions are from recognizable sources. The often used "Stair Loop" or "Danger Theme" is actually a vari-speeded section of Badalamenti's score for Lynch's "Clean up New York" public service announcement.

Included in this bundle are six key tracks presented in their full-running length.

49. "Half Speed Orchestra 1 (Stair Music/Danger Theme)" **Scott Pick**

This first orchestra cue is probably the most famous "scary" track in the series, remarkable not just because it played in an ad Lynch directed, but also because it is used quite a few times in the series, always creating immediate dread. This is one of the most classic *Twin Peaks* tracks not released on vinyl; it may be scary and unsettling, but that's why we love it. It was used in the Pilot and many times after. I wanted to understand exactly what the process was to create the songs, so I asked Dean Hurley.

Scott Ryan: Can you explain to me the origins of the slow-speed orchestra and the half-speed orchestra songs?

Dean Hurley: This is a very important technique for how David goes about stuff. It's a tool he uses in all his films, probably starting in *Eraserhead*. Every tape machine has an IPS [inches per second] setting. But on some 24-track machines, you can go into a free mode and adjust the speed. Here is a pedestrian example for you. I am sure you are familiar with *Home Alone 2*.

Scott Ryan: [Laughs.] I gotta say out of all the things I thought we were going to talk about today, *Home Alone 2* wasn't one of them.

Dean Hurley: [Laughs.] There is a scene where Kevin has the Talkboy, and he is at the hotel, and he calls the front desk, and he makes a reservation for himself, and he records him saying, "I am the father. Here is the credit card." But when he plays it over the phone, he drops the pitch so he sounds like an adult. It is that concept of recording something on tape at normal speed and then slowing it down to get a robust timbre. We called it dropping an octave or two. When you have something playing at fifteen inches per second and you drop that to seven and half inches per second, you are going to get something that is an octave lower. It is going to be running much slower. David realized that, probably from Alan Splet, who probably taught him all of that; it is Classic Sound Design 101. You can go back to *King Kong* [1933], where they recorded a lion; then they played it an octave lower and it sounds like a giant ape. So you get those bigger and scarier sounds by doing it. With music, David started experimenting with it willy-nilly. "Play that at half speed and see what it sounds like."

Scott Ryan: And he's used this in so much more than just *Twin Peaks*.

Dean Hurley: If you listen to "Gone Ridin'" in *Blue Velvet*, there is a cue in there where they are driving in the car, and it's a Frank Booth scene. You've got the Chris Isaak song instrumental, because Chris gave David the 24 track of that song for *Blue Velvet* and said, "Have at it." David basically took the vocal out, made an instrumental of the track, and slowed it down. Not a full octave, but just enough to make it more meaty. Listen to the version on *Silvertone* and then listen to the *Blue Velvet* scene, and it's noticeably lower in pitch and sounds beefier.

Scott Ryan: Does he do this with songs with vocals as well?

Dean Hurley: The most famous version of doing this on a song is the other Chris Isaak song in *Wild at Heart*, at the Iguana motel scene. The song "In the Heat of the Jungle" is a very fast song. If you go to the scene, it's like the most incredible Tom Waits-on-cough-syrup kind of music cue, but it's literally the song slowed down at half speed. It is an octave lower, and it's the most incredible transformation of music I have ever heard. I even thought he must have remixed it, but when you listen to "In the Heat of the Jungle," there is an instrumental part and sound effects of birds and stuff, but the way that stuff smears and turns into something else when you slow it way down is like "wow." There really should be an audio plug that is just called David-Lynch-a-fy.

Scott Ryan: And the "Stair Music" track wasn't written for *Twin Peaks*, right?

Dean Hurley: The famous stair climb one ["Half Speed Orchestra 1 (Stair Music/Danger Theme")], that cue is Angelo's music from his New York rats PSA ["From Rats to Riches"]. Listen to that, and it's the same cue. A lot of people come to the idea that music for film has to be this composition thing. But in a way, there is this backdoor entrance where David is looking at what he has available. They did this PSA cue that Angelo wrote. So play that half speed and see what it sounds like. "Wow, that sounds like a slow plodding up the stairs." David loved to say "action and reaction." Do something and then see what it sounds like, and then react to it. He is always looking for something to give him an indication of something. The music in *Twin Peaks* is like these little mosaic pieces that are like a quilt, and it's woven together in an interesting way. The other directors are essentially, by necessity, doing the same thing. "What do we have to work with?" That is the secret to a good score. You sit down in the edit bay, and you have an Avid with different takes from the actors, but rarely do people sit down with the finished music and start building the score in the same way. They, most of the time, Frankenstein together a score from other scores as a temp track, and then the composer is hired, and in the worst-case example just mimics that score. But if you have a library of all this original music, in all the configurations, you can build a score.

This is certainly one of the most iconic "scary" tracks in the entire series. It is hilarious to me to find out that it was used in a New York City rat PSA. But this does show how Lynch and Badalamenti used everything they could get their hands on to fill the score of the Pilot. It truly backs up Slusser's claim that there just wasn't a lot of new music to use when scoring the two-hour episode. It means that it is very likely that some of these other tracks could have come from many other projects. I promise you I tried hard to get diaries from the Badalamenti estate to try to piece these things together. I guess Leland got there first and tore them all up. Maybe in twenty-five years someone can find a few of the pages in one of the doors in the men's bathroom stalls at Dirt Fish. (That may be a deep-cut joke, but I stand behind it.)

50. "Half Speed Orchestra 2 (Dark Forces)"

This cue always reminds me of when Cooper and Major Briggs went fishing and Briggs disappears. Horns start off the cue, but then the unsettling synth starts bringing in all the creepiness around 1:11. The pulsating sound of the strings rising and falling is when Cooper is relieving himself and the owl is seen. This is another classic "scary track" that has not been officially released, but I only picked one of these tracks for space because I am pretending this vinyl is actually going to happen.

51. "Half Speed Orchestra 3 (Windom Earle's Motif)"

Somehow "Windom Earle's Motif" debuts in Episode 14, which is many episodes before his arrival. When this track was used, the directors usually just played the front part of this cue. There is a bouncing synth sound that takes over halfway through the track, but I don't recall this ever being used in the series. I think they just looped the front part of this song. At around 1:13, the strings come and go like howling ghosts. This is an enjoyable cue for fans of the darker side of the music, although I'm not sure it was ever used much. You know where they did use this one? During what many think is the ultimate low point of the series. This cue, which again for some reason was called "Windom Earle's Motif," is used in Episode 19 when Caleb Deschenel zooms in on Andy's face and Little Nicky appears as a devil surrounded by flames. That is when they chose to use this cue. So let's call it "Devil Nicky's Motif" from here on out.

52. "Slow Speed Orchestra 1 (24 Hours)"

This cue plays for just two minutes in Episode 16 when Cooper asks the sheriff for "twenty-four hours to finish this," but the entire track is over eight minutes long. I have no proof of this, but I think Lori Eschler and David Lynch used this cue in *FWWM* at different speeds buried in the mix. It really has the sounds of the slowed-down music used for Teresa Banks and the confrontation between Leland and the One Armed Man. Lori did say they used orchestra pieces in reverse and backward. This opening scene of Episode 16 is so important; Cooper is so lost and feels he isn't close to solving the mystery, but we know he is closer than he thinks. This long cue sets the tone. Despite its "24 Hours" title, the cue debuted in Episode 8 when Cyril Ponds (who cast that guy?) reports on the mill fire, so the track must have come in with the other new tracks for Season 2.

53. "Slow Speed Orchestra 2 (Unease Motif/The Woods)"

This slow build of a hovering sound that grows more and more centered is called "Unease Motif/The Woods." Well, later on in this release there is a track called "Back to Fat Trout" that has the same subtitle. I have listened to both tracks, and they don't sound the same to me, so I am going to say they are different cues. This cue was often mixed within a different cue to create a sense of danger. All things being the same, I'd rather listen to "Back to Fat Trout" than this one.

54. "Slow Speed Orchestra 3 (Black Lodge Rumble")

This is an almost seven-minute cue of a rolling, dark, synth sound as a knocking sound effect pops up randomly throughout the track. This "rumble" sound was used many times throughout Season 2, but in *The Return* was replaced with an ominous woosh. I believe this is a prime example of what Lynch and Hurley refer to as firewood. It is hard to say this should be on a vinyl release because it is over six and a half minutes long, but it sure is one of the main nonmelodic tunes that we have come to know as one of the primary sounds of the series. The main difference between the Black and White rumbles is this version has that knocking sound. Maybe Bob is trying to get out? But would he knock?

August 4

Hurley wrote: The origins of this short piece hearkens from a nine and a half minute take of raw material labeled simply "Vinnie Bell Guitar Chords." Most of what transpired in the recording were single guitar chord sustains probably intended to be used as transitional material. (At least one can be heard in the Deer Meadow Sheriff's Department early in the film.) The recording gets off to a slow start with a number of false starts complete with Bell's own verbal count offs, but around the three-minute mark the sequence of chords for "James Visits Laura" appear nonchalantly. This slowly strummed sequence of minor chords is brief; then Bell shifts toward a major chord and stops. Badalamenti's voice interrupts the silence by asking, "Is there like lower-sounding chords, Vinnie?" Bell then drop tunes his guitar, but the remaining minutes of the recording yield unused and uneventful material. Much like the life of *Twin Peaks* on-screen, it's almost hard to believe that more of this composition doesn't exist. It's also a ripe example of the ability Lynch and Badalamenti had to somehow zero in on a small, improvisational musical idea and reframe it in a way that conjures a poignant cinematic moment.

55. "James Visits Laura" **Scott Pick**

I love the story that this was found as a cue among minutes of Vinnie Bell improvising. The pulsating guitar chords mixed with his strumming constantly create anxiety, which scores the scene of Laura panicking when James shows up at her house unannounced in the daytime, which could lead to her father discovering who her secret lover is. Not cool, James. I also love that they again used a guitar sound to score a James scene in the film. More than any other character, James's theme songs are all connected to the baritone guitar. The guitar brings to life "Just You," "Night Bells," and "Americana," all associated with James. This might be a short track, but it needs to be released. Vinnie Bell's contribution to the music of *Twin Peaks* is as substantial as those of Kinny Landrum and Al Regni.

It is impossible to hear these strums and not see Laura standing on the front porch of the Palmer house at the beginning of this scene. Ron Garcia placed the camera at street level, and the lighting on her makes her appear tired and scared as the shadows fall across her face. At the end of the scene, Leland stands on the porch and gives James the same stare that Mary Reber gives me whenever I show up at the Palmer house.

August 11

Hurley wrote: Laura Palmer's diaries serve an undeniably important role to much of the beginning half of the television series. They provide a vehicle for her voice from beyond the grave by offering secrets, clues and personality insight into what is the show's simultaneously omnipresent, yet absent character. The keeper of Laura's second diary, the agoraphobic Harold Smith, receives an appropriately delicate musical theme (included on the *Season Two Music and More* soundtrack), with an even more fragile melodic structure and timbre. This haunting melody is showcased here in a version of this theme designated "The Living Novel." Similarly, "Laura Palmer's Theme" receives a number of variations with similarly wistful and ethereal tonal treatments. Three different "lighter" versions of this ever-present, chameleonic theme are included additionally within this bundle: the angelic "Ethereal Pad Version," "Ghost Version" (of which the later half was used during James Hurley's first sighting of Laura's cousin Maddy), and a version dubbed "Letter From Harold." As a bonus, an additional half-speed version of "Harold's Theme" is included as it appeared in Episode 18 of the series.

56. "Harold's Theme (Josie's Past)"

This cue has the same melody as "Harold's Theme," which is on the *Season Two* release, but this cue has both a different synth sound and wind chimes. It is played when Josie first tells Harry about Thomas Eckhardt. If you ever run into me at a *Twin Peaks* event and you like inappropriate humor, ask me to do my bit about Eckhardt planning revenge on Andrew Packard by dispatching his girlfriend, who is fifty years younger than Andrew, to have unlimited sex with him. I wish someone hated me like that.

57. "Harold's Theme (The Living Novel)"

Lara Flynn Boyle doesn't always get many kudos for her portrayal of Donna Hayward. Some of that is on her, but this is a scene in which she really shines. This cue plays after "Love Theme (Dark)" as she recounts the night she and Laura met up with some boys at a stream. The cue's melody is the same as those of the other Harold's themes, but after Donna takes the notebook that Harold wrote her story in and runs outside, the music turns dark as Harold struggles once he realizes he is outside. This proves

Angelo did play to some scenes in the series, because the music in the scene matches exactly to the way it plays on this release. It is fascinating how people I interviewed constantly said Angelo was not open to writing music specific to a scene, while so many examples prove that he did, and this is one of them. The change in the cue could not have been done in editing; it is a performance change. There are a few versions of "Harold's Theme," but this one is the best because of the dramatic ending.

58. "Laura Palmer's Theme (Ethereal Pad Version)"

There are almost twenty versions of Laura Palmer's Theme in the *TPA*, but this is such an important version because of the scene it scored and because of how different it is from all of the other "Laura" cues. I love Angelo's improvisations. This is played in Episode 16 when Donna and Cooper visit Harold Smith's neighbor only to find Mrs. Tremond, though not with her grandson. (Of course, Mary Reber is my favorite Mrs. Tremond.) This cue scores the scene until Donna reads the page about Laura's dream. Then the scene is scored with "Laura Palmer's Theme (Vibraphone)," but this short introduction cue really sets the tone for the great scene in which Cooper finds out that he and Laura shared a dream. (But remember, I don't believe it is Cooper's dream, so I think Laura and Cooper had a vision of the future.)

59. "Laura Palmer's Theme (Ghost Version)"

This cue skips the synth buildup and just starts at the ascending part of the theme, producing a ghost-type vocal sound. Only the middle of the song plays, followed by vocal pads of an oooing choir sound. The end of the track is the moody synth part, but again with a different sound. All and all, it's just another version of the same tune.

60. "Laura Palmer's Theme (Letter From Harold)"

Same song, but with a different synth sound. This track is used a few times in the series, and the sound is recognizable. One nice touch that had to come from Lori is that it is used when Pete runs into the mill to save Catherine, and then again when Catherine recounts her version of that night to Harry. Connections like that are so damn cool, and it's why respect has to be paid to the score of *Twin Peaks*.

August 19

Hurley wrote: Another highly signature sonic stamp of the series comes in the form of this solo saxophone version of "Dance of the Dream Man" (previously released in-part amidst the montaged "The Bookhouse Boys" track from the original soundtrack). The artfully-long plate reverb effect on this distinctive version manages to transform Al Regni's sax into a symphonic ensemble of harmonic overtones and lush chordal accompaniment. The sonic treatment additionally has the effect of embedding a ripe sense of place or location into the recording. Even when divorced from the images of the television show, this recording seems to carry with it a detailed description of the abstract environment it represents. Coupled with the strong sense of melody and musical technique, we are presented with one of the more mood-rich pieces of the series to be executed on a solo instrument.

61. "Dance of the Dream Man (Solo Sax)"

This cue is used in the series to connect Agent Cooper to the viewer. It is so aligned with him that it is also used for the first appearance of Cooper in *FWWM*. This is basically Al Regni playing the solo from "Dance of the Dream Man," and that is all you hear on this stem. While it is great in the series, it really isn't the kind of cue you want to listen to on its own. It is great when mixed in with something else, but isn't better than hearing the original version off the first CD.

August 25

Hurley wrote: Most of the jazzy-cool pulse to the musical sound of *Twin Peaks* can arguably be attributed to one man: drummer Grady Tate. Tate's own slick, sizzle-cymbal-infused bop sound was defined long before the series took shape, and ultimately brought a large portion of the "cool jazz" sonic equation to the table. Tate's style has been often referred to as "hard bop": a style that developed in the mid-1950's jazz landscape and can be traced back to its own extension of the bebop sound about a decade earlier. His style is so distinctively layered with nuance, swing and a musical use of the kick drum that it is little wonder that he is featured so often with accompaniment through the series. Three of Tate's solo percussion tracks (all utilized in the series) are presented here, showcasing this unique drum sound and performance style. Solo Percussion 3 even reveals a bit of Tate's own vocalizations, a frequent occurrence that illustrates the level of soulful investment that went into his performances. As an additional related track, this bundle also includes the sparsely-arranged "Audrey's Dance" for Percussion and Clarinets.

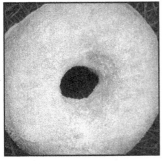

62. "Solo Percussion 1"

This is probably the most used drum cue in the series. It is used several times in the Pilot, including during our introduction to Audrey: the iconic scene in which we glimpse just her black-and-white saddle shoes as she slides into a car. This cue just sets up a nice beat and doesn't have a ton of movement, so it was useful in scoring lots of scenes when the director wants to suggest that something cool or fun was going on. It is used mostly for comic relief. This is one of the few cues also used in *The Return*, specifically in Part 2 for the Las Vegas establishing shot, but it's a blink-and-you'll-miss-it moment.

63. "Solo Percussion 2 (Grady's Waltz)"

Another great cue from Grady. This cue was used for the rock-throwing scene in Episode 2, as Cooper sets up the test while Harry measures the distance to the bottle. I have done this event at many a festival, and it is much harder than you might think. The drums move around a bit more on this cue, so it isn't used as much Solo Percussion 1.

64. "Solo Percussion 3"

This percussion cue is much slower than the other two. The first time we hear it is when Albert makes his initial trip to Twin Peaks. After that, it is used mostly to score Andy.

65. "Audrey's Dance (Percussion & Clarinets)"

We certainly have David Slusser to thank for this cue. This is one of the stems he recorded from the complete "Audrey's Dance" so that he would have only the drums and Al Regni's clarinet performance. This stem is even used in the Pilot when Cooper and Truman watch the Roadhouse from across the way. "You know why I'm whittling?"

September 1

Hurley wrote: Another quarter has been deposited into the RR jukebox. This time, one of the most commonly rotated tunes in Twin Peaks' premiere diner is heard; the slow-tempo, western-soaked "Northwest Gulch."

66. "Northwest Gulch"

Only sixteen miles out of North Bend, where the actual RR diner (Twede's Cafe) is located, is the Rockhound Gulch, by Denny Mountain. So Rockhound could also be known as the Northwest Gulch. It is a great place to find some rocks worn down by the falls right outside the Great Northern (the Salish Spa in the real world). I have collected a handful of really soft worry stones from the bottom of the falls. During every interview I conducted for this book, I held one of those rocks in my hand. The rocks that come from the Snoqualmie area are incredible. If you need a definition for a gulch, here you go: a gulch is a narrow, steep-sided ravine marking the course of a fast stream. I like that Angelo named this song after a gulch and that there actually is one in the area. This track was used in six RR diner scenes over the course of the series, and it really makes you want to share a piece of cherry pie with the Log Lady. (Pitch gum not welcome.)

September 15

Hurley wrote: *Twin Peaks* was the start of a longstanding working method between Badalamenti and Lynch of composing and recording a portion of a project's musical ideas before principal photography began. From *Twin Peaks* onwards, musical ideas, themes and variations were collected by the pair as one might collect wood for a fire. "Firewood," as a term, became synonymous with musical building-blocks. Creating multiple versions of an idea became the standard practice while Lynch and Badalamenti were creating the music and, eventually, the various versions and stem isolations would find their way into usage . . . sometimes being collaged and assembled as late as an episodes's final sound mix (typically the last stage in an episodes's creation). Since there were a number of working directors trading duties throughout the cycle of a season, a music educator "kit" was made which cataloged all the various mix combinations of a cue and made it easy for directors working on an episode to use and build their own combinations of music.

Inside this small excerpt from a music editorial kit are five versions or components for "Dance of the Dream Man": a drum and bass only version, a solo bass stem version, two takes of solo clarinet and a solo flute version.

67. "Dance of the Dream Man (Drums and Bass)"

David Slusser strikes again. These five versions of the same song are the exact same song with the other instruments muted so the music editor had options for scoring. None is better than the original, so the one you'll desire to listen probably depends on whether you are a crazy fan of the solo bass, clarinet, or flute. As I said, I prefer the mix of all of them, and I'll take the original, but having each one released as an MP3 is pretty damn cool. Surely no other television series has done it.

68. "Dance of the Dream Man (Solos Bass)"
69. "Dance of the Dream Man (Solo Clarinet)"
70. "Dance of the Dream Man (Solo Clarinet 2)"
71. "Dance of the Dream Man (Solo Flute)"

September 15

Hurley wrote: Although a majority of the music for the television series was recorded at Excalibur Sound in New York, "Just You" was one of the few sessions for series music recorded in full in Los Angeles. Highly recognized as one of the more memorable vocal performances of the show's second season, this instrumental version of "Just You" actually does get utilized a handful of times (to less quirky effect) in a few subsequent episodes. The instrumental backing track was the first to be recorded, with the actors overdubbing their vocal performances at a later date. In fact, it is in part because of the instrumental's original key, and this separate addition of the vocals, that attributed to the eventual vocal-pitched effect and distinctive usage in Episode 9. In order to accommodate the three actors' performance to the prerecorded track, the tape speed was reduced during recording, and later returned to its original speed. Incidentally, the other material from Season 2 recorded the same day as "Just You" was the oft-used "Night Bells" guitar and bass track, as well as "Drug Deal Blues," which was originally designated on the tape job as "Just You: Blues Version."

72. "Just You (Instrumental)" **Scott Pick**

Now this is a damn fine track. If we didn't have this, then how would drunk fools at *Twin Peaks* events karaoke to "Just You" in front of all their friends? For all you haters out there who don't like James Marshall's performance, here you just have Angelo's music to focus on. I actually love both, but there is something really nice and relaxing about this instrumental. This simply must be on the vinyl, because while you want to pretend in public that you don't like this song, you want to be able to sing along to it in the privacy of your own home.

September 23

Hurley wrote: It seems as though prior to *Twin Peaks*, criteria for quality television music was simply "having a memorable theme song." Although *Twin Peaks* managed to fulfill that category with "Falling," it also managed to establish a new benchmark in TV music by laying forth an entire catalog of memorable instrumentals. One of these memorable instrumentals is yet another crucial pillar in the formulation of the *Twin Peaks* sound: the distinctively-austere "Bookhouse Boys." Once again, Vinnie Bell's guitar work is foregrounded here, commanding the most responsibility for the tonal flavor of the piece (evident in the frequent usage of the track in it's solo guitar form), but the importance of this track seems to be in its Frankenstein hybrid of both cool "finger-popping" jazz combined with a Duane Eddy/late 50s-style guitar rock. This mode of genre mixing hybrids is an important umbrella under which most of *Twin Peaks* operates . . . both the music and the general conventions of the show itself. It is in these hybrids that 1 + 1 does not equal 2, but 3; a resulting whole that is greater than the sum of its many parts.

Included with this download "Bookhouse Boys" is the drop-key, solo guitar version of the track also featured heavily in the series.

73. "Bookhouse Boys" **Scott Pick**

As I pointed out when I covered this track on the original soundtrack, "Bookhouse Boys" was basically created in an editing bay. Here we get two versions of the actual recording. If you listen first to Track 73 and then the soundtrack version, you will hear all the cues that were mixed in. This five-minute version has just the "Audrey's Dance" bass played over the Vinnie Bell guitar that is so associated with Bobby and Mike. It does tend to go on for a while, but I really don't mind at all. In that way, it has a "Pink Room" feel to it: you can almost lapse into a meditative state with the repetition of the cue.

74. "Bookhouse Boys (Solo Guitar)"
This is only Vinnie Bell's guitar part. Many times this cue was used to punctuate a scene in the series. Again, it was just plain genius of Slusser to mix out the cues. Luckily, we get only a little over a minute of the repetitive guitar. It is nice to have as an MP3, but I prefer this guitar mixed with other cues.

October 4
Hurley wrote: With all of the *Twin Peaks* music that has been released thus far, it is particularly noteworthy that we have continued to see new character-based themes come to light that have previously remained absent from soundtrack releases. This is a testament to not only the extensive quilt of characters in the show, but also of the approach in the score to musically identify so many secondary elements within the show. One could argue that this is a large factor in the way the show's music helped create such a strong sense of viewer familiarity with characters, even after as little as their second on-screen appearance. While clearly the themes and recurring motifs presented in this release are not necessarily flagship moments in the show's musical identity, they do serve as important stitching to the great fabric of the show's storytelling.

Presented with this bundle are ten tracks that compile supporting character themes through the show (among these are "Hanks's Theme," "Wheeler's Theme," "Leo's Theme," "Earl's Theme," "Lana's Theme," "Josie's Web," ["Horne's Theme"] and the theme from *Invitation to Love*).

75. "Earle's Theme" **Scott Pick**
Before Windom Earle joined Season 2, the only real danger in *Twin Peaks* was the show getting canceled by ABC. So it was nice to finally have an actual villain. Kenneth Welsh was such a great actor (and a really nice person). The second half of Season 2 gets a bad rap, but I think once Windom joins, most of the issues are solved. Cooper is best when he has a worthy opponent. This track, played on a woodwind, is used whenever Earle is around. It is haunting and airy and feels almost primitive. Earle

represents evil from another time, and this theme sums him up perfectly. The fact that he used a musical instrument to beat Leo illustrates his disdain for anything artistic and beautiful. He also uses poems, cards, and games against his enemies. I bet he never donated to his local PBS station even once. For most of these bundles, I don't have the actual price anymore, but this one was $3.99 for ten tracks. That is a crazy deal, way below worth. The *TPA* was certainly economical; by no means was Lynch trying to fleece his fans. It was a more innocent time on the internet.

76. "Half Speed Orchestra 5 (Leo's Theme)"

This cue is another creeping orchestra piece that moves slowly up the scale, creating tension and never letting go. "Leo's Theme" is used in Episode 1 and is always associated with danger.

77. "Hank's Theme"

Hank is another character who is not really one of my favorites, but I sure do recognize this cue as his theme song. It has the same sound that is used at the end of "The Bookhouse Boys" mix on the original series. This is a short piece that is used when Norma goes to Hank's parole hearing and he threatens her. Sometimes I wonder if maybe he was a bad husband.

78. "Hank's Theme (Version 2)"

This is a thirty-second alternate version that has the part usually played for Hank.

79. "Invitation to Love (Lover's Dilemma)"

This track really kills me. It is two minutes long; you hear like four seconds of it in the series, and it is so quiet you never really hear the melody of it during the scene. The fact that Angelo spent so much time on this track is something I would have loved to have asked him about. The theme is definitely trying to spoof "Nadia's Theme" from *The Young and the Restless*. Yes, this track is a little cheesy, but also it's kinda filled with such campy goodness that I have an affection for it. Angelo really was a master at doing things like this. This is played in Episode 4 when Lucy is watching *Invitation to Love*. When Harry asks her what is going on, she tells him what's happening on the fake show, not at the sheriff's station.

80. "Invitation to Love Theme (Bumper)"

This is just an eight-second bumper used when *Invitation to Love* comes in and out of the series. This is a fun one, and if I ever did a *Twin Peaks* podcast, I would use this as my theme. I am assuming a million people already have. Also, if I ever do a *Twin Peaks* podcast, please be a dear and kill me.

81. "Invitation to Love Theme" **Scott Pick**

Here we get the full theme song of *Invitation to Love*. This track, campy as well, comes in at under a minute, but it should be preserved because we fans are the opposite of Season 2—we actually remember *Invitation to Love*. I picked this as my first track on the vinyl set because after over thirty years of having to hear "Falling" as the first track on so many releases, we're giving *Invitation* a shot at being first.

82. "Lana's Theme" **Scott Pick**

Here we have another one of those times when the theme is better than the character. This song, played on a flute, evokes feelings of the love Robin Hood has for Maid Marion. (And yes, I am talking about the Disney version only.) Lana is supposed to be a character who can make men do anything for love, and this theme hits it right on the nose. We can't say for sure if this theme was just lying around or if Angelo wrote it for Lana, but because it is so short, I tend to think he wrote it directly for her character.

83. "Horne's Theme"

This starts with a bit of "Audrey's Dance" but then adds that pulsing Packard and then goes into the "Dreams are made of" buildup. It is funny that when this cue was first released it was called "Josie's Web," but Dean changed it to "Horne's Theme." It comprises parts and pieces of several themes. It was most famously used when Ben and Jerry Horne are presented with a bevy of sex workers; Ben starts quoting Shakespeare to Blackie at One Eyed Jacks, and Jerry interrupts with "Where's the new girl?" Hence the dramatic ending. It makes more sense to call this "Horne's Theme," since this is where the cue originated.

84. "Wheeler's Theme" **Scott Pick**

The western feel of this song is a welcome reprieve from the language of most *Twin Peaks* music. This fits John Justice Wheeler quite well. Doesn't it just make you wanna wear a big wool sweater? John has that sheriff-in-a-cowboy-town-trying-to-do-right vibe. This cue was just the beginning of Angelo demonstrating his range with themes based on the acoustic guitar. This is certainly a precursor to his work on *The Straight Story*, which sounds nothing like any of his other work, and is just as brilliant.

November 10

Hurley wrote: In as so much as "Freshly Squeezed" is an all-too-familiar composition from the *Twin Peaks* discography, hearing all of its variations can open a listener up to a more broad understanding of its various musical incarnations. Specifically, it is revealing of the instrumentalists involved . . . several of whom are presented here on solo track versions, improvising on what were (more often than not) single recorded takes. The level of musicianship tapped for the show's music is unquestionably high, and listening to these alternate versions back-to-back has the unique effect of lowering one's aural barometer in order to create appreciation of notes and not just tracks.

Nine tracks in total make up this "Freshly Squeezed" themed bundle. Included are recordings of solo bass, flute, clarinet and bass clarinet, as well as alt. versions of clarinet and flute with full ensemble. Additionally, a "Fast Cool Jazz Version 2," "Mid-tempo," arrangement and full unedited version of the original cut are included here for download.

Here are a bunch of "Freshly Squeezed" takes that will certainly make you say there isn't much of a difference between this song and "DOTDM." As with other bundles of the exact same cue with just instrumentation changes, it pretty much depends on how you feel about each instrument as for which of these cues is your favorite. None is critical to me.

85. "Freshly Squeezed (Clarinet)"
86. "Freshly Squeezed (Complete Version)"
87. "Freshly Squeezed (Fast Cool Jazz Solo Bass)"
88. "Freshly Squeezed (Fast Cool Jazz V. 2 Clean)"
89. "Freshly Squeezed (Flute)"
90. "Freshly Squeezed (Mid-tempo Version)"
91. "Freshly Squeezed (Solo Bass Clarinet)"
92. "Freshly Squeezed (Solo Clarinet)"
93. "Freshly Squeezed (Solo Flute)"

November 18
Hurley wrote: Certainly one of the premier iconic images to the show's visual legacy, the Packard Sawmill also embodied the most complex storyline amidst the entire *Twin Peaks* saga. Its plot involved a small multiple of players and can be thought of as the foundation to the more "soap opera-ish" flavors of the show. In reality, the lumber mill that was featured as the Packard Mill in the series was demolished and downsized only a few months after the show's Pilot was filmed. The old mill would remain in tack, however, as images of the original building and its working hardware would be replayed week after week during the show's opening titles sequence. In a way, this is very analogous to the life of *Twin Peaks* itself. Although "dismantled" from a broadcast perspective, the show has continued to live on in a kind of suspended montage, romantically existing always as it once was . . .

Included within this bundle are "The Mill Deal" as well as "Josie and Jonathan" (a half-speed version of "The Mill Deal" utilized in the second season). Additionally included is "The Mill Fire," which is one of the rare action-oriented tracks of the series that actually resembles some of the more typical television music of the period. It offers a good comparative reminder of just how different from its contemporaries a majority of the music of *Twin Peaks* was.

94. "The Mill Deal"
Episode 4 has so many new tracks in it. That is how you know it was directed by Tim Hunter. This track is played when Ben meets Leo in the woods to talk about burning down the mill. This cue has a bit of the eighties in it and isn't as brave or new as the rest of the score. But then again, what song could you write to the dialogue of "You were in business with a couple of glue-sniffing squish heads, Leo?"

95. "Josie and Jonathan"

If you want to understand the entire concept of the half-speed versions that Lori Eschler created for the series, there is no easier way than cuing up "The Mill Deal" and "Josie and Jonathan" back-to-back in your iTunes. When you switch back and forth between them, you can tell they are the exact same song, just played at different speeds. The original runs eighty-seven seconds, and the new one is 123 seconds. That means the song was slowed down thirty percent. You can tell the orchestrations are exactly the same, but the feelings they evoke are totally different. "Josie and Jonathan" sounds much more uneasy, not quite human, or man-made. Everything feels just a little off. This track is played when Josie's life is becoming more unsettled itself. When "The Mill Deal" was originally played, Josie felt fairly confident she had bamboozled Ben Horne out of the land and was on her way to running off with Thomas Eckhardt. (Damn, she had a low bar for success.) But by the time Lori started using the track "Josie and Jonathan," it was pretty much all lost for Josie. She probably knew that not even a barbeque-smoked pig with an apple shoved down its throat could save her. Although I doubt she knew she was destined for a drawer. What a knob! (That joke is Ben Louche's; I happily borrow it and suggest you all play Twingo with the Double R Club to hear more comedy of such high esteem.)

96. "The Mill Fire"

I bet even you can guess which scene this cue was written for. Just like "The Mill Deal," this is one of the few dated-sounding cues. It is really hard to listen to this cue and not giggle at its silliness. Despite the name and sound, it is used again when Truman and Cooper rescue Audrey from One Eyed Jacks. I asked Mark Frost, who directed the episode in which the track was first used, about how it came to be.

Mark Frost: I told them I wanted this to be scored to picture, and then they did it, and then they played me the finished product. I didn't attend the scoring session because I was busy doing other stuff. I wasn't involved until the final mix.

Kinny Landrum: That was a big, long cue. That took all day.

It had drums and everything else on it. I did play on that, positively. That was a pretty complicated sync issue. Art didn't have any way of literally synching audio and video in his studio, so it became a pain in the ass.

Dean Hurley: I remember this was a very straight-ahead classical cheesy television movie cue. Think *X-Files*. It sounds like somebody banged out a symphonic cue on a synth. Those were the kind of things Angelo had to do for an episode.

December 8

Hurley wrote: Although most of the original music for *Twin Peaks: FWWM* saw release with the film's 1992 soundtrack album, there were a considerable amount of musical passages from the film that didn't see release. Of these passages, a majority were a familiar blend of slow speed orchestral music that surreptitiously wove in and out of scenes, aurally unifying portions of the film in a similar way cement mortar is used to bond bricks. Most of this music was created in the same fashion as like-sounding music from the series; a "collage approach" that layered and combined vari-speed recordings of re-purposed music. In fact, much of it *is* the same music in different configurations (the previous archive releases "24 Hours," "Unease Motif/The Woods," "Stair Music/Danger Theme," etc. can all be heard here, swimming together with newer motifs unique to the film). Much of this type of music was created directly on the dubbing stage . . . cut and assembled in the same fashion sound effects are combined and mixed during the final stages of finishing a film. As a result, some of the excerpts here are reclaimed from the film's music stem and do not, unfortunately, represent longer compositions.

Included within this bundle are eight screen examples of slow speed orchestral passages from *FWWM*. Additionally included are an alternate sax version of the "Theme from FWWM" (the opening bars which should be recognizable from the screen version of the composition) and an unedited, 11-minute version of "Circumference of a Circle" (a synth improvisation which was used as a collage element during the film's train car sequences).

97. "Back to Fat Trout (Unease Motif/The Woods)"

After focusing so much time on the original series, the *TPA* finally gets back to where my heart truly lies: the music of *FWWM*. This cue combines all the feelings of being between two worlds that Laura and Teresa experience throughout *FWWM*. There are tons of countermelodies playing frontward and backward throughout this cue. This plays during

Cooper's appearance at the Fat Trout trailer park. "Two Chalfontes. Weird," says Carl Rodd while this Black Lodge Rumble-esque cue plays. Truthfully, this isn't as complex and layered as some of the other cues from *FWWM*, until about two minutes in. That is when Cooper sees "Let's Rock" written on Desmond's car. After that, Cooper stands at the river and says, "Who knows where or when?" This cue scores this entire scene, which means Dean pulled this directly off the *FWWM* finished film. I am sure Lori Eschler and David Lynch created all these sounds and combined a few stems to create "Back to Fat Trout."

A fun side note is that when Lynch was editing Part 12 of *The Return*, he used the same cue from *FWWM* when Cooper sees "Let's Rock" for the moment when Diane says "Let's rock" after Albert explains what the Blue Rose means. Although would it have killed Albert to plug the magazine at this point?

98. "Behind the Mask"

This is the cue that plays while Laura slowly climbs the Palmer stairs to find "the man behind the mask [who] is looking for the book with the pages torn out." Watching Sheryl Lee confidently but tentatively climb the Palmer stairs and open her bedroom door only to see Bob jumping out could make just about anyone forget that music was playing at this point. One of the main differences between the "Behind the Mask" release and the film version is that there is no sound of a fan spinning on this cue; in the film, that is another layer of sound that was added. Also, when Laura sees Bob, the music in the film is so much louder. The cue actually does have a crescendo, but you really can't hear it above all the other sounds. It does play, however, because the cue continues as Laura runs out of the Palmer house, and that music is exactly the same in the film as on this cue.

99. "Circumference of a Circle"

This eleven-minute cue is quite a cacophony of sound that plays during Laura's murder in the train car. I couldn't verify this because of all the other sounds playing during that scene, but according to Ross Dudle, only 7:10-7:53 is used from this long cue. I would never argue with Ross, who's *Twin Peaks* Soundtrack Design website has helped me time and time again. This is a very disturbing, long piece of music. It would be hard to say this needs to be released, but like many of the firewood-type cues, it sure is nice to have.

100. "It's Your Father" **Scott Pick**

"It's Your Father" is a much more layered track compared with "Back to Fat Trout." This plays in the scene in which the One Armed Man approaches Leland and Laura in the middle of the street. Lori and Lynch faded in all those whooping sounds associated with MFAP at around 1:15. "I am the arm and I sound like this." While there is no doubt that this cue was created by layering all kinds of music, it was the sound effects supervisor who had a lot to say about it on the *Sound Effect Podcast*.

Doug Murray: The whole scene is louder and the music is more powerful. It's like it's all coming through; it's finally bursting through, and whatever is happening here—and it's so intense. The music is what pushes it into that magical realm of this Red Room otherworld bursting through into the real world that is the cause of all Laura's suffering. It's happening most powerfully here in the movie until the end, when it's fatal. The music—which is the same musical elements that were in ["Teresa's Autopsy"]—there are some backward guitar sounds, little niggly little kinds of sounds, and then you have various other sounds that are probably stems from other cues that have been used earlier in the film to identify some kind of bleed from the Red Room space into the real world.

Lori Eschler: That was a very intense segment that we worked on. It was like a dance or a painting almost in regard to the audio, the music, and the sound. There's the sound that Doug brought and the dialogue that was manipulated, then all these musical sort of stems from different sources. I had my digital editing system set up to the right of the mixing board, and David was mixing the music.

Scott Ryan: So are you giving the cues to David frontward and backward, and he's deciding which ones are used?

Lori Eschler: No, I had preprepared them. There were different textures, like there was a backward track of ponticello violins.

Scott Ryan: It sounds to me like someone has a bow, and they're just sawing on it.

Lori Eschler: Yeah. The technique, as notated by an orchestrator, is called the Italian word, ponticello. Let's say this is the bridge right here, and here are the strings, and so you take the bow right next to the bridge and you're just sawing, literally, right next to the bridge, at that point on the strings, then you'll get that sound.

Scott Ryan: And was it done on a cello or a violin?

Lori Eschler: Those were violins, and I slowed them down and made them backward, because that's what we did. It was so abstract.

Scott Ryan: To me, that sound signifies that what is going on at that moment connects to the Red Room. Would you agree with that?

Lori Eschler: No, I think it's part of a mood that a specific track is almost like cousins with other string sounds that are also used. I think it was Ron Carter playing bass on one of the tracks. Those sounds gathered together fit the mood.

This day of filming that scene was a rare combative day for David Lynch. When I interviewed Ray Wise and then later Al Strobel about filming this scene, both mentioned that Lynch yelled at them on this day. There is so much noise, tension, fear, and anger captured in this scene that it makes me wonder if Lynch did that to provoke them. Or was he just having a bad day?

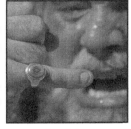

Al Strobel: I don't think he lost his cool, but I know I scared the shit out of him when I was stunt driving. He was in the Cadillac convertible. And I started having fun with my little camper. I even got it up on two wheels at one point. And that scared David. He was on the walkie-talkie with me, and I could tell I scared him. And then we did the scene where I stopped the camper close to the Palmers' car. I think it was done in one take. David asked me to rev the car a couple of times, and he had a couple of grips jump up and down on the back bumper. So my camper was rocking up and down. And he said, "Don't worry about being heard above all this noise because we can always dub back in in post." Using all my techniques, I was able to be understood well enough above all the ruckus that we didn't have to dub it in. My focus during that scene is on Laura because I want to tell her she is driving with a murderer and a rapist. I am shouting past Ray because he was in the driver's seat. I could tell out of the corner of my eye that he was kind of spooked too.

101. "Jacques's Cabin / The Train Car"

This cue plays from when Leland grabs Ronette and Laura at Jacques's cabin until Laura puts on the ring in the train car. (He said DON'T take the ring. She never listens.) This track is then combined with a classical piece of music, "Agnus Dei" from *Requiem in C Moll*, that takes the foreground as the murder is actually committed and is reprised during the credits after "The Voice of Love."

Doug Murray: David found this piece of music, Cherubini's *Requiem in C-Moll*, conducted by Riccardo Muti. He had this recording, and he decided this is what is going to go in there. They tried to get the rights, and Muti said, "I never let my music be in a movie; it degrades it." Lynch had to make a direct appeal to Muti and explain to him what he was doing and why it was so important, and Muti relented. But it was touch and go there because Lynch couldn't imagine any other piece of music being there. (*Sound Effect Podcast*)

Scott Ryan: There is a classical piece called "Agnus Dei" that you used in the train car scene. I bought the vinyl that it comes from, but I can never find the exact moment that you took the music from.

Lori Eschler: When you were playing the vinyl, did you try putting it at half speed and backward?

Scott Ryan: [Laughs.] I did not.

Lori Eschler: That's your clue. Remember how we started doing things backward in the Red Room? That was part of the music vernacular. It was okay to play things backward. Isn't it beautiful? I have goosebumps from just remembering that scene. It was really hard, although it is really fun to talk with you about it because you know so much about it, and you have such great insight. I am not being triggered whatsoever. I got to meet Sheryl Lee, and she is a very deep person and just as sweet as she seems. She brought so much light, which is the opposite of what she is playing. She is like an angel.

Scott Ryan: Speaking of angels, what about the angel in *FWWM*?

Lori Eschler: I love that scene. I remember we were so close to the end of the job and thinking this is the end of *Twin Peaks*.

Scott Ryan: Ha. *Twin Peaks* never ends. Where did "Agnus Dei" come from, because it is rare for Lynch to license a song for *Twin Peaks*?

Lori Eschler: David was flying back from somewhere while we were editing the film, and a woman sitting next to him told him he had to listen to this piece of music. She had it on a little audio cassette, which he brought to the stage, and I had it digitized and then slowed it down, and the producers had to scramble to get it cleared. It was a little dramatic, because it was like one of the last days. So we have to have this.

Scott Ryan: And you really took it from a cassette? So what we're hearing in the film is from a cassette?

Lori Eschler: Yeah.

Scott Ryan: Wow! That's awesome. What were the temp tracks in those scenes before this song was put there?

Lori Eschler: Nothing. We hadn't gotten to that scene yet. Nothing was ever locked in before the film was finalized.

One last thing on the *Requiem in C-Moll*. I bought the vinyl on Discogs because I really wanted to have this piece of music. It really is incredible how you just can't find it on the recording. Never does it actually sound like it sounds when the end

credits kick in and Lynch freeze frames on Laura's sad but smiling face. So if you are wanting to get the song, you are better off taking it directly off the DVD, over buying the record. I sort of wish that this track would have been a *TPA*, but of course, they wouldn't have had the rights to it. The reason I decided to cover it here is because of how intertwined it is with the cue "Jacques's Cabin / The Train Car." It also is one of the best examples of how much Lori and Lynch were manipulating every aspect of sound heard in *FWWM*. For years it has been easy to lament that Sheryl Lee wasn't nominated for an Oscar for this film, but rarely does anyone talk about how Lynch wasn't nominated for sound on *FWWM*. Yes, Sheryl Lee was most certainly robbed, and so was Lynch.

102. "Laura Visits Harold"

Here is another cue used in *The Return*, although it isn't one many people would recognize. In Part 10, when Gordon opens the door and has a vision of Laura Palmer crying to Donna in *FWWM*, this cue is played. The part of the cue that is reused can be found at 1:30, when the song has a scary apex. The scene in *The Return* which they overlay Sheryl Lee is from a scene in *FWWM* where the "Best Friends" cue is playing, so these musical cues don't connect properly. In *FWWM*, this same apex is used when Laura says to Harold Smith, "Fire walk with ME!" So in reality, if Lynch wanted to use this cue again, he should have shown Laura say this line, or he should have scored *The Return* scene with "Best Friends." But again, this would be true only if he had wanted continuity. But that is not of any importance in *The Return*.

Going back to the original use of "Laura Visits Harold," Lenny Von Dolen talked about how Lynch made him feel this scene in which Laura visits Harold was the most important scene in the film, but he wondered if maybe that wasn't just what Lynch does for every actor in every scene.

103. "Phillip Jeffries" **Scott Pick**

David Slusser: The "Phillip Jeffries" cue has hallmarks of Angelo's harmonic palette. It's also a reversed recording and seems to be synthesized strings. If you can reverse it, you may recognize it from somewhere.

I decided to take Slusser up on his task for me. "Phillip Jeffries" and

"It's Your Father" are actually just the song "Slow Speed Orchestra 1 (24 Hours)" in reverse with random saxophone solos added (not from "Freshly Squeezed" or "DOTDM."). So here we have another cue that was manufactured like a Dougie. Lori and Lynch created this cue to fit David Bowie entering the FBI office and returning to our world for a bit. It's hard to decide which of the *FWWM* sonic moments should be released on my pretend vinyl, but I pick this one because it has elements of some of the other pieces, but the "We're not gonna talk about Judy" scene is so classic and I have studied this scene for clues so many times that this cue seems like a must own to me.

Lori Eschler: That is a layer of a whole bunch of things processed. It was little bits and pieces from *Twin Peaks* and some stuff from Angelo's studio and some sound effects. That was part of the stuff where David was mixing the music live and I would feed him tracks. He was mixing a bunch of stuff together. I can't tell you specifically what they were. I remember the low drone and the sloweddown cello thing. There were sound effect samples, drones, and it turned out really scary.

104. "Teresa's Autopsy" **Scott Pick**

This is played during the autopsy of Teresa Banks. The cue really kicks in about a minute into the track. That is when all the Red Room noises start infecting this cue. You can hear a bit of the fan, some electricity, and the ponticello violins. This is a real mix of noises that represent the world of Bob. During the autopsy, the Red Room noises really start to play with the discovery of the letter T under Teresa's fingernail. This is a sign that Lynch, back in 1992, connected these musical cues to the place where there is always music in the air. That music was silenced in *The Return*, but it is alive and well in *FWWM*.

That being said, "Teresa's Autopsy" is used in Part 12 when Sarah Palmer sees the turkey jerky and storms out of the store. This is another time when the musical cue doesn't totally match its original use. It could match in that there are certainly Black Lodge forces at work within and around Sarah. One could also say that the actress Zoe McLane, who is playing the store clerk, sort of looks like Pamela Gidley, who played Teresa Banks, so maybe that is the connection, but most likely, Lynch just likes the cue because of all the funky sound effects he and Lori dumped onto this track. But this grocery store scene has little to do with Teresa's autopsy. With the few *FWWM* cues used in *The Return*, I sure would have preferred having this cue on the score release from *The Return* over "Audrey's Dance" again. This is why I am picking it as one that should be released now.

Doug Murray: The scene where they are inspecting under Teresa Bank's fingernail in the morgue there is this really creepy music that is several layers of backward and slowed-down pieces from different score elements from the movie. (*Sound Effect Podcast*)

105. "Theme from Twin Peaks: FWWM (Saxophone)" **Scott Pick**

I will never get over how beautiful this version of the theme from *FWWM* is, and it makes me angrier than Mr. C was when he was redirected from the Palmer House to the sheriff's station that this piece of music isn't released, isn't on vinyl, isn't preserved for the future. This is my all-time favorite *TPA* release and the most beautiful recording in the entire canon of *Twin Peaks* music. We are here. This is the best one. The fact that this piece of music will disappear when all the original *Twin Peaks* fans are gone breaks my heart. So why do I love this specific track so much? Where do I begin?

Because the first sound we ever hear in *FWWM* is the beginning of this cue. This saxophone, which blows a haunting riff, plays over the New Line Cinema logo. So the very first thing I heard in that theater in August 1992 was the sax version of "Theme from FWWM," and that alone means it should be released. The cue then fades from the sax version to the trumpet version that plays during the opening credits. The trumpet version is released on the official *FWWM* soundtrack, but this sax version exists only as an MP3.

This is the version that Big Ed and Norma listen to in the back seat of Ed's truck during the *Missing Pieces* scene. They tune this song in on the radio and the theme plays: not the trumpet version, but the sax version. For so many people, this is their favorite scene cut from the film. I know Big Ed and Norma are fan favorites, but I would once again submit that the real reason this scene works so well is because the song matches the mood and fits the dialogue. Norma herself tells Big Ed, "It's you and me, Ed. You can barely hear us." It gets worse than that, Norma; your song was never even released for anyone to hear it. But I guess Norma is fine with waiting; she waited over forty-five years to marry Big Ed.

This version is a wonderful example of how important instrumentation is when orchestrating a song. Julee Cruise sings this song on her *Voice of Love* album. It is called "She Would Die for Love" but it's the trumpet version. It is a similar mix that plays during the *FWWM* opening credits, although on her version the bass is turned up a bit more. It makes perfect sense because the trumpet version, with Jim Hynes on trumpet, is the Laura Palmer version. It represents her. I personally would not want a saxophone to be associated with Laura, because that instrument will always be closely aligned with Agent Cooper. The lyrics are surely a tribute to Laura Palmer, although I did read an interview with Julee in which she said her second album was going to be a bunch of songs about someone trying to kill her. She said this in an early nineties interview, and I'm sure that idea changed, but "She Would Die for Love" would have fit that motif. This sax version is much more associated with the love between Big Ed and Norma, and that longing sax fits them perfectly. This was a track that Al Regni, who played the lead on the sax version, remembered:

Al Regni: There was a sax solo that wasn't used in *FWWM*. I thought it was quite beautiful, and they didn't use it. They used the trumpet version. Maybe it fits better with the scene. That is me playing the sax. I got lucky on that one. Angelo wrote a couple of bars, and then I played along with the chord changes and what would be appropriate for that song. I tried to play what fit in with the premise of the show. "*FWWM*" and "Dance of the Dream Man" were soloistic, and I remember both of those quite vividly.

Man, would I love to know which was recorded first, the trumpet or the sax version? The melodies are similar, but the moods are completely different. I wonder who followed whom. More questions we will never know the answers to.

An alternate version of this track is one of the bonus songs Dean Hurley released after the *TPA* was completed. He released a version called the "Theme from Twin Peaks: FWWM (Deleted Scene Futz)." This was also released on the Sacred Bones *Floating into the Night* mixtape release, but there it was called "AM Radio Broadcast." That version is a shortened version and was not released on vinyl.

The beauty of the original track gets me every time I hear it. I do love the trumpet version, but I love the sax version just as much. Both should be released and protected.

106. "Wash Your Hands"

This cue is used in *FWWM* when Leland tells Laura that she didn't wash her hands before sitting down to dinner. When Ray Wise tells you to wash your hands, you better do it. This track was also used in *The Return* in Part 11 when Miriam crawls out of the woods after little Lord Horne boy beats her up. (Sorry, I just think Richard Horne is the least scary villain in any Lynch project ever.) It is fascinating how many of these *FWWM* orchestra tracks Lynch reused in *The Return*. What makes it fascinating is that almost all of them are generic cues that would not be recognized by casual fans. It wasn't that he wouldn't use older cues; he just didn't use those that were widely known.

December 16

Hurley wrote: A clean "studio" version of this very unique composition can be heard here in a running time considerably longer than the original version. Although the show seemed to favor usage of the ethereally-murky dictaphone recorded version (most commonly heard in the show's Log Lady introductions), this traditionally recorded take is certainly audible at several points throughout the show. The clarity and presence of this direct version allows for a more revealing examination of the distinct synthesizer sound that forms the core of the very composition itself.

Additionally included with this version of "Dark Mood Woods" is One Eyed Jack's parlor piano music, as well as the seasonally-relevant bumper music used for the show's promotional holiday greeting.

107. "Dark Mood Woods (Studio Version)"

Scott Ryan: There is a "Dark Mood Woods" dictaphone version, and then there is a "Dark Mood Woods" studio version. Is the one really from a dictaphone, because the quality is actually pretty good?

Dean Hurley: No, I wouldn't call it good. We are not talking about an Agent Cooper micro cassette. It was a regular cassette player, one of those big, bulky things. The "Dark Mood Woods" two versions is a great example. It was a big revelation for me when I pieced that together. My memory from when I saw the series, before I was working for David, was that piece of music. It definitely has a soul-esness in the last episode of Season 2. It is relied on so heavily. There is a certain essence of the show that comes across on that piece of music; it is a very distinctive sound. When I came across the work tape for that song, I realized, "Holy shit! David *used* the work tape even though there was a studio version." They were both recorded at the same time. They had the dictaphone running at the time to make sure that nothing was lost idea-wise. But Angelo is also running straight to DAT out of the keyboard. So both versions are the same. But when you listen to them back-to-back, we are talking about timbre. The timbre of them is so different, and there is so much mystery and extra sort of grit, and something that you can't quantify in that dictaphone recording. That is just hugely  illuminating to me from a working standpoint, and a magic trick standpoint, when you don't know how something was captured. That is the thing about audio: when you don't know how it was captured, it completely eradicates itself from context. You can hear it as magical. What the hell is that?

Knowing that, I even wonder about my own thinking. If I was in that situation, and David told me to get "Dark Mood Woods." I might have reached for the DAT recording, the proper version. I'd say to him, "I don't understand. You want to use the cassette recording?" But when nobody knows how it was captured, there is a certain quality in how you experience it. It is a very interesting thing. When I was working for David early on, he had a phrase he loves to use, "Money can't buy that." You can't pay someone well enough to fuck up on purpose. There were no parameters or archetypes of logic that dictated to him how something should go. It was purely a childish reactionary kind of thing that a lot of other practitioners in their field might get tripped up by that.

108. "One Eyed Jack's Parlour Music"

It is always fun to get a cue that was never used, and here we have one. This was supposed to be for a One Eyed Jack's scene, but no one ever picked this cue, so it wasn't used. It's a fine piano track, but I think it feels more like it would be in a western saloon than a place where you might bump into Laura, Ronette, or the new girl.

109. "Twin Peaks Christmas Greeting"

This is a silly twelve-second bumper that has sleigh bells playing on top of the bass notes from "Falling." This also ends the first year of the release.

January 12, 2012

Hurley wrote Cooper's first monologue to Diane from Episode 1 and then wrote: It is important to rewind for a moment and spotlight the very first musical cue which began the first season of *Twin Peaks*. The quicker-tempoed soprano clarinet version of "DODM" is recognizable from its use in the opening scene of episode one: Agent Cooper awakes having just spent his first night in Twin Peaks, and his musical accompaniment is this specific "rise and shine" rendition of his own theme.

Two additional tracks are also presented here alongside "DODM." "Laura Palmer's Theme (Baritone Guitar Punctuation)" borrows a sonic character from the show's main theme, infusing the signature three-chord riff with an even higher dosage of ominous dread. Additionally, "Leo's Return" is included a singularly synth-based cue that supports the narrative arc of Leo Johnson's return from vegetative state amidst late Season 2.

110. "Dance of the Dream Man (Fast Soprano Clarinet)"

This fun version highlights Grady Tate's drums, mixed higher here than on other versions. Then the clarinet does take some liberties with the melody, which makes this version quite different from the released version. It is probably the second-best version of this track. It really swings. I have been careful to not pick tracks that have already been released, but if there was extra room on my made-up vinyl, I'd pick this just because Al Regni's improvisations are so much fun, especially after the three-minute mark. Since the drums are mixed higher, you can actually hear Grady Tate scatting as he plays. I love that. The mixers should have left that in every version. As Dean points out, this is the first musical cue from the first regular episode of *Twin Peaks*; that in itself makes it worthy of remembering.

111. "Laura Palmer's Theme (Baritone Guitar Punctuation)"

What sets this apart from other versions of this cue is Vinnie Bell's baritone guitar. He hits the bass notes, and it gives the cue a bit of a "Bookhouse Boys" feel to it. The guitar drops out at the apex of the piano, after which it is the same mix of the theme. The guitar comes back in after the piano section. It repeats it all again, making this an almost-five-minute track. Most of the other "Laura Palmer" cues are shortened. This is a nice track to mix in if you don't want to listen to the same old same old. More Vinnie is always good for me.

112. "Leo Returns"

This track wins for the most dramatic beginning in the *TPA*. It is so over-the-top and feels so eighties that you would expect this track to be from *The A-Team*. It debuts in Episode 21, which really is a shocker because that means it was written toward the end of the series. By this point, it really shouldn't sound this eighties, because it was 1991. It plays when Leo comes back to attack Bobby and Shelly and then escapes into the woods. I gotta be honest: this cue sounded really harsh after listening to so many beautiful tracks, so I decided to watch this scene. Shelly is moving slowly along the side of her fridge when Leo throws a jar of *jam* at her head and just misses. Maybe this is the correct music to score a lethal jam attack. I stand corrected.

January 20

Hurley wrote: Laura Palmer bound so much of the *Twin Peaks* universe together. Her presence—and to an even greater extent her absence—managed to summon a collective, community-wide emotional pulse. For the music of the series, this was reinforced by the "double duty" of this singular composition . . . acting as both "Laura Palmer's Theme" as well as the "Love Theme." Whether characters were conjuring up memories of Laura specifically, or channeling emotion in general, one unifying theme ascended and descended over all.

Included within this bundle are a number of remaining unreleased versions of "Laura Palmer's Theme." Some are full expressions of the familiar composition while others are truncated portions. At the risk of over-saturation, every take of one series of "Laura Palmer's Theme" for solo piano has been included here. Although not all of these were screen-used, it does sound as though a majority of them were. Beyond piano, versions of the theme for vibraphone, clarinet and synthesizer are additionally presented here.

113. "Laura Palmer's Theme (Caroline)"

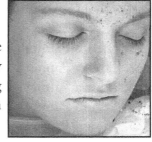

As I have stated before, every once in a while Angelo picks a synth sound that just hurts my ears, and this is one of them. There is something unpleasant about this sound; luckily it goes on for only just over a minute.

114. "Laura Palmer's Theme (Clarinet Bridge)"
This is a short version that plays only the apex section on clarinet.

115. "Laura Palmer's Theme (Clarinet Strings Bridge)"
This sounds like Laura fell into a Casio synthesizer in 1984.

116. "Laura Palmer's Theme (Dark Synth)"
This is by far the darkest version of the theme. It never plays the apex section and is only the synth part at the start of the song. It is really dark, and approaches a Super Mario Brothers sound. This cue is used in Episode 3 when Cooper goes to the Bookhouse for the one and only time, when it wasn't a built set. This scene was filmed at the greatest place to have breakfast in all of LA, maybe the world. It is called The Old Place and is located in Cornell, California. I have had many a breakfast here with my fellow *Twin Peaks* friends. Right around the corner is the place where Andy gets the twine. Both are fun places to visit.

117. "Laura Palmer's Theme (Letter from Harold)"
This has that vocal/ghost feel that is associated with Harold.

118. "Laura Palmer's Theme (Piano A) TK1"
As a piano player, I love these cues. This take is a one-note-only version of the song until the apex section. But it never fully develops. It's a very lonely, solo piano version.

119. "Laura Palmer's Theme (Piano A) TK2"
120. "Laura Palmer's Theme (Piano A) TK3"

I have to give a special shout-out to this version because this is the one used when Laura says the subtitle to my *FWWM* book, "Your Laura Disappeared."

121. "Laura Palmer's Theme (Piano A) TK4"
122. "Laura Palmer's Theme (Piano B) TK1"
123. "Laura Palmer's Theme (Piano B) TK2"
124. "Laura Palmer's Theme (Piano Bridge)"
125. "Laura Palmer's Theme (Solo Piano)"

126. "Laura Palmer's Theme (Vibraphone)"

This version finishes out the scene in which Donna reads Laura Palmer's last page from her diary. While I love the cue in the episode, it isn't the most pleasant one to listen to because of the wavy sounds the synth makes. The cue is played while Donna reads, "February 23: tonight is the night that I die." Wait a minute, Laura, we have all been celebrating February 24; don't mess with us. Also, do Hawk and Frank Truman know about this hidden page when they are looking for the missing pages or are they just looking for Miss Carrie Page? "Goddamn, these people are confusing."

February 3

Hurley wrote: Many will recognize "Abstract Mood" as "Night Bells" from the *Season Two Music and More* soundtrack release. Originally recorded during the "Just You" sessions, "Abstract Mood" was one of the few tracks for the series to be recorded in Los Angeles and with players different from the usual contributors. Recorded at 1541 N. Wilcox Ave. in Hollywood, "Abstract Mood: Slow"—as it was labeled on the original tape box—was the last cut of the session and most likely a largely unplanned improvisation . . .

"Abstract Mood" is presented here unaltered in its original version. Additionally included is a slower, near-half speed version of the composition.

127. "Abstract Mood"

There is something different about this version versus "Night Bells," and it has something to do with the mix. "Abstract" plays just a little louder and clearer, whereas "Night Bells" seems to have a filter on it. But in the end, I think they are the same actual performance. "Abstract Mood" plays a few seconds longer. Push comes to shove, I'm gonna go with "Night Bells" on *Season Two* over this one, but I can't really justify why.

128. "Abstract Mood (Slow Speed)"

This really is just the same track slowed down. It is used when Major Briggs wanders off in the woods.

February 10

Hurley wrote: Tempo is a powerful element of any musical composition. Changing the speed or pace in a given piece of music can have a direct-affecting relationship with the music's mood or energy. Dramatic temporal changes can yield some of the most fascinating results. It is this territory—straddling the threshold between music and sound design—where much of the slow-speed orchestra material resides amidst the series and feature film.

Originally titled "Lowest Circle of Hell" in the archive, "White Lodge Rumble" is just that . . . the lowest, most moody, bass-rich of the slow-speed material employed in the series. There are also additional elements at work in this unique track that somehow aid in its sounding like the mysterious gateway it is intended to signify: Ominous percussion peppers the track almost like distant cannon blasts or mammoth wooden knocks. These, along with a patina of analog tape noise, act to render an impressionistic sonic landscape that seems almost three-dimensional . . . even without synchronous visuals . . .

"Slow Speed Orchestra 4 (White Lodge Rumble)" is presented in its complete running time of 12 minutes, 13 seconds.

129. "Slow Speed Orchestra 4 (White Lodge Rumble)"

Scott Ryan: The opening scene of Season 2 is incredible, with Cooper having been shot and the Giant appearing. There is so much sound in those scenes.

Lori Eschler: Oh my God, I love that scene, and that drone that is playing underneath, and oh, it is so beautiful. David was really specific about what he wanted. For that scene, we were working digitally, and all my cues were readily available, and I could just bring up anything I wanted as quickly as he wanted to hear it. He had to weed out a lot of sound to isolate what he wanted to hear. That was how the entire team worked. It was like "Have everything ready, and then let's try to do a rough mix and show it to David." Then he would come in and say, "Let's take that out." It was a process of subtraction where he would come up with this beautiful mix of sound and music. He had an amazing ear for that.

Scott Ryan: I remember that when I watched it live on TV back in 1990, whenever the Giant would show up, the sound would cut out on his dialogue. It really pissed me off.

Lori Eschler: That was because of the way the network would compress the signal. That was standard, but we were working in surround sound, but it was early days, and we would play back the mix on the lowest mono speakers and try to make it sound good in both worlds, but once you handed it over to the network it was like "God only knows what they are gonna do with it."

Was I the only one who thought the sound cut out every time the Giant appeared on screen? It always drove me crazy, but it was nice to finally understand why from Lori. This is a cue that is probably mixed under so many scenes of the series that it would be really hard to find them all. This scores the beginning of Season 2 when Señor Drool Cup comes in with the warm milk. I listened to the scene, and it certainly is the rumble that plays throughout the time Cooper is lying on the floor, although it does seem like it is mixed with other sounds as well.

February 17
Hurley wrote: This split-theme bundle features two secondary versions of themes primarily known for their previously released versions. "Harold's Theme" is presented here in a unique composition for harpsichord and synth. "Audrey's Prayer" gets "Windom Earle" treatment in a slightly stilted variation for synth-based flute.

130. "Harold's Theme (Harpsichord)"
Here is a different version of "Harold's Theme" that is slower and more dramatic. This cue is used when Harold confronts Maddy and Donna with the rake and just before he drags the hand rake over his face, which is pretty dramatic. So the score fits the scene. I am sure this is one of

the occasions when they asked Angelo to play a theme on the synth to match Harold's outburst. This track doesn't play very long in the scene, as director Graeme Clifford and Lori Eschler use the "Living Novel" version for the majority of this scene. (Also, anyone else notice that a bit of the blood drips off the handle of the rake and is on Lenny's cheek *before* he cuts himself? TV was simpler back then.)

131. "Audrey's Prayer (Flute)"

Here we get another version of the main theme from Season 2. This cue takes the melody of "Audrey's Prayer" and interprets it on Windom Earle's pan flute. The nice thing about this cue is that it is the most different "Audrey's Prayer" of any of the versions. As I said with "Freshly Squeezed" and "Laura Palmer," what is the point of having the same tune again and again? Answer: when the version is completely different. This flute version is different, not just because of the pan flute but also because of the improvisation of the melody. I really like this track because of its improvisations. Don't skip this one.

March 8

Hurley wrote: The character of Audrey Horne provided quite an interesting array of musical motifs for *Twin Peaks*. Whether it be the off-kilter sensuality of "Audrey's Dance," the playful mischievous of "Sneaky Audrey," the optimistic bounce of "Freshly Squeezed" or the lush emotion of "Audrey's Prayer," the entire gamut of music owes credit to the show's sweetest troublemaker: Miss Audrey Horne. Like many of the themes from *Twin Peaks*, these motifs were not simply reserved for a single character or particular location, but instead cross-pollinated and conversed with a multiple of different people and scenarios, making the dialogue between story and music far more layered and interesting . . .

Included within this bundle are eleven tracks in total that feature a number of variations and components of "Audrey's Dance": the often-used "stripped down" version for Rhodes, bass and drums ("Clean"); versions for drums and bass and solo Rhodes; as well as hybrid "Audrey's Dance/Dance of the Dream Man" versions for clarinet, flute, and sax. Also included are three additional variations/versions of the composition "Sneaky Audrey."

Editor's note: the additional "reprised" version of "Sneaky Audrey" that appears in Episode 4 of the series was not located for this release.

We've gotten the data dumps of many of the main themes: it was time to get "Audrey's Dance." As with other bundles like this, pick your favorite and proceed. I'm gonna stick with the original on the soundtrack.

132. "Audrey's Dance (Clean)"
133. "Audrey's Dance (Drums and Bass)"
134. "Audrey's Dance (Solo Rhodes)"
135. "Audrey's Dance (Synth and Vibraphone)"
136. "Audrey's Dance (Clean Fast)"
137. "Audrey's Dance/Dance of the Dream Man (Saxophone)"
138. "Audrey's Dance/Dance of the Dream Man (Clarinet)"
139. "Audrey's Dance/Dance of the Dream Man (Flute)"

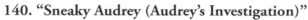

140. "Sneaky Audrey (Audrey's Investigation)"

This cue is used in Episode 5 when Audrey spies on Catherine and Ben through her hiding place. "Sneaky Audrey" was never released as its own piece of music. A portion of it was used on the original soundtrack in the mix of "The Bookhouse Boys." So this cue gives fans the full version of just "Sneaky Audrey."

141. "Sneaky Audrey (Solo)"

This is just the whimsical clarinet part of "Sneaky Audrey," without the other instruments. Just another stem track.

142. "Sneaky Audrey (Alternate)"

They may call this an alternate, but I don't see how this isn't just the synth part of "Laura Palmer's Theme." If the cue doesn't have the clarinet melody that is "Sneaky Audrey," then don't put that title in the name.

March 15

Hurley wrote: As evident from this stripped-down recording, the clarinet solo that became the "One Armed Man Theme" originated as an improvisational take over "Audrey's Dance" (a closer listen will reveal a floor of headphone bleed from the original basic track). The track serves as an excellent testament to the experimental atmosphere under which the show's session musicians must have been allowed to operate. Exploration and improvisation seem to be not only allowed, but encouraged; paving the way for loads of music that might not have otherwise manifested itself . . .

As was typical with a considerable amount of music from the series, the included track found itself both combined and alongside other passages of music. It is presented here, however, as it was found with the archive: as a solo component.

143. "One Armed Man Theme (Solo Clarinet Improvisation)"

That this is an important track in the series is proven by the amount of times Lori Eschler was able to pop it into scenes to create an unsettling feeling. That doesn't mean anyone would really want to listen to a five-minute track of a duck being strangled.

March 22

Hurley wrote: The Great Northern is subject once again in this themed bundle of eight additional tracks from Twin Peaks' premier hotel lodge. "Great Northern Big Band," "Attack of the Pine Weasel," "Great Northern Piano Tune #4," "Twin Peaks Theme (Harp)," as well as 4 tunes that appeared in the Milford Wedding and reception are included here.

144. "Great Northern Big Band" **Scott Pick**

The things that I have gotten to do within and around the world of *Twin Peaks* are truly mind-boggling, maybe none of them crazier than dancing with Ray Wise (Leland Palmer) on stage to this song. In the series, Leland hears this song at the Great Northern party with the Icelanders and starts crying and dancing as he covers his face with his hands. Catherine Martell mimics his hand motions as a dance move, and a Macarena/Twin Peaks dance craze is born. I have done this very dance move with Ray Wise on stage in Indiana in January 2020 at a screening of *FWWM*. Ray and a few of us that were still around after the event danced to the entire 1:45 of this track. Did I mention that Sheryl Lee was sitting off to the side watching us and shaking her head? I was also able to sing with Ray Wise, two Broadway showstoppers that he likes to sing: "Getting to Know You" from *The King and I* and "On a Clear Day" from the Barbra Streisand movie of the same name. I don't know when I sold my soul to Bob to be able to have these unique musical experiences,

but I do know I got the better bargain. My soul isn't worth the fun I had singing and dancing with Ray Wise. [See photo above.]

Lori Eschler: I think Angelo found that piece in a library, and it may have been public domain. I remember that track because the temp music was some Glenn Miller tune.

So maybe Angelo didn't write it. We will never know for sure, but it still is one of my vinyl picks because of how classic the scene is; plus it was something I always wanted to own.

145. "Wedding Hymn"

Just like with the Miss Twin Peaks tracks, I find it beyond fascinating that Angelo, assumingly, had to write four brand-new music cues, from scratch, for the stupid Milford wedding plot. I'm telling you, the worse the storyline, the better the music. This is just some organ music that plays as Dougie, who we later learn, in *The Secret History of Twin Peaks*, is the single most important American ever born, and his bride Lana get married.

146. "Wedding Song #1" **Scott Pick**

As silly as this wedding is, this track is a classic one and must be released on vinyl. It starts playing after the cutting of the cake and continues while Denise explains some life changes to Cooper. Fix your hearts or die if you can't get behind them. The cue is used not just here, but again in Episode 25 by Duwayne Dunham in the "happy scene," when Gordon tells Harry his cure for a hangover. This cue loops for a while in that diner scene until Annie correctly recognizes the bird that Cooper sees through the window; then the music transitions to a repeat of "Hook Rug Dance." Back-to-back these tracks create pure happiness. I truly love the tracks from the Milford wedding as much as I abhor the storyline. Because this is one of my favorite tracks, I asked Kinny if he was on the keyboards or if it was Angelo . . .

Kinny Landrum: I'm not sure if I am playing this or not. It is very old-fashioned sounding. Piano seems a little ornate for Angelo to play.

147. "Wedding Song #2 ('Stranger Nights')" **Scott Pick**

This cue plays as Pete tries to salvage the dinner conversation at his table while sitting with the Log Lady, the Mayor, and Catherine. I guess it wasn't too lively. I totally agree with Pete when he says "The music turned out pretty good." So good that I want this on my vinyl. Then we see Cooper and Audrey dancing, which is one of the few times these two characters interact in the back half of Season 2, but probably Andy and Denise steal the scene as they dance cheek to cheek. The subtitle of this track is "Stranger Nights" because, I am sure, someone told Angelo they would like to have a "Strangers in the Night" type of song and didn't want to pay to license it. So Angelo wrote a tribute to it. The main instrument is the sax, so I asked Al Regni if he remembered whether he was the one playing it . . .

Al Regni: That sounds like it could be me playing in the style of a wedding band.

148. "Wedding Song #3 (Accordion)"

This could have also been an M.T. Wentz track—it has that feeling—but is just another wedding track. There actually is a background actor with an accordion shown on screen as Cooper enters the reception and heads over to talk to Denise. When the track ends, the audience applauds. I always love when the cues are heard by the TV viewers and the characters as well. This is another cue that was slipped into *On the Air*, in the Lynch-directed Pilot episode for just a few seconds when a homeviewer is shown tilting their heads to watch the upside-down scene.

149. "Attack of the Pine Weasel" **Scott Pick**

Here we come to one of the best of the hidden gems in the entire bunch. I freaking love this cue. It couldn't be more fun. The melody is played with a kazoo. A KAZOO! (Said with the same inflection as David Patrick Kelly's when he says "Chopping wood *inside?*") Go ahead and try to top this cue, Hans Zimmer. Again, this scene is so juvenile you would think it would be from *On the Air*. The Save the Pine Weasel event goes awry, and everyone screams and runs, and this cue plays. It has energy, fun, zaniness, and everything else one loves about Angelo's music. This sounds like something that would be on a Herb Albert and the Tijuana Brass album, and by golly, it should be. When I asked Kinny Landrum about it he said, "I don't think it's us. Sounds like an actual old record." It really does sound like an old record, but I think it is the band, because I don't think the producers would have paid to license a track for this cue, especially considering that for the rest of that scene, before the  weasel is set loose, James Foley used typical *Twin Peaks* music. I would be remiss if I didn't point out that here is another quality track that is used for a massively less-than-quality scene. This song is too good to have been played just once and then forgotten.

150. "Great Northern Piano Tune #4" **Scott Pick**

As I said, this track has the same beginning as "Tune #3," but it is a different recording. I pushed play on "Tune #3" on my laptop and "Tune #4" on my phone at the same time so that I could see if they were *exactly* the same tunes. The notes at the beginning are the same, but from different recordings. The reverb on this track almost sounds like the piano player is making mistakes and double hitting notes, or that there is an overdub, but there is something screwy about the beginning of this take. Then, at about twenty seconds into the tracks, they veer into different performances. It's like both are structured the same but aren't played exactly the same. They are improvisations within the same song, but with just enough differences for each to be its own thing. This cue was used when Annie and Cooper have a drink at the Great Northern and in the first wine tasting scene. I decided to send the track to Kinny and see what he thought.

Kinny Landrum: I'm not positive this is me playing. It sounds like it could be me, and it seems a little too well played and jazzy for Angelo, though it could be him too. A few things I notice: These are based on the same tune, though they are not the same tracks. You can put them on top of each other, and they veer away fairly immediately. At about 1:44 in "Great Northern Piano Tune #4," there is a long, low, out of key synth drone that comes in, obviously to indicate something ominous or sinister is happening. The other does not have this. It also has some reverb on it that sounds like Art's AKG spring reverb that the other doesn't. The more I listen, I'm not sure it's me, because I think I would have remembered. Must be Angelo, because there are a lot of liberties taken that a session guy might not have done. But hey, you never know.

The ominous synth that comes in for about ten seconds in this track matches Cooper seeing Annie's scars on her wrist, which means this track came directly off the mix of the episode from this scene. The track has the exact same ending as it does on-screen before it cuts to Windom Earle in Owl Cave.

151. "Twin Peaks Theme (Harp)"

This is truly just "Falling" played on the synth sound of a harp. It runs 1:03, but the scene it scores lasts for 1:08, so Lori had to slow it down to fit the scene. Um. Hmm. Okay. I guess you are waiting for me to tell you the scene? Do I have to? It is in Episode 21. Is that good enough? No? Fine. It is Doc Hayward telling Dick and Andy the back story for Little Nicky. I will be totally honest with you and say I have watched the Little Nicky storyline only twice in my life. I always fast-forward through the Little Nicky stories, James and Evelyn, and basically anything with Ernie. So I hadn't heard this dialogue in a long time. I think Warren Frost should have won an Emmy for getting through his monologue. I mean, did you all know that Little Nicky was conceived during a back-alley rape by an undocumented immigrant who fled through the border immediately after committing the crime? What is it with Frost/Lynch and this topic? It is the same thing with Mr. C and Audrey. Can they get a new story already?

March 29

Hurley wrote: Included within this bundle are the track and elements that form "Ben's Battle," the "fife and drum" soundtrack to Benjamin Horne's Season 2 psychotic breakdown. The four tracks comprise: the full track itself as well as solo elements/stems of marching drum, flute and trumpet. Additionally included is the campfire synth-harmonica track "Ben's Lament."

152. "Ben's Battle"

Bad storyline = good music cues. Maybe it is because the assignment was so specific for Angelo. He knew exactly what kind of music needed to be written for a Civil War scene. A fun fact about this track is that while Dean Hurley never wanted to release these cues, it was the only bundle that Kinny Landrum had purchased from DavidLynch.com. (Someone really should give him these all for free.)

Kinny Landrum: I love the one with the fife and drums. I paid for those when you could download them. That was the only one I bought. That is an example of when some music cue needed to be specific, and we did it.

153. "Ben's Battle (Solo Percussion)"

These next three cues are just the stems contained in "Ben's Battle." You can get the drums, flutes, and trumpets as separate entities for when you play Ben Reenacts the Civil War at home. You have the correct stems to mix it up some.

154. "Ben's Battle (Solo Flute)"
155. "Ben's Battle (Solo Trumpet)"

156. "Ben's Lament"

Kinny Landrum: That is me doing a harmonica like it was around a campfire. I made that up on the spot.

April 6

Hurley wrote: The final remaining archive slow speed orchestra cuts are presented here in the "Black Lodge-" themed bundle. Although each is only a minute to a minute and a half in duration, their brief run-times are testament to the "building block" nature of much of this style of music woven throughout the series. Four additional tracks sans overdubs that appear in the latter half of *FWWM*, "The Culmination"—a largely unheard full-length track also known as "The Owl," as well as a distant train horn tone-pad used to musical ends in *FWWM*.

157. "Half Speed Orchestra 4 (Dugpas)"

"Dugpas" is a really unremarkable dark track. It has the rumbles like other orchestra tracks, but is a pretty simple cue and really doesn't stand out. While it is used in Episode 27, when Windom Earle talks about the Dugpas, it actually made its debut in Episode 12 when Cooper and Ben receive the ransom instructions. I always love when a song has a title from a later use. As Lori explained, Lynch often changed the titles after she filled out the cue sheets.

158. "Half Speed Orchestra 6 (Bob's Dance/Back to Missoula)"

This cue builds as it ends, so it has a little more oomph than "Dugpas." It is used when Leland murders Maddy and "sends her back to Missoula." In the televised version, there is the clicking of the end of the record skipping, but honestly, there isn't any layered music in this scene. It truly is just this cue. That speaks to the power of this moment in Ray Wise's acting as he yells at Sheryl Lee, who was having a really horrible day. Bless both of them for giving their all for one of the most terrifying scenes ever to air on network television.

159. "Half Speed Orchestra 7"

This was never used in the series, but it would be hard to prove it. It is a typical "ominous woosh" track that sounds like so many of the other half-speed orchestras.

160. "The Culmination"

I will never understand how a composer can create a sound that immediately enables the listener to visualize an actual object in their mind's eye. Angelo is a king at doing this. When "The Culmination" begins, all I can see are fire sprinklers going off from the ceiling of the interrogation room. Somehow he made that sound. This cue is used when Bob takes his final spin in Leland Palmer's body. If you skipped over Tim Hunter's interview earlier in the book, you missed a wonderful story about this scene. Shame on you.

161. "Distant Train"

This is always one of the *TPA* releases that makes me wonder if I am a bit too obsessed. Why would I want this MP3 on my phone? It really is just the sound of a train howling way off in the distance. But when I hear it, I think of Ray Wise's acting in *FWWM*, and it makes me think how lucky I am to have met him and spent a few days with him. He is an incredible actor, but a nicer human being. This train sound is heard as Leland sits on the side of the bed and we see, through only Ray Wise's acting, that Bob has left him, and Leland is back. I asked him how he achieved this level of acting . . .

Ray Wise: It is putting yourself in the right mood to start it off. It takes an intense concentration and a whole sense memory thing. A myriad of things are going on in my brain to come up with the right emotion, and then I have it register on my face and on my person. It's a mechanical process, but it is an emotional and psychological one. I am able to physicalize a sense memory.

162. "Laura's Dark Boogie (Clean)"

This version is the track before Lori Eschler and David Lynch got their hands on it. The two tracks are the same length, but this "clean" version has all the "fucks" bleeped out. No, that's not what "clean" means; I am thinking of rap songs. Both versions have the ponticello violins, which to me is what makes that sawing sound on the strings, but the "clean" version has less saxophone. So that is something they added to the film version, which was released on the *Season Two* vinyl. Personally, I like the extras that they added. It is nice that when they were doing the album, they went back to the film to get that version, as it is what we are used to hearing. But it is nice to have the original version too. That is why these archives are such a gift to fans.

163. "The Red Room"

This cue has never been released officially without being mixed with "Dark Mood Woods." So here we get "The Red Room" part of that medley on its own. When you compare the time frame on the medley, it comes out to right around 5:34, so we basically have the entire "Red Room" track in the medley, and this track was released on vinyl on the score for Season 2. So while I love this track, there is no reason to pick it because it has already been released.

April 12

Hurley wrote: After stripping back several layers of "Love Theme From Twin Peaks," we arrive at this sparse "dark" version of the composition. The intro section here has been reduced to a solitary low-register Rhodes (heard below flute in previous versions of the track). Flute then joins the bridge section almost like a single candle in a light-less room . . . brightening the overall timber of the track as it compositionally ascends. High synth strings finally arrive in unison at the crescendo, creating perhaps the most intense tonal contrast between A and B sections when compared with other versions of the composition. The result is an unassuming emotional punch that is delivered without the track's traditional employment of its signature piano.

164. "Love Theme (Dark)"

This is pretty much another version of the same old same old. It has a different sound, but that's about it.

April 19

Hurley wrote: Four tracks are presented here in this James Hurley/Evelyn Marsh-themed bundle. The sparse, screen-used version of "James & Evelyn" as well as "Evelyn's Mourning:" a dirge-like composition that initially hints at, then ends with direct quotations from "Laura Palmer's Theme." "La Speranza:" an incredibly convincing operatic piece with an ever-so-subtle Badalamenti stamp across it, and perhaps the highlight of the bundle, "Trail Mix" (archive title): a 9+ minute, largely unheard track that easily sits atop with some of the more widely known improvisation-based tracks from the series.

165. "James & Evelyn" **Scott Pick**

The storyline of James and Evelyn is soap opera, pure and simple. It doesn't really help the James character overall. He loves Laura, he loves Donna, he loves Maddy, he loves Evelyn, he loves Donna, he loves that married chick in the booth. But again, plots have no bearing on the music. Angelo wrote a cue that has so many connections to other cues, but they all come together in this track, which really should be released on vinyl. It has the pulsating feel of "Packard's Vibration." It has the guitar of "Abstract Mood," but combined they create a new piece of music that is glorious. It almost makes watching James and Evelyn do it on top of a car in broad daylight worth it. I said almost.

166. "Evelyn's Mourning"

These next two tracks are the same cue, just one is longer than the other. This cue begins with the same octaves of C in the bass, just like "Laura Palmer's Theme," but then goes off into a different piano piece. It connects enough to the original theme to let us know the song is all about death, but it's different, actually with a new melody, but certainly a cousin to the original theme (so much so James wanted to date it). Speaking of death, Diane Keaton directed Episode 22, which focuses on the end of the Evelyn story, and this theme is used quite a bit in the episode. Lori Eschler remembered what it was like to work with Keaton.

Lori Eschler: She is a genius and really playful. She came in on Saturdays to just work on the music. There was a scene with Evelyn in her veil, and I played the dark theme, and she jumped on the couch up and down and said, "Yes. Death. All death." [Laughs.] She had a lot of hand in the music.

167. "Evelyn's Mourning (Extended)" **Scott Pick**

Not a lot of differences between these two, so we might as well release the longer version. Dean found a better version, so he released this as a free version to downloaders. I am telling you the deals were real at DavidLynch.com back in the day. "You want to hear about our specials?"

168. "La Speranza"

I find it hard to believe that Angelo busted this track out of nowhere for Episode 1. It is used to score the Briggs' family dinner, the one where the major smacks the cigarette out of Bobby's mouth. (Man, do I love nineties television. Now that character would have been canceled before Episode 8, and the redemption of Major Briggs would never have occurred.) This is used again, and I think more effectively, in Episode 22—Diane Keaton strikes again—when Donna meets James at Wallies bar. The exterior of Wallies was actually a truck stop called Santa Susana Cantina. I would have bet real money that I went there on one of Melanie Mullen's LA tours, but she and Courtenay Stallings told me I have never been to Wallies, and I have to believe them because otherwise they will kill me. Plus I have always relied on Courtenay to be my *Twin Peaks* events memory.

169. "Trail Mix"

This is a long work session from the band where the bass part became the cue "James & Evelyn." This is a seven-minute session. If you are a fan of Vinnie Bell's baritone guitar, this is pure heaven. It is strange that Lynch never used more of this as "firewood" for scenes in other films. It is the kind of layered track that would really bring out the creepiness of a scene. Again, it is incredible the amount of wonderful music that came out of a story about an older woman seeing a biker and thinking, I bet I could pin the murder of my husband on this dude. Let's invite him to stay with me and my butler lover, who can pretend he is my brother.

May 3

Hurley wrote: The label "Dark Intro" is used a lot in the archive to denote the 3-chord intro section to "Laura Palmer's Theme." In fact, many versions of "Laura Palmer's Theme"/"Love Theme" are split into "Dark Intro" and "Laura Palmer's Theme" separately . . . the latter beginning with the piano scale ascend. Somewhere among the myriad versions of "Dark Intros," the popular pattern starts to be twisted into a number of variations. Several of these can be heard in previously released versions of "Laura Palmer's Theme:" "Letter From Harold," "Ethereal Pad," and "Caroline" versions are all variants that fell under the label "Dark Intro." The versions presented in this bundle, however, were never used in the series . . . yet, with echoes of the show's most prominent theme it is easy for the mind to imagine the scenes they could have accompanied . . . Included within this bundle are 6 versions of "Dark Intro."

Not much to say about these six tracks. They are basically just the beginning of "Laura Palmer's Theme" six times in a row on a normal synth. Nothing special or necessary about any of these. They are just for completists.

170. "Dark Intro #1"
171. "Dark Intro #2"
172. "Dark Intro #3"
173. "Dark Intro #4"
174. "Dark Intro #5"
175. "Dark Intro #6"

May 10

Hurley wrote: Presented here is the screen-used version of the Packards' primary theme, bundled alongside "The Mill Durge": a brief, unused cue that echoes elements of the "Packard's Theme" chordal motif.

176. "Packard's Theme"

This is another version of "Packard's Vibration." This cue is a few seconds shorter than the version that came out on the *Season Two* vinyl. The two cues are virtually identical, but there is something about the mix of this one that makes me like it more than the official release. I still wouldn't select it as a pick

because it is already released, but when I am making a playlist, I'd choose this cue over the other. The thing that surprised me about working on this book is how similar this cue is to the "James & Evelyn" cue. They have a lot of similarities, which makes me think they were written at the same time and got divided by Lori and the directors, one becoming associated with the Packards and the other with James and his love of the moment.

Kinny Landrum: Things like the "Packard's Theme" were scored to picture after the fact as a separate session. Angelo would come in with a lead sheet, and then I would say, "Well, strings, but maybe this would be good too." We would start and stop at the right place.

177. "The Mill Durge"

This is another unused cue, but it is basically "Packard's Theme" on a synth for thirty seconds. This seems like another demo release, which is great for the *TPA* but not for my fake vinyl.

May 31 (Odds and Ends Bundle Vol 1)

Hurley wrote: As the list of remaining unreleased material from the *Twin Peaks Archive* dwindles, we are left with a few final release-bundles of assorted miscellany. Volume 1 of these last releases features several remaining sought-after tracks: The extended, film version of "The Pink Room": an epic 6 minute 44 second extended mix of perhaps the most striking blues-rock instrumental to emerge from the *Twin Peaks* universe. Several of the remaining Badalamenti muzak oddities are also included here: "Llama Country," "One Eyed Jack's Country," and "Dick Tremayne's Swing." Lastly included are "Jean Renault's Theme (Solo Bass Clarinet)," as well as a number of shorter cues briefly used in the series: "Earle's Theme (Audrey's Walk)," "'Such Stuff as Dreams are Made of'," and "Leo Attacks Bobby."

178. "Jean Renault's Theme (Solo Bass Clarinet)"

While I compared the One Arm Man's theme to the strangling of a duck, this track is much more palatable. I guess candy really is dandy. This improvisation by Al Regni is all over the place, but it is kind of enjoyable and certainly makes you think of Michael Parks's incredible performance as Jean Renault. I am always surprised when people don't give the Season 2 any props. While we hate to see our beloved Audrey kidnapped and drugged, at least Jean was a worthy adversary for Cooper during a stretch of the series when there wasn't a lot of danger going on. This cue may go on a bit long, but it really shows off the talent of Al Regni and what he could do with a clarinet. It also is a great example of how much of the score for the series was made up of bits and pieces that combined to make something much greater.

179. "One Eyed Jack's Country" **Scott Pick**

Here we have another example of how versatile Angelo was. This track doesn't have a sliver of the sound of *Twin Peaks*, and it shouldn't. It sounds like an overture for a Dolly Parton musical. (I mean, she did star in *Best Little Whorehouse in Texas*, so she could have worked at One

Eyed Jacks.) I am not sure why a house of ill repute located in Canada is playing country music from the South? Maybe Blackie came from Georgia? I will always associate this track with Big Ed saying "Own a gas station. I'm an oral surgeon." It was dialogue like that that made Season 1 of *Twin Peaks* untouchable and a perfect example of how to write good television. The fact that the writers let Big Ed mess up, but save himself is why we love the character so much.

Here is a strange thing about this cue: it was brought back later on, in the Double R when Gordon Cole and Shelly Johnson have pie with Annie and Cooper. So I guess this song is in rotation on Muzak in the great Northwest, because it also plays at Wallies when Evelyn and Donna meet up. Since this is a cue that was used quite a lot, I picked it for my vinyl box set.

180. "Dick Tremayne's Swing" **Scott Pick**

Just like the "Pine Weasel" cue, I absolutely love this song. It is so much fun and makes you wanna snap your fingers, put on dress shoes, and take your partner out dancing. It is suave and elegant, and if it could use a fork, it would totally use it the "European way." The thing about this cue is that the bridge is actually quite sophisticated. Angelo didn't just phone this one in; the purpose of a bridge is to give the listener a break from the melody but still be audibly connected to the blueprint of the song. Next time you listen to this cue, pay attention to the bridge; it's aces. As a point of trivia, the first release of this cue had a screen edit in it; Dean fixed it, and then released the version that is now out. He was so diligent with these releases, and I am forever thankful.

We first hear this cue the very first time we meet Dick, as he comes into the sheriff's station to escort Lucy to lunch. I am not a fan of Dick Tremayne, although Ian Buchanan is a very sweet man and is in my documentary about the last fan-run year of the *Twin Peaks* Festival, but the three songs associated with him are honestly in my top ten: 1. "Pine Weasel" 2. "Mr. Snooty" 3. "Dick Tremayne's Swing."

181. "Llama Country"

This is another track that is so good it makes you wonder if Angelo had created it for something else or if he wrote this complete song just to have Cooper go face-to-face with llama in a veterinarian office. I mean, this could totally be a song that you would hear in an elevator filled with businessmen whom you don't want to talk to. It really doesn't play very long in the scene, but by golly, this track made me feel like I was once again part of the happy generation.

182. "'Such Stuff as Dreams Are Made Of'"

This cue is used as Ben Horne walks in to "greet" the new, new girl, who just happens to be his daughter. It is a pretty short piece of music and was used for just this one scene. This track plays for the exact length of the scene and builds to a dramatic ending, so Angelo had to time it out. It is pretty much just a punctuation note, but I want to point out again how Mark Frost's episode really seems to have the most music written specifically for scenes. It pays to be the boss.

183. "Earle's Theme (Audrey's Walk)"

I love the arrangements of all of Windom Earle's music. Associating him with the pan flute is such a great idea. I mean, it works, but I don't know why. I guess because they gave him one to have on set. Director James Foley transitions really nicely from Windom playing the flute to a pan up of Audrey walking the Great Northern runway. I know we are all modern, evolved individuals and we live in a time where we are not to mention anyone's looks, but I am telling you, in the history of the world, no one was as beautiful as Sherilyn Fenn in the later half of Season 2. I think I watched her do this walk in Episode 24 more times than anyone should. And I think I'm gonna go watch it again right now. Cancel me.

184. "Leo Attacks Bobby"

This cue plays when Norma sees Nadine at the store buying cotton balls. I'm just kidding. I thought it would be funny if a cue with two characters' names in the title was about two other characters. Sue me; I've been writing about the *TPA* for weeks now. This is another action-adventure type cue that I am not sure is really in Angelo's top bag of tricks. This scores the scene in which Leo attacks Bobby in Episode 7. Wait, is this another track scored to picture for Mark Frost's episode? Who does he think he is, Tim Hunter? This cue is done in a competent way, but not really in a *Twin Peaks* way.

185. "The Pink Room (Extended Version)"

The extended version begins with a drumstick countdown before those opening guitar riffs welcoming Laura, Donna, and two dudes totally playing out of their league to Canada in *FWWM*. This version is the exact one that plays in the film. If you cue up this track and the film

side by side, you can tell this version plays for the first 4:42 of the Pink Room scene. The remaining two minutes of this track are not heard in the film. So this is just the full version from countdown to abrupt ending. The version on the *FWWM* soundtrack fades out after 4:06, whereas this plays for 6:44. Both songs have the exact same ending, so somewhere within the soundtrack version, someone cut directly to the

end. It might have been interesting if the medley version of this song and "Blue Frank" had also been released. I think it would have been a cool release to show listeners how that scene does, in fact, have two distinct songs in it. I am grateful for this extended version, because even though this song truly is the same chords played again and again, whenever the song is over, I wanna hear it one more time. I should get sick of it, but I never do. I have never been to a club like The Power and the Glory, but if I go, I sure hope they play this song. Although I sure hope I don't end up dancing topless with Buck.

June 14 (Odds and Ends Bundle Vol 2)

Hurley wrote: Though we are nearing the end, the *Twin Peaks Archive* is not quite over . . . Volume 2 of Odds and Ends presents a number of alternate versions of previously issued material. The *FWWM* cut "Half Heart" is included here in an alternate mix (employed briefly in the film), which removes the original's guitar and percussion for a softer arrangement of saxophone, synth and upright bass. Also from *FWWM* is a slower and noteworthy version of "Voice of Love" (which likewise appears briefly in the film). "Dance of the Dream Man" can now be coveted in its purest form: playing here without the additional vibraphone on the final measures of the original soundtrack release. Similarly, "Audrey" is included here without its various soundtrack editorial additives. A full-length version of "Great Northern Piano Tune #2" finally receives its proper release, replacing a truncated version previously released by the Archives last year. A mix of "One Armed Man's Theme & Jean Renault's Theme" reduced from Season 2's music stem is also included here: a stellar example of the highly layered musical combinations that were crafted at times during the final mixing stages of the show. Lastly, and in close relation to the previously released "Distant Train," the musical sound effect creation "Log Lady Presence" is included from *FWWM*; a track that seemingly utilizes distant train brake "squeals" through infinite-decay reverb to create an incredibly ominous quiet chorus of tones.

186. "Half Heart (Solo)"

Far be it from me to disagree with the Archivist, but if you can hear a difference between "Half Heart" and "Half Heart (Solo)," you have better hearing than Gordon Cole with his volume cranked all the way to eleven. I even played the two tracks at the same time on my computer, and they are precisely the same. I don't know if someone messed up when they released it on vinyl or on the *TPA*, but this track does have a bass and guitars; somewhere there might be a solo version, but it sure isn't this one.

187. "Dance of the Dream Man (Original)"

I have written about this track more times than Leo had to copy a legible poem to Audrey, Shelly, and Donna. There really isn't much of a difference from what was released on the CD in 1990.

188. "Great Northern Piano Tune #2 (Full Version)" **Scott Pick**

I wrote about this piece, first released as Track 29, earlier in this chapter. Because this is a minute longer than the other version, I select this track for the vinyl release or for your playlist.

189. "One Armed Man's Theme & Jean Renault's Theme (TV Mix)"

This is a cool track to have but is never much fun to listen to. It can be really jarring if it comes up on shuffle. I imagine this is the sound that Fred Truax's wife made when her husband came home from work on February 24. Luckily, it runs for just two minutes, but these two unmelodic saxophone riffs can seem like the longest two minutes in the history of time. I mean, even Fred Madison said, "Hey, tone it down."

190. "Audrey (TV Version)"

This is a strange one for me to figure out. This is called the TV version, as it should be because it is used in Episode 14 when Audrey tells Cooper she is in possession of incriminating information about her father. Curiously, the version on *Season Two* has this cue mixed with "Sneaky Audrey." Why mix those two just for *Season Two* when the choice could have been made to release just this studio version, especially given that "Audrey" was never mixed with "Sneaky Audrey" in the scene? Also, it wasn't like "Sneaky Audrey" was previously unreleased, because it was mixed with "Bookhouse Boys" on the original soundtrack. So someone (probably Dean Hurley) was tasked with extra work on that one when the decision could have been made to use this version. Maybe it is just a case of following the hard-and-fast rules of *Twin Peaks*: have the names be confusing, and if it has already been released, release it again.

191. "Voice of Love (Slow)"

This is a slower version of the final instrumental that plays when Laura is in the Red Room and sees her angel. This slower version plays earlier in the film when Laura looks at her painting with the angel. I like to call this cue sound foreshadowing. It is such a cool thing that Lori Eschler and David Lynch did throughout the film. The music

cues not only set the mood of the scene, but also connect later scenes to earlier scenes. If you are ever lost in a Lynch film, just pay attention to the music; it is your guide. This instrumental was played by Kinny Landrum.

Kinny Landrum: Yes, I remember these string parts. I probably played them on a combination of my Roland Super JX rackmount and Roland D-50 analog strings. As I said, Angelo never liked sampled stings, only analog.

192. "Log Lady Presence"

This track from *FWWM* plays when the Log Lady appears to Laura Palmer outside the Roadhouse and warns her about the fire within. This was one of the tracks that Dean Hurley wasn't sure should be released, but anything that involves the Log Lady must be released. This is the only appearance of the Log Lady in the film; one of the *Missing Pieces* that really breaks my heart is when the Log Lady looks up to the sky in pain as Laura is being killed. It wouldn't have made the film any longer to use this shot, and it would have connected nicely to the scene in which she tells Cooper about this evening.

June 28 (Odds and Ends Bundle Vol 3)

Hurley wrote: Volume 3 of Odds and Ends presents a number of remaining rarities as well as partial tracks. Easily Grady Tate's most enjoyable solo percussion artifact: "Solo Percussion 4" (also known as "Grady Solo Ride") finally joins the series of solo drum stems previously released by the archive. Similarly, "Solo Percussion (Arbitrary Cymbals)" is included, giving a spotlighted showcase to Grady's cymbal array—in particular his signature sizzle cymbal used so prominently throughout the show's music. Sadly, only a partially complete recording of "Freshly Squeezed (Fast Cool Jazz Version 2 Clean)" was located amidst the contents of the archive . . . tape starts are included on both "Version 2 Clean" and "Love Theme (Light)" to indicate the obsolete beginnings of the "as-is" recordings discovered. Lastly, a second take (take 2) of "Wheeler's Theme" is included as well as the *FWWM* cue "You Killed Mike." "You Killed Mike" is also partial in nature as it is extracted from the film's music stem and therefore unavoidably combined with "Night Bells." The original recording was not to be located for release.

193. "Solo Percussion 4"

This cue is so similar to "Grady's Groove," which is used in *The Return*, that it is really hard for me to say they are different. I can say that "Groove" is ten seconds longer, but that is about it. Maybe Ringo could hear the difference, but I can't.

194. "Wheeler's Theme (TK 2)"

This is just a shorter version of the other release. It is basically the same melody. It sounds to me like this is mixed a little louder, and it feels a little more alive, but it is hard not to go for the longer version. This cue is thirty seconds shorter, but I kind of like the ending of this cue better. So do we like it big or does size not matter? I'll leave that up to you.

195. "Solo Percussion (Arbitrary Cymbals)"

Here we have 1:14 of just random cymbals. It feels like a great place to grab a cymbal sound if you are ever telling bad jokes. Again, for the completist, it is nice to have, but not sure it is that much fun to actually listen to.

196. "Freshly Squeezed (Fast Cool Jazz Version 2)"

If you can really tell the difference between this song and "Dance of the Dream Man (Clarinet)," you are better than I am. To me, they are the same. But this track does conclude the wonderful work in the *Archive* of Al Regni, who played the woodwinds on all of these songs. He wasn't just a master of the music of *Twin Peaks*; he had an incredible career outside of the show. Getting to talk on the phone with someone of his level, who created such iconic music, was an absolute treat for me. When I found out he knew Sondheim, you know I went crazy.

Al Regni: *Twin Peaks* was an important part of my recording. I was busy from the seventies to the nineties. It was toward the end of my recording days. In the nineties I was busy with jingles and *Twin Peaks*. I did a lot of work with Angelo on different projects. I also was in the orchestra pit for *Funny Girl, Company, Follies*. So I did lots of Broadway shows in the sixties and seventies. Jonathan Tunick, who arranged all of Sondheim's shows, would call me often. I play the flute on one of the tribute albums to Sondheim.

197. "You Killed Mike"

A person could spend their entire life picking out scenes that Sheryl Lee crushed in *FWWM*, but the "You Killed Mike" scene is certainly near the top. I bet Dana Ashbrook wanted to pop Sheryl in the nose as she annoys him nonstop during this violent, scary moment in the woods. The score for this scene has this new theme but then gives us a moment of "Abstract Mood" from the series. Dean Hurley was sad he couldn't find the original recording, without those guitar refrains at the end, but I like having this version because it plays exactly as it does in the film.

198. "Love Theme (Light)"

This is just another version of "Laura Palmer's Theme." I can't possibly hear that track again. This sounds like a million other versions we already have.

July 12th

Hurley wrote: To end at the beginning seems an appropriate destination for the year+ journey that has been the *Twin Peaks Archive*. Before the myriad versions, before there were variations on themes, before there were mix minus and stem extracts, there were the original musical *ideas*: the "demos" that were recorded to capture fledgling compositions. Most of the demos included here are from a single cassette recording dated February, 1989. Listening to these Fender Rhodes demos, one is able to hear the soundtrack to *Twin Peaks* just as Badalamenti and Lynch initially heard it. As demos go, Rhodes piano was an incredibly suited compositional choice as it has an inherently mellow sound over that of an acoustic piano. This, in addition to its built-in vibrato controls enabled demo recordings to be made that contained far more information than simply chords and melody... it served as a document of tone and mood as well. Most interesting in some of these early recordings are the hybrid versions of "Falling" and "Laura Palmer's Theme" . . . on several occasions, the two compositions are actually merged into one. (Separately included is a later demo of "Questions in a World of Blue" sung by Badalamenti himself.)

From here, we are left with the spinning world beyond *Twin Peaks* . . . *On the Air* would be the subsequent Lynch/Frost follow up, premiering on ABC a mere months after *FWWM* debuted at Cannes in 1992 (although replaced after only 3 aired episodes). The composition known in the *Twin Peaks* universe as "Half Heart" would later double as a brief love theme for the newly created television compositions that were recorded specifically during *On the Air* session dates, the mood is undeniably *Twin Peaks* in origin ... a subtle nod at continuing the music's life beyond the finality of a singular television series ...

Today what has been left behind is a staggering volume of original music for what was ultimately a relatively short series (in the world of serial television). Hopefully, these archives releases have helped and will continue to help service the continued life of an imagined place ...

May there always be music in the air ...

199. "Falling into Love Theme (Demo)"

I can't lie to you. I don't like any of these demos. They are interesting, but unpolished. It is nice that they were released, but they are just the beginnings of what is to come. I am a Bob Dylan fan, and I love all his work—post 1997. But he releases these bootleg versions that have every version of every song he ever recorded. I know completists want that stuff, and I know that all masterpieces have to start somewhere, but I am not one of these people who needs to know where it all started. These are the demos from when it all began, and I'm so glad they released them, but I never listen to them.

200. "Love Theme Slower and Darker (Demo)"
201. "Slow Cool Jazz (Demo)"
202. "Chinese Theme (Demo)"
203. "Wide Vibrato Augmented Chords (Demo)"
204. "Night Walk (Demo)"
205. "Low Wide and Beautiful (Demo)"
206. "Wide Vibrato Mood to Falling (Demo)"
207. "Love Theme to Falling (Demo)"
208. "Love Theme Light (Demo)"

209. "Questions in a World of Blue (Demo)"

Here is a really sweet demo of Angelo singing "Questions in a World of Blue." It is nice to hear our maestro's voice and hear him play the song live. It really shows you what a moving piece of music this is. I am glad they released this demo. I am always a fan when a composer sings his own songs. I wish Dean would have done a few other ones. It would be great to have heard Angelo sing "Just You" or "Sycamore Trees."

210. "Love Theme from On the Air (Take 4")
I recently watched all seven episodes of *On the Air* for the first time. I was underwhelmed. The theme song is inspired and fun; it would have been nice if Dean had slipped that into this bundle. Angelo used "Half Heart" in the Pilot. This take is as close as a release gets to sounding like what is actually in the first episode. It only  plays for a very short time. This is the same melody as "Half Heart" from *FWWM*. Lori confirmed to me that the track was written for *FWWM* and then just reused here.

211. "Love Theme from On the Air (Slow Jazz Version)"
It seems really unlikely that this version was ever recorded for *On the Air*. The bass is too dark for anything that would have been used on that show. Also, this is a seven-minute track. I am sure this is a work track version for *FWWM* that morphed into the beauty that "Half Heart" became. But I have no firsthand knowledge of that; it is just my guess based on the arrangements and the tenor of the series.

212. "Love Theme from On the Air (Clarinet Strings)"
Same "Half Heart" theme, played on a clarinet.

Oh, don't you just wish we were done? But we have four bonus tracks to cover. These cues were not officially released during the *TPA*, but Dean Hurley found them after it ended, and he, or someone like him, leaked them to Dugpa, who then shared them with the world.

Bonus 1: "Hotel Tango"
The main reason this cue wasn't released in the *Archive* is because the *TPA* happened before the *Missing Pieces* were released. Since this scene was cut from *FWWM*, Angelo never scored it. This is a track that Dean Hurley

wrote to fit the tango scene in Buenos Aires when Phillip Jeffries checks in to meet Judy, who was supposed to be Josie's sister, according to Bob Engels. This was all before Judy became Jooday or whatever nonsense it became in *The Return*.

Scott Ryan: You wrote the "Hotel Tango," right?

Dean Hurley: It was the David Bowie scene where there were these on-screen musicians miming playing along while Phillip Jeffries checks into the hotel in Buenos Aires. There was no preconceived notion of what music was going to go there. It was the musicians just straight up, miming it to a tempo, and so I remember being quite excited, like, "Oh, I have to make something that fits the tempo." So I just made that track.

Bonus 2: "I'm Hurt Bad (Clean)"

A version of this song was already released through the *TPA*, but this is the studio take, without the sound effects from *Industrial Symphony*.

Dean Hurley: *Industrial Symphony* is the intersection of *Wild at Heart*, *Floating into the Night*, and *Twin Peaks*. I just know that when David talks about that show, he talks about it as a real whirlwind affair. Angelo and David didn't have a lot of time. They were just in the midst of working on all these different projects.

This was a cue Dean really wanted to release, since it is this version that Bobby and James select on the jukeboxes in the series, but all Dean could find was the version used for *Industrial Symphony*.

Bonus 3: "The Swan (Instrumental)"

This track was covered in the *Floating into the Night* chapter. This isn't an instrumental on Julee Cruise's album, but this was a cue Lynch used while editing the Pilot, probably because he didn't have a lot of options and he was working on her album at the same time, so the song was fresh in his mind. Dean Hurley couldn't locate this cue while compiling the *TPA*, but he subsequently found it and even released it on a Sacred Bones mixtape along with the following bonus track....

Bonus 4: "Theme from Twin Peaks - FWWM (Deleted Scene Futz)"
This was also released on the Sacred Bones mixtape, but before that it had sneaked out onto the internet. It is really just the sax version of "Theme from FWWM" run through a filter that makes it sound like it is playing over the radio. The beginning even includes the sound of Big Ed tuning the radio to the song during the *Missing Pieces* scene with Norma. This is a much shorter version of the song, and the entire track sounds like it is coming through the AM radio of Ed's truck. It is cool, but the original is much better.

Dugpa really wanted me to include bootleg versions that fans have pulled off laserdiscs, DVDs, or edited themselves. I didn't want to do that because the focus of this book is on the songs that actually were released through David Lynch. On the next page are the tracks that I suggest Warner Bros. releases on a vinyl box set, produced by Dean Hurley and Sabrina Sutherland with linear notes by Scott Ryan. In the end, it came to thirty-nine tracks, which seems perfect for a four record box set. I was careful not to pick any of the really long tracks. And if you are mad at me for picking all four of the Great Northern piano cues, then throw your book away because I don't like you anymore. Come on Sabrina and Dean, let's make this happen. Here is my potential album cover:

From The Series:

Invitation to Love Theme
Laura Palmer's Theme (Piano and Rhodes)
The Norwegians
Bookhouse Boys
Half Speed Orchestra 1 (Stair Music/Danger Theme)
Dick Tremayne's Swing
Mister Snooty
Attack of the Pine Weasel
One Eyed Jack's Country
Western Ballad (RR Tune No. 5)
Great Northern Big Band
Great Northern Piano Tune #1
Great Northern Piano Tune #2 (Full Version)
Great Northern Piano Tune #3
Great Northern Piano Tune #4
Audrey's Prayer (Clarinet & Synth)
Annie and Cooper
Owl Cave
Earle's Theme
Lana's Theme
Wheeler's Theme
Americana
Just You (Instrumental)
James & Evelyn
Evelyn's Mourning (Extended)
Wedding Song #1
Wedding Song #2 ('Stranger Nights')

From The Film:

Theme from Twin Peaks: Fire Walk With Me (Saxophone)
Teresa's Autopsy
Hotel Tango
Phillip Jeffries
Mysterioso #2 (film version)
RR Swing
James Visits Laura
Nightsea Wind
Girl Talk
It's Your Father
Sycamore Trees (Instrumental)
Birds In Hell

TRACK 10

"The Fireman"

Dean Hurley (Reprise)

If in my introduction to Dean Hurley for the *TPA* I called him the Archivist, I better come up with a new name for him for his work on *The Return*. The Fireman is definitely what I am going with. The Fireman, who was previously known as the Giant, stands by and watches over the activities. When things get out of control, he responds to the alarm and dispatches Laura Palmer to the world. You will learn in this interview that Dean Hurley stood aside and watched as Angelo Badalamenti and David Lynch reunited to create music once again, this time over the internet. When things got out of control, he had to tend to the alarm and fix the connection. But that wasn't the only reunion he witnessed. Dean was also there when Lynch reunited with another long time collaborator, but just like his Fireman avatar, he didn't get involved directly, just watched from afar. (Wow, I wonder if this somehow makes me Señorita Dido? Probably not.)

We begin this interview while Dean and I are talking about streaming music and the difference between owning music over letting it come down from the cloud as ones and zeros.

Dean Hurley: I got so fatigued with streaming music that I went back to my old original iPod, which still holds a pretty good charge and everything. It was so amazing to kind of be freed from internet listening.

Scott Ryan: I'm one of the only people left on the planet who doesn't stream music. My phone is full of MP3s. If DavidLynch.com had only streamed the *Twin Peaks Archives*, those tracks would be gone now.

Dean Hurley: The thing I was bowled over with my iPod is that I'm like "Wait a minute. I've spent my whole life collecting the music that I respond to, and that I resonate with, and it's all here. I don't have to search for it."

Scott Ryan: Right, that's how I live my life. I can't imagine asking a corporation if I'm allowed to listen to Barbra Streisand or Bob Dylan or Tom Waits today. I'm going to listen to them, and there isn't anyone who's going to track what I'm listening to.

Dean Hurley: It's very cool, and this is why I think, as generations fold into other generations, these old paradigms of life start to be lost, and that's why the oral history tradition is so important, and why I was enthused to see that in your *Lost Highway* book, it's basically like the Bible, isn't it? It's like you're seeing Peter's perspective. And Luke's perspective of the same events, you know?

Scott Ryan: Yeah, except *Lost Highway* actually happened. Ba dump bump.

Dean Hurley: [Laughs.] Well, I'm not a proponent for the Bible. I'm just saying historically, it's a good technique.

Scott Ryan: I know, but if you pitch one like that, I'm gonna swing. What's the beginning, for you, of starting work on *The Return*?

Dean Hurley: My job is with David every day. So it starts like any project. It's just a little whiff in the air. There's no announcement. David rekindles his relationship with Mark Frost, and that happens at a lunch. It's like "Oh, did you hear, David's having lunch with Mark Frost?" It's like "Oh, that's really cool." And then maybe a few weeks later, it's like "Oh, Mark's gonna come up, and we want to screen the last episode of Season 2." And then, a little while later, it's like "Mark's coming up to the house today." "Oh, interesting." They'd go up to David's painting studio and talk for a while. Then, all of a sudden, it became a regular thing. He's there in subsequent days, day after day. And it's like "Okay, they're obviously writing."

Scott Ryan: Now, there are secrets in the world. I'm sure senators and presidents and dignitaries have secrets. And then there are SECRETS. I mean, you had a secret. How was that for you?

Dean Hurley: I'll tell you how I live my life, and I wish more people did. Some people put too much emphasis on things. Putting the cart before the horse really can ruin a thing. This is exciting. But I'm not gonna get too excited about this, because I run my life on disappointment. I've been disappointed so many times that this is where I've come to this philosophy of not trying to let something build up too much in my mind. And it's honestly sort of a creed that David works by and why he's so protective of information getting out. When things come out too early, people build it up in their mind. And they're overwriting what something is going to be. Expectations can ruin what an experience could be.

Scott Ryan: Having expectations for any Lynch project can be deadly. What was it like knowing they were in the studio and you were outside working. Did you ever get to help out on anything?

Dean Hurley: Sometimes they called down. I remember one time they both called down to me needing research. David said, "Dean, what kind of recording technology would have existed in, let's say, 1939 or 1940?" I don't know what they were thinking about, but clearly that was something in the Phillip Jeffries traveling through time thing of just figuring out how something would have existed. I never saw any evidence of that conversation in the script. I wish I could have been a fly on the wall to see how those ideas got onto the page from their conversation.

Scott Ryan: When did they start working on the music?

Dean Hurley: In July of 2015, we set up the source connect session with Angelo. That's when they started writing new music for the series. David's in his studio, and we've got a studio-quality synth output from Angelo's New Jersey studio piping in. It's like pumped up in volume so David can really feel what's going on. They've got video so they can see each other and talk to each other while the full-bandwidth-resolution music comes through. So it was like "Okay, this is how they can work together." Because ever since I had that job I'd heard, year after year, David make an offhand comment of, "Yeah, I'd work with Angelo every day if he lived next door." I kept thinking, "Man, this is so sad." So David's like "Okay, I want to work with Angelo. No offense, Dean, but I just want it to be me and Angelo in the room." We set up the session, probably on a weekend, and it's basically two days with them, working in four-hour chunks.

Scott Ryan: What was the process?

Dean Hurley: David came with basically a list of words. They were all strategically related to specific scenes in the new series. It'd be like electricity, romance, beauty, night, turmoil, death, euphoria, stuff like that. Once they did these sessions, I'm going back in to sort out the music. It was the true magic of the job for me, because it's like this spiritual archaeology. You're trying to go through and organize what they've generated. I'd say probably like 75 percent of what they did in those eight hours wasn't even used.

Scott Ryan: I like knowing there is more music out there that they worked on.

Dean Hurley: At the end of the session on day two of them working together, David says, "Just play "Laura Palmer's Theme." Jim Bruening, Angelo's assistant, is rolling Midi on his end. Even though I'm recording the broadcast version, Jim sends me all the MIDI session tracks just to insert back into the Pro Tools session. We have all the MIDI notes under everything. So I get a bird's-eye view of the session where I see the MIDI notations. And I'm like "Huh, it graphically looks like a long stretch of mountain ranges." When I zoom in on a single "Laura Palmer's Theme" instance, I see that the Midi for the song forms twin peaks. Think about it. It starts out with the pedal tone bass of the back-and-forth motif, and then, when he starts climbing for the crescendo part of the song, he climbs up the scale, it tips, and then it descends down. It descends down, goes back into the A-B pattern. The composition itself literally forms twin peaks. It's in the fucking DNA of the fucking music, like unbeknownst to them.

Scott Ryan: Tell me about all the cymbal sounds that are used in *The Return*.

Dean Hurley: Before I even worked for David, I remember my biggest takeaway in listening to the original *Twin Peaks* music was Grady's sizzle cymbal. That sound leapt out to me so much. What the hell is that? Why is that sound so cool? And it's everywhere over that series. And actually, you'll hear it in the sound design. I tried to make my own sizzle.

Scott Ryan: Is that the cymbal sound that begins every episode? On your *Anthology Resource Vol. 1*, I think it is called "Intro Cymbal Wind."

Dean Hurley: Totally. I did that because I thought the coolest element, sonically, was the sizzle cymbal. It has something so energetic about it. If you strike that sizzle cymbal, it cascades out. It keeps going as you're doing little fills or flourishes. So I would start working in that sizzle in some of the reverse ramps, like little stingers that we would make for *The Return* because it sounded like *Twin Peaks*.

Scott Ryan: I love thinking that every episode of *The Return* starts with a tribute to Grady Tate. There are many scenes that don't have any score, like so much of Part 18 when Cooper and Carrie are driving to Twin Peaks.

Dean Hurley: When they were driving, David had Angelo score underneath. It doesn't even sound like music. There would be some times in those online sessions where he would prompt Angelo to do more like sound design stuff. He had Angelo attempt to do a whole electricity thing which didn't get used, but there was some of that low driving stuff he used. It's so low and sort of a cluster tone that sounds like a sound effect. It doesn't sound like music. It's kind of like this tonal air kind of thing that happens in the driving sequences.

Scott Ryan: So how was it to play the drummer for "Snake Eyes" in Part 5?

Dean Hurley: It's cool. I'm not much of an on-screen performance guy. So I really had to kind of psych myself up for that, but I remember Duwayne saying he really appreciated me drumming in that scene because, and I remember thinking it too, watching Riley and Alex stand somewhat motionless in that scene. I thought, "You gotta have some sort of energy." So I'm the one flailing around the sticks. That will provide enough visuals.

Scott Ryan: That was a long day of everyone performing. Where did you fall in the lineup?

Dean Hurley: We were the first Roadhouse performance that was filmed. They used us as the guinea pigs to test the lighting. We did that the day before. Peter Deming was figuring out where he wanted the cameras. He was discovering what coverage he was going to get with the three cameras and was testing the lighting and just showing David at the monitors what it was gonna be like for that whole next day. That way they could iron out the issues by using us. We ran through the song like three times.

Scott Ryan: The music for Part 8 is incredible. It has some of my favorite tracks from *The Return*.

Dean Hurley: Well, Part 8 is a masterpiece. The music really comes together. And think about those scenes too. There's no dialogue in those scenes. They're literally music, set pieces, and visual set pieces. That's why it's funny seeing people try to emulate David's style. They don't realize that to do it, you really have to have big, long sections without any talking. That's how you can sink into the sort of quicksand of that thick mood. He lets that stuff be the center focal point, as opposed to just exposition.

Scott Ryan: On your release *Anthology Resource Vol. 1.*, you have some of the sound-design songs on it, but it doesn't have a song called "Sub Dream" that was used a few times in *The Return*. What can you tell me about that track?

Dean Hurley: "Sub Dream" harkens back to *Inland Empire* time, as does "Night Electricity Theme." I would make these sampler patches that trigger stuff from my sound effects library. It was a way of live performing and having some musical elements in there like cymbals and other things. "Sub Dream" in particular is probably a forty-five-minute recording. It goes back to David's idea of firewood.

Scott Ryan: What about "Night Electricity Theme?"

Dean Hurley: On "Night Electricity Theme," there's something really cool that relates to the DNA of that song. It was written in the *Inland Empire* era, in 2006. I had made a patch from an electricity hum. That song sounds like it's a synthesizer, but it actually is a recording of this electricity hum that I mapped on all the keys of a keyboard. You can play it like a synth, but you're actually playing electricity. It might have actually been Duwayne who worked it in somewhere, or it might have been David. *The Return* is steeped in this electrical theme. The first moment it was used was when Cooper and Richard drive up to the coordinates and Richard gets electrocuted. I mean it's called "Night Electricity Theme," and that's the original title too.

Scott Ryan: Those sounds were just as important as the score. There is a similarity to the slow-speed orchestra stuff that was used in *FWWM*, but it's not as musical in *The Return*.

Dean Hurley: What I did for *The Return* was I made a lot of sounds by slowing down records that David and I had done so we would own the rights. And it's funny, because I noticed there was an instance of some people speeding shit up on YouTube to figure out what was underneath scenes. There were some hilarious ones where people were speeding stuff up, being like "If you speed up the sound from Sarah Palmer watching the TV of the wild animals going at each other, you'll hear David Lynch's voice." And it's because that's how I would achieve what they were achieving on the original series, because they were probably slowing it down with tape, and I have a slow-speed record player, and I was putting on a vinyl that David and I had done.

Scott Ryan: I found out from David Slusser a little more about "Sycamore Trees." He says Koko Taylor sang it in *Wild at Heart*. He remembers it because of her saying "Sick-y-mo trees." Any thoughts on that?

Dean Hurley: Okay, so a thing like this is one of these stories that rings true to me, even though I have no evidence to back it up, because I've never heard that version. But I believe it, because it's around the same time where you've got Koko Taylor singing "Up in Flames," and the same song falls on Julee Cruise's album, where she's singing "Up in Flames." David is constantly reusing and repurposing. Nothing is sacred from his perspective. But that's interesting. Gosh! I wish I had that little nugget to ask David about it back when I was working on the *TPA*.

Scott Ryan: Well, it could be a deleted scene from *Wild at Heart*.

Dean Hurley: Having worked on the *Wild at Heart* deleted scenes and having seen all the material, I didn't see any material where she was singing that song. It's like the classic case file where a detective gets a new shred of information, and you're like "Let me go review all my materials." I'll take a look at what I have here and just see if anything's there. Ideas cross-pollinate, and the ones for the projects that aren't used get folded into new ideas. So it is hard tracking this stuff down. I'll take a look with my limited amount of stuff and see if I can find any evidence of that.

Scott Ryan: Don't you feel all this music should be preserved for future generations?

Dean Hurley: Eventually a university might get all of these tapes or the Library of Congress or the Museum of Motion Pictures, where you can go to the museum and look this stuff up and have audience with it. It becomes a library.

Scott Ryan: I am glad to hear that you think it won't be lost, but I want a CD/vinyl box set. I'm going to keep pushing it, knowing that I have no power, but I'm going to do what I can to make other people say, "Yeah, why isn't there an Angelo Badalamenti box set?"

Dean Hurley: Yeah, I think a vinyl box is a hard one to do with this. It has to have a certain framework to make sense, because as a vinyl box set, it would be like fucking twelve LPs long.

Scott Ryan: Well how many discs is that *Twin Peaks Z to A* Blu-ray release, which is now sold out and going for hundreds of dollars because they let it go out of print? Plus, someone like me could curate it. It doesn't all have to come out. There is a difference between having nineteen versions of "Laura Palmer's

Theme" and having one version of "Josie and Truman" released. Going back to *The Return*, why do you think there was so much less score than in the original series?

Dean Hurley: When David and Mark screened that last episode of *Twin Peaks* to kind of bring themselves up to speed, it always struck me as so odd that David's big takeaway coming out of that was the wall-to-wall music. He said, "I don't know what I was thinking. I used too much music." And I was like "You're fucking crazy." I didn't say that to him. But that was cinematic television. The music in that episode is without match. The song they used in the Red Room was called "composite," with the bass and the organ. That mood was amazing. You've also got "Sycamore Trees" and "Dark Mood Woods," but he was convinced that he used too much music. I found this evident on "Mulholland Drive" as well. When I looked at the original mixing session, there were scenes that had music hard muted in the Pro Tools session. His first pass would have too much music, and then he would go through again and drop the cue.

Scott Ryan: But if you are going to do an episode that has twenty minutes in the Red Room, you are going to have twenty minutes of score because "Where we're from the birds sing a pretty song."

Dean Hurley: Well, that is why *The Return* was so sparse with music, because his emotional memory of rewatching that episode was "I used too much music." I remember when we started mixing *The Return*, it's like Part 1 and as soon as we hit the exterior of the sheriff station I'm like rubbing my hands. "Okay, are we dropping some Grady Tate brush drums here?" I was really overzealous at first, and then I put it on there. He's like "No, lose it."

Scott Ryan: [Sighs]

Dean Hurley: But that made it all the more impactful when that Bobby scene comes up and you hear the "Laura Palmer's Theme" in all its glory. That's the first moment in *The Return* where it's like "Oh, shit! This feels like we're back." But it's funny how you see Laura Palmer's aged photo, and everything's in a box. It's kind of like him looking at the old show and saying, "We can't go there. We can't fully go there."

TRACK 11

"Shadow"

Twin Peaks Music from the Limited Event Series, 2017

Here I will once again exercise my Giant-given right to complain as an original *Twin Peaks* fan: why can't things from the world of *Twin Peaks* ever have logical names? I mean, the name of this next album is *Twin Peaks Music from the Limited Event Series*. Rolls right off the tongue, doesn't it? This should have been called *Live from the Roadhouse* or *The Bang Bang Bar*. The other album is called *Twin Peaks Limited Event Series Soundtrack*. There really isn't anything in the title that speaks to the differences between them. And if they are both just a potpourri of songs, then they should have been combined and been released as a double disk called *Twin Peaks: The Return Soundtrack*. But I doubt that very many obsessive fans of *The Return* could properly name these two albums. I can be honest and say every time I have to type one of the titles in this book, I have to go back and copy it from my table of contents just to be sure I am using the correct title. Even as I am writing this very sentence, I can't remember what the Bang Bang album is officially called.

Dean Hurley: With Season 3, David said, "I want to do a whole day with music. We will film ten bands in a day. I don't know where they are gonna go. I don't know how I am gonna use them. I want to have them." It is the building blocks, the firewood. We can work these in. It gives you an extreme latitude of how

you can circumvent problems. He is sidestepping all the issues traditional shows have of "Well, this episode has to be forty-two minutes." He is like "The narrative is this; I am two minutes short. Well, I have a band I can throw in at the end." He figures out these unique working methods that allow for flexibility and creative boundless freedom, where a lot of people think there is a rigid architecture to how you do something. Bear in mind, a script is very important.
He has always worked in a manor where there is enough of a coming together of elements at the right time because he has saved these things in his pocket.

"Twin Peaks Main Theme (edit)"

Edit or not, there is no earthly reason for this to be on the soundtrack. We have this song many times over. This cover has the picture of the reflection of the Bang Bang Bar's neon sign in the mud puddle that comes directly from Episode 14. If they knew they were going to have two soundtracks released from *The Return*, then it would have been nice if they had stuck to a formula for it. This album should have been all the songs from the Roadhouse, and the other album should have been songs from the score or background. "Falling" did not play at the Roadhouse, so it shouldn't be here.

I will point out the songs that should or should not be on this album. At the end of the following chapter, which covers the other *Return* soundtrack, I will include a new track list that actually adheres to the concepts that the two albums were supposed to follow.

"Shadow" by Chromatics

With only a few minutes left in the end of Part 2, Lynch cuts to the Bang Bang sign. We get our first glimpse of James Hurley and Shelly Johnson. It starts to really feel like we are back in Twin Peaks. At the same time, a band starts to play a song on the Roadhouse stage. The music feels similar to a Julee Cruise song but is a touch more modern than the Badalament/Lynch/Cruise music from the original series. That is because it isn't Julee Cruise singing on stage; it is the Chromatics, singing lines like "And now you're just a stranger's dream. I took your picture from the frame." They may have kept repeating the refrain of "for the last time," but it was actually just the first time. A pattern would emerge that almost every part would end at the Roadhouse with a band performing. This was the new way Lynch brought music into the series. It used to be music was in the air; now it was music on the stage.

"Mississippi" by The Cactus Blossoms

"Mississippi" is an enjoyable song, but I have never been able to make any connection between this song and the feel of Part 3. The pleasant harmonizing and Buddy Holly feel doesn't evoke the feeling of the Mansion Room, where Cooper meets Naido. If "Shadow" has the breathy Julee Cruise, synth pop feel, this track has the mood of a Chris Isaak song. But Chris Isaak never sang in *Twin Peaks*, he just fell asleep bending over for a ring and then dreamed all of *Twin Peaks*. (Tony Stanic and I call this the reverse dream theory.) The Cactus Blossoms are fronted by Jack Torrey and Page Burkum. They were interviewed for *The Blue Rose* magazine and had this to say about the experience . . .

Jack Torrey: They were testing out having an MC introduce the bands. When he did that for us, he said, "We'd like to welcome The Cactus Blossoms." And Lynch said, "Cut!" He goes, "Is it The Cactus Blossoms or Cactus Blossoms?" And we go "The Cactus Blossoms." And he goes, "Roll it!"

Page Burkum: They made it deceptively simple. They knew our instrumentation, and they were all set up for us. There was gear on the stage, and the mics were in position exactly like every other show we play. It said a lot about their planning. We just stood where we always stand. They weren't telling us "Move over a foot," you know? They made it feel weirdly normal. (*Blue Rose* by Matt Latterell)

"Lark" by Au Revoir Simone

It was nice to have an all-girls band in the series. This is a fine song, but again, doesn't really connect to anything in the series. This plays at the end of Part 4. No disrespect intended, but I got nothing on this one. In 2018, Melanie Mullen put together a location tour in LA for *The Return*, and I was able to visit the location where they filmed all the bands for the Roadhouse. It is called the South Pasadena Women's Club [See photo below] and is tucked away in a little neighborhood. It was fun to get to stand on the stage where all this wonderful music was captured. I, of course, grabbed a broom and started sweeping, but even I knew not to do that for too long before it got old.

"I Am" by Blunted Beatz

This is not the kind of song that I would ever have on my phone, but for some reason, I really like it. It truly sticks in my head. That being said, it really shouldn't be on this vinyl. It is more of a score song, and this album should have been only the Roadhouse songs. This is basically Ike the Spike and Lorraine's theme and is used in Parts 5 and 6. Sabrina Sutherland told me in an interview that she had to track this song down after Lynch heard it and really wanted to use it. I can see why: it is catchy, and it fits Spike quite well.

"I Love How You Love Me" by the Paris Sisters

I defy any fan of Season 3 to hear "I Love How You Love Me" and not picture the smiling face of Amanda Seyfried. Becky Burnett may not have been a completely fleshed-out character, but the scene in which this song plays certainly was one of the best cinematic moments of Season 3: that smile, that freedom, and a pure moment of elation from a character who is drowning in sadness. Drugs and rock 'n' roll combine in an explosion of happiness as Becky listens to this song while the wind blows her hair in the car. Having a bad day? Turn the radio on and lose yourself in the moment. Something that Sailor and Lula would totally agree with.

The most interesting thing about this track for me, and fans of the television series *Psych*, is the use of this song in the *Twin Peaks*-inspired episode titled "Dual Spires" from 2010. One of the shows stars, James Roday, is a huge *Twin Peaks* fan, and he cowrote an episode that has over a hundred references to *Twin Peaks*, and he cast it with a few actors from the original series. But if someone happened to watch this episode today, they might say, "Wow, look at that; they did a references to *The Return* as well." But that would be impossible because this episode was broadcast in 2010, and *The Return* came out in 2017. But when Shawn and Gus walk into the diner in the small town of Dual Spires, playing on the jukebox is "I Love How You Love Me" by the Paris Sisters. If James Roday really is that big of a *Twin Peaks* fan, he must have really lost it in Part 5 when the song he picked to play in his episode was now playing in the series. Is it future or is it past?

"Snake Eyes" by Trouble

"Trouble" plays in Part 5 and rocks the Roadhouse for the only true time. This song has a fun, repetitive beat with a saxophone that immediately connects to the musical world of *Twin Peaks*. Also, there is something fun about hearing a song in a Lynch movie performed onstage with the saxophone taking the lead. Let's get Bill Pullman up there and bring it all home. This song is performed by David Lynch's son Riley and is cowritten by Riley and Dean Hurley.

Dean Hurley: Riley's a PA on the show. So he's working on production every day. He comes to me one day. And he's like "I hear my dad wants to do a day of filming bands. It'd be so cool if I could get a song in there." I said, "Okay, let's just try to write something. But it's your dad. So it has to be really fucking cool for

him to use it. He's not just gonna be like 'Oh, Riley wrote a song, so we're putting it in there.'" We got together one day, and nothing was prepared. He just starts playing that little very simple riff that he has for the song. It had a hard-edged vibe. It had one chord the whole song. People like James Brown did similar stuff, like a really bulletproof funk groove and would just fucking vamp on a single chord and never stop. I was on drums. Riley was on guitar. We recorded a fifteen-minute version of it. I invited my friend Alex Zhang Hungtai from Dirty Beaches to come up because he was starting to play sax, and he jammed on top of our jam.

We were at a point of figuring out who was going to be the Roadhouse acts. There was a lot of pretty stuff. There was the Chromatics, Sharon Van Etten, and Au Revoir Simone. We were lacking stuff that was going to be kind of hard. I don't think we'd received the Trent Reznor song yet. I remembered there was this fight scene that breaks out with Freddie and the dudes at the bar, and I was thinking we were writing the song for that scene. Technically the song was called "Trouble" at that point. I named the file "Trouble" because there's trouble at the bar. Duwayne had all these performances, and he was pairing them up. He had the scene with the introduction to Richard Horne, and that's where the song ended up. I remember walking in, and he's got that scene built around "Trouble," and I remember my first instinct was "Oh, fuck! No, that's supposed to be for the other scene." I had written it in my head, and it took me a good day and a half to even come around to the idea.

"Tarifa (Roadhouse Mix)" by Sharon Van Etten

Part 6 ends with "Tarifa," and it's another pleasant song, but just like the lyrics say, "I can't remember" anything connecting this song to that episode. But this is a good time to talk about the bonus feature on the *Z to A* box set of all the Roadhouse bands edited together as music videos. I love that JR Starr introduces most of the bands, and how actors were swaying on the floor and waitresses were carrying beers as they navigated through the crowds. It would have been nice if we saw some of the townsfolk of Twin Peaks dancing here. Like couldn't they put Alicia Witt in the crowd? We all know Gerstin is too cool to stay in that crappy apartment at night. She would be out getting it done. Remember that the two times the original series had scenes in the Roadhouse with live music onstage, our cast members were there to enjoy the music. Having Ed and Norma listening to "Falling" in the Pilot and James and Donna swaying to "Rockin' Back Inside My Heart" made those scenes classics. And I am not counting all the randos in the back booths. I'm talking about the mosh pit. I bet if someone gave Dr. Amp a shovel, he would mosh.

"She's Gone Away" by Nine Inch Nails

Part 8 is all about breaking the conventions of *The Return*, and one of the first things Lynch and editor Duwayne Dunham did in this episode to throw us for a loop was have the Roadhouse music scene early in the episode. I really think it is funny to hear the intro "The Roadhouse is proud to welcome the Nine Inch Nails." I mean who is the NIN booking agent? That person got fired the next day. And I know earlier I said it would be nice if there would have been shots of the townsfolk in the crowd, but I am thankful that during "She's Gone," we don't have a cut to Dick Treymane headbanging with Catherine Martell. Although Catherine did boogie with Leland at the Great Northern, so who am I to say? I have to give props to the lighting for this scene. When you are aware of the fact that they recorded all of these performances in one day, you understand how creative and versatile Peter Deming is, lighting most of the bands one way but then pulling out something completely different for Part 8.

This song is most certainly not my kind of music, but there is no doubt that it is perfect for the feel of the episode, and it's nice to have a little variety in the type of songs picked. This loud, violent performance felt way out of place on first viewing. Why were we being hit with a sonic baseball bat? On second viewing, it makes perfect sense. Lynch was setting us up for the nuclear explosion, an actual assault on humanity, and preparing our ears for "Threnody to the Victims of Hiroshima." With Deming's lighting, the performance of Trent Reznor almost appears to be in black and white, which sets up the following forty minutes of Part 8. Whether this is your type of music or not, it would be hard to argue that the song doesn't set the proper tone. Of course, having Trent Reznor back with David Lynch is great fun for *Lost Highway* fans. Reznor's work on that legendary soundtrack makes him a welcome addition to the series. For me, *The Return* always succeeds the most when it collides with Lynch's legacy. I look at the series as the cherry on top of Lynch's film career.

"My Prayer" by the Platters

It is a definite talent that Lynch has in taking a sincere song from the past and making it feel sinister (see also "Blue Velvet" or "Crying"). From the opening lyrics ("When the twilight is gone"), there is something unsettling about the chords, vocals, and images that lets you know Lynch is setting you up for trouble. This song plays twice in the series. The first time is in Part 8, in which everything is meant to be studied and analyzed for clues. The second time "My Prayer" plays is when Diane and Cooper (or Linda and Richard or Jeffery and Sandy) have sex. Again, the song doesn't seem to fit the action. It sure doesn't appear that anyone's prayers are being answered in this sex scene. For Part 8, the song sets up the sleepy, innocent town where a kid at home, a waitress in a diner, and a mechanic all listen to a song on the radio. That's when a woodsman crushes people's skulls, and then logically, a frog moth goes inside a teenage girl's mouth. You know, just like the Platters envisioned when they recorded this track in 1956. All that being said, this shouldn't be on this soundtrack because the song isn't a Roadhouse performance.

"No Stars" by Rebekah Del Rio

This track is one of the most perfect fits in the entire series. The

Roadhouse songs work best when they emotionally and historically connect with Lynch or *Twin Peaks*. "No Stars" is written by Rebekah Del Rio, John Neff, and David Lynch. Rebekah famously sang "Llorando" in *Mulholland Drive*, which one could argue might be the greatest musical sequence in any of Lynch's films. John Neff was Lynch's sound man before Dean Hurley came around. Neff worked on many projects with Lynch, but my favorite is when he combined two different tracks to create "The Jitterbug" cue in *Mulholland Drive*. He was also a friend of mine. He passed away in 2022. In 2017, he told me this about working on "No Stars" with Lynch and Del Rio.

John Neff: It started off as a *Blue Bob* song. The chord progression that I wrote was initially to be for a second *Blue Bob* album. Brian Lox brought over Rebekah Del Rio to meet us. We were toying with the idea of doing an entire album. So David really loved those chords. He wrote the English lyrics, and Rebekah wrote a Spanish translation and the vocal melody. David and I both played guitar on the record. I played the guitarchestra, which is a big, guitar-driven synthesizer, orchestral rig. I played drums and recorded and mixed it. It sat on the shelf for a long time. There is a version of it on Rebekah's *Love Hurts, Love Heals* album from 2011. The version you hear in the series was something that we did some years ago. Oh, and I played guitar on it, not Moby.

Moby does a nice job pretending to be John Neff in the episode. Moby is connected to Lynch by sampling "Laura Palmer's Theme" on his hit song "Go." Kevin Laffey told me in our interview that he helped Moby not get sued over that sampling; Moby hadn't gotten permission to use it, but then he met Lynch, and they hit it off.

I think this is the best song in the entire Roadhouse selection. It sounds like *Twin Peaks* because it is written by a longtime Lynch collaborator. It has that fifties sound that all the Julee Cruise songs have. Also, Rebekah truly gives her all in her performance. She isn't phoning this in. She isn't trying to be "too cool for school" on stage. She is feeling this song. Many of the performers at the Roadhouse have a stage presence, like they were inconvenienced just being there. Rebekah is living in the moment. Add in the fact that this song coincides with the death of the Log Lady, and it all makes perfect sense. For those of us who knew Catherine Coulson in real life and for the characters in the town of Twin Peaks who loved the Log Lady, the combined death in real life and fake, there really are no stars. There is only darkness left. Catherine meant the world to me. She was such an incredibly kind person. There was no one in the world who gave more to *Twin Peaks*. She spent the last days of her life filming her scenes from her house. From her literal death bed. The Log Lady represented the good and the innocent in a town where there was no innocence. She spends her last moments of life trying to pass on her information to the only comparable spiritual leader left in the town, Deputy Hawk. She knows her time has come. The sky will be blank and there will be no stars left once she passes. We are left with the fear that all goodness is in jeopardy. What an absolute display of perfection of song and scene. This is what Lynch does best and why *The Return* is a marvel.

[Okay. Sorry that I did that to you, but we are way too far in this book for you to have fallen for that. I just wanted to pretend for a moment that "No Stars" was used as it should have been. For some reason, Lynch didn't pair this song with the Log Lady dying. He used it in Part 10 instead. I didn't get it then; I don't get it now. So I decided to just write it like he used it that way. If it's all a dream and we don't know who the dreamer is, I guess you can at least rule out that it is me who is the dreamer because I sure as hell would have used "No Stars" for the Log Lady's death.]

"Viva Las Vegas" by Shawn Colvin

This cover of the classic Elvis Presley song plays in Part 11 and is the biggest head-scratcher in all of Lynch's filmography, not just *Twin Peaks*, but all of it. I don't get the use of this song. I remember watching this scene the first time and just being gobsmacked. It was like Nora Ephron took over the directing. Lynch used a lackluster cover of "Viva Las Vegas" to have someone literaly drive across Las Vegas. I am sure I don't know the exact number of films that have used this song as their main character goes to Vegas, but Lynch might just as have had Dougie say "Vegas, Baby." Maybe Ike the Spike could have said "What happens in Vegas stays in the Black Lodge for twenty-five years." The song plays for almost two minutes, with just stock footage of the Vegas strip, and it couldn't be more ordinary. It just doesn't fit in the world of Twin Peaks or a David Lynch movie. I love Shawn Colvin, I love the song, but I will never be able to say this jives with the feeling or purpose of *The Return*.

"Just You" by James Marshall

"Just You" might just be the most controversial song in the world of Twin Peaks. Some fans love it, and some think Bob came over the couch in Episode 9 just to stop James Hurley, Maddy Ferguson, and Donna Hayward from singing. However, playing at the end of Part 13, "Just You" occupies a new space. It was a shocking moment to see James (Marshall and Hurley) sit there and sing the song (or, more accurately, lip-synch to the exact same version) again. Here the song doesn't summon Bob; it summons fans' memories, as well as the character's history. Think of the pain this song must bring to the character of James. Maddy was murdered just days after singing it, and he and Donna never reunited. This was a perfect use of nostalgia. It reminds us of the past, but colors it with the current state of the town and the characters. While Donna Hayward doesn't make an appearance in *The Return*, this version of the song is the exact recording that was used in Episode 9. So while there are two women on stage backing up James, they are actually lip-synching to Sheryl Lee's and Lara Flynn Boyle's vocals. So in a way, Donna did return. The song is intercut with shots of the character Renee from Part 2, who has feelings for James. Don't get too caught up, Renee. James falls in love quicker than CBS shuts down a fan selling an Audrey doll made out of yarn.

"Green Onions" by Booker T. and the M.G.'s

There are a few tracks that just don't feel like *Twin Peaks* to me. This is one of them. This classic rock instrumental is from 1962, which doesn't even fit the fifties vibe Lynch usually goes for. This song is played as we watch Jean-Michel Renault sit at a bar while some guy sweeps the floor. There has been much talk about this scene, and some people feel it's a waste of time. This scene plays from 47:37 to 49:58. So that is 141 seconds. To me, the problem isn't that Lynch wastes our time for those two minutes; it is the music choice that causes the controversy. I can quickly think of another classic scene that involves an extended shot of a floor. It is the hook-rug dance sequence in Episode 15. That scene played from 6:28 to 7:44, which is 76 seconds, and no one has ever complained about the hook-rug dance sequence. That is because the music was Angelo's, and it fit the series. It also lands with one of the best final lines of dialogue in any scene: "Lord, what's become of us?" What if the sweeping scene was scored to the sax version of "Theme from FWWM" or one of the unreleased tracks? Then we could have connected it to the past, and it would have made more sense to have a Renault in the scene. Anyway, this song shouldn't have been on this album anyway because it wasn't performed on the Roadhouse stage.

No one is going to be inspired by hearing "Green Onions" for two minutes. The scene feels like a way to give Walter Olkewicz a chance to come back to the series, which really is a slap in the face to fans, since he spent years fleecing many of them out of their money. I had to block him on Facebook, as he constantly hounded me for cold hard cash, and I am hardly the only one. It is difficult to justify bringing him back and leaving Piper Laurie and Joan Chen out. I love *The Return*, but much of what should be open to criticism can be found in this very scene and song selection. To top it off, Part 7 ends with a 1959 rock instrumental, "Sleep Walk," which was left off both soundtracks. This one should have joined "Sleep Walk," and we maybe could have forgotten either was ever used.

"Wild West (Roadhouse Mix)" by Lissie

From old rock that doesn't work to current rock that does. In Part 14, we get Lissie singing "Wild West," and it is the best uptempo song in the entire Roadhouse collection. This song has so much life, and Lissie actually looks like she is having fun performing it. This is the track from *The Return* that I listen to the most, and always at full volume. Andrew Hageman wrote in *The Blue Rose* #15 that the MC had a rough time pronouncing Lissie's name correctly, and that could be why he says it with such gusto in the take Duwayne Dunham used, because he finally got it right. Superfan Aaron Cohen has seen Lissie in concert three times, and she never performed this song at any of those concerts. He asked her about it, and she said the backstory of her writing the song for her personally makes her not want to revisit it in concert. That is a shame, because it really is a great track.

"Sharp Dressed Man" by ZZ Top

Scene: we see a couple who are not married but are in love. A man just wants to say hi to a girl, but the man who is with that girl won't allow it. Before we know it, a fight breaks out as the music plays on the stage of the Roadhouse. Now my question to you is this: What song is playing? I'll answer that in a moment.

MC Starr introduced each band at the Roadhouse. Some of them are used in *The Return*, and some are just on the bonus featurette. Here, for some unknown reason, MC Starr introduces ZZ Top even though they are not there. He calls it a playlist song. "Sharp Dressed Man" plays, and once again, we get a major missed opportunity. This song kicks me out of the mood of *Twin Peaks* every time. This is played in Part 15 when James and Freddie get in a fight and use the green glove on Renee's husband. Lynch is so famous for matching the perfect pop song to the scene he is crafting. Using a hair band hit from the eighties just doesn't fit the scene or the series.

It doesn't pack the punch that "Love Me Tender" does in *Wild at Heart*. It doesn't mesh like "The Locomotion" does when a group of women start dancing in front of Laura Dern in *Inland Empire*. When "I've Told Every Little Star" plays in *Mulholland Drive*, we feel happy and inspired, even though we are rooting against Melissa George getting the part. Lynch took a song from the fifties hit parade and built one of the scariest on-screen villains of eighties cinema, Frank Booth. What song did Frank love? "Blue Velvet," which was hardly a creepy song until Lynch got a hold of it. He has been a master at matching a story with a pop song. "Love Me Tender" is probably the best example, because when Sailor starts singing it to Lula at the end of the *Wild at Heart*, audiences don't have to wonder why; we know why. It was set up earlier in the film.

In this scene for *The Return*, we have a song that doesn't fit and a story of a man in a green glove who can punch someone's brains out. This isn't hyperbole; that is the plot. Could any song have fit? Well, now let's go back to my earlier question. What song was playing at the Roadhouse when a fight broke out? "The Nightingale" by Julee Cruise. The scene I described was from the Pilot, not Part 15, but they sure would have been connected if MC Starr would have said, "Next on the Roadhouse playlist, here is Julee Cruise." Lynch wouldn't have had to film Cruise twice; "The Nightingale" would have connected the fight in the bar in the original series to the fight in Part 15, and the song would have actually fit in the world of *Twin Peaks*. I know I've been harsh with a few songs from this album, but no other song is as bad as "Sharp Dressed Man." I am not saying "The Nightingale" would have saved the green glove storyline, but it sure would have given it a fighting chance. The connections would have also been the fact that Big Ed was attracted to Norma, a married woman he shouldn't be with, and James making time with Renee, a married woman. Then we add in that in the Pilot fight, Bobby started the fight and now he is the deputy who locks James up in jail. But instead, we get ZZ Top. "It's a world of truck drivers."

"Axolotl (Roadhouse Mix)" The Veils

Here is another example of where the sound and the feel fit perfectly with what we've come to expect from David Lynch. The arrangement and repetitive bass make it feel like an identical cousin to "The Pink Room." This song came out in 2016, and even though it was current at the time, it doesn't feel out of place. There are current songs that can fit in the world that Lynch created, and it's not about being classified as rock, dance, or pop. It is about the feel. This scene in Part 15 also has momentum, which most of the Roadhouse scenes don't. We bond with Ruby in a second, and she doesn't have to have minutes of pointless dialogue to make us care. When the bullies plop her on the floor and she starts to crawl, we immediately think of Dougie crawling across the floor to the plug. The lights flicker, and there's wires in the air, and the dance floor is all around her. This is what we want from the Roadhouse songs. It would have been better to jettison the songs that were forced in and let moments like this happen organically.

"Out of Sand" by Eddie Vedder

MC Starr introduces Pearl Jam's front man by his real name, Edward Louis Severson. When the series started, I tried really hard to connect the song to the part, but then I realized that was mostly a pointless endeavor. But this song really seemed to fit the situation so well. I asked Dean

Hurley if there was any reason that was so, and of course he knew the answer.

Dean Hurley: His song was composed for the series. Everyone else was a needle drop. It was a song that we told the band we wanted them to play. Eddie was a friend of Ben Harper, and Laura Dern was married to Ben Harper, and Laura's the one who said to David that he should put Eddie in there. He had already done the benefit concert [*Change Begins Within*] that happened at Radio City Music Hall in 2009. Paul McCartney and Ringo Starr reunited for that benefit. So Eddie had already done that, but his connection to that whole world was Laura. David gave me Eddie's number, and we had a conversation where Eddie was asking me what the series was about. I remember trying to explain it, but we were still filming at the time, and Sabrina Sutherland was like the prison warden saying, "If anybody breathes anything to anybody, you will be shot and killed." He asked if there were any themes for this show in general. I said that the overarching theme was time. I saw the series as a poetic sort of rumination on time. You've got the element of time travel. You've got like the whole twenty-five years later. When I heard the song come in I was like "Wow, that's perfect." He hadn't seen a frame. He didn't know anything about anything, but he just took this concept of time and made something perfectly suited for that moment.

The lyric of "Running out of sand" is exactly how we all felt knowing that there were only two parts left and so much story to go. Even though we knew there would be no wrap-up, it was hard not to hope for some conclusion. Either way our fun summer of watching *Twin Peaks* and discussing it on podcasts and weekly phone calls with our friends was coming to an end. We were all running out of sand.

"I've Been Loving You too Long" (Live From Monterey Pop) by Otis Redding

Norma's hand appears out of nowhere on Ed's shoulder, and Big Ed lets a smile appear on his face. Just moments before, he had asked Shelly for a cup of coffee, and . . . what was it? Oh yeah, a cyanide tablet. You know, a Norma Plate Special. "I've been loving you too long," howls soul singer Otis Redding live in concert. The two star-crossed lovers kiss, and Norma accepts his proposal. It is just an average love story coming to completion. It only took forty-five years. Remember it was

twenty-five years ago that they were meeting at the Roadhouse in secret to talk about trying to steal a moment together. Six weeks after that, they thought Nadine was ready for a divorce, but she got her memory back, and the two stayed apart for the twenty-five years in between. How do you bring a love story like that to completion? You do it with a passionate performance by Otis Redding. The song is all about singing with soul; the pain and desire in Otis's voice infuse the entire song. Lynch even uses a live version because there is so much rawness to both the scene and the recording. "My love is growing stronger as our affair grows old."

This is an affair that has caused much damage for Nadine, Ed, Norma, and in some ways Shelly, whom we see moved to tears by their engagement. Ed and Norma's unwillingness to put love first reverberated throughout the community, emitting waves of negativity and collateral pain. It has been a long time coming, and this song isn't in any hurry either. Otis, just like Ed and Norma, takes about forty-five years to get through the chorus. He asks the band to do it one more time, then one more time, then one more time as the band hits the chords at each request with a bam, bam, bam. The crowd goes wild because everyone is waiting for that climax. This kiss is the only resolution allowed any of the original *Twin Peaks* characters. I have said for years that to Lynch, their love story was the heart and soul of the series. I made this claim in my *FWWM* book by pointing out that the themes to the series and the film are the love theme used to score Norma and Ed. "Falling" is used in the Pilot and "Theme from FWWM" is used in the *Missing Pieces* scene in which they make out in a car and listen to the radio. In *The Return*, Lynch gives them the great Otis Redding singing his heart out, with soulful sighs echoing the emotion of fans who watched these two finally get together. Well done, Mr. Lynch. Perfect song choice, and great job on a story with closure. Only complaint is that it shouldn't be on this vinyl, as it isn't performed at the Roadhouse.

"The World Spins" by Julee Cruise

Each week fans of Cruise waited to see when she would be one of the bar bands. It finally happened in Part 17. Besides this song being the last Roadhouse song from the series, it would serve as the last time we see Julee Cruise in the world of Twin Peaks. This song will always be strongly associated with Julee and will resonate on a deep emotional level with fans of *Twin Peaks*. It is impossible to hear those first notes and not be overcome with emotion. The use of "The World Spins" in Episode 14 may be the best use of music in the entire series. The song plays like an anthem of hopelessness as Cooper sits there and wonders why the owls are in the Roadhouse. Compare that with Part 17, where we just spent the last twenty minutes watching recreated scenes from *FWWM*. Laura is a teenager once again, walking in the woods with Agent Cooper, and then "The World Spins" starts to play. Our emotions are triggered not by the new scenes, but by our memories of the scene in Episode 14.

I wish Lynch didn't have Julee sing "The World Spins" again, because it had been done before. It doesn't pack the same emotional punch that it did back in 1990, as Cooper looked up wondering what he missed. So why play it again? The song doesn't even play to completion. "She Would Die for Love" or "The Voice of Love" (both instrumental tracks from *FWWM* that include lyrics on Cruise's second album) would have matched the experience of seeing Laura Palmer again from *FWWM*. To have Julee Cruise sing "The Voice of Love," which we last heard (with no lyrics) as the final scene in *FWWM* as Cooper stood over Laura, would have fit with Cooper standing above Laura on a hill before she disappears. This would have connected to the final scene in *FWWM*, when Laura laughs with tears of joy. When Part 17 aired on September 3, 2017, fans jumped online to say Cruise was angry about her placement and the use of the song. When I interviewed her in 2018, she had this to say about it:

Julee Cruise: Everyone thought I was angry at the end of Part 17 because I didn't get enough airtime. That is not it at all. Really. David does things that will make me look good. He would not ever do anything to compromise his work. Hell, no. It was a glance at the past. It was beautifully done. I was hyper and nervous and didn't know what to expect, and I did get quite a weird direction before I started. I have a photo of what I'm doing. It is quite different from what you see. That is not my face. I am not sad during that song. I am not exuberant. The song is hope. The song is reality to me. I had it played at my mom's funeral. This isn't a sad song. This is life—afterlife. It is very Carl Jungian. It is a simple way for this complicated person to live.

Devery Doleman: "The World Spins" always puts me in a trance to sing it, and it's so vulnerable. I really think "a dog and bird are far away" is one of the most moving, sad lines ever written. There's something so pure about the grief and love in that song. I've cried singing this song, just alone in the practice space. I remember just crying a lot learning "The World Spins" because it is so pure and moving and achingly sad and beautiful. My marriage had also ended that year, and I think "a dog and bird are far away" really hit the core of having lost someone who had been the only person in my life who ever felt like my real home, and that lyric is the only way to really communicate exactly what that felt like to me. It's almost as simple as a hieroglyph.

The Missing Music Pieces

As I pointed out a few times, there are tracks on this album that shouldn't be here because they weren't played in the Roadhouse. But even stranger, missing are songs that *were* performed at the Roadhouse. Here are those tracks:

"A Violent Yet Flammable World" by Au Revoir Simone

While I didn't have much to say about this group's first song, I really wish this was on the Roadhouse album. This song has a little more oomph to it, and I don't understand cutting any of the songs performed at the Roadhouse. But if you were going to choose one of the two Au Revoir Simone songs, this is the better of the two for matching the type of song that connects with *Twin Peaks*. The drum beat has that Phil Spector feel that Lynch loves and reminds me a lot of "Pinky's dream" from Lynch's *Crazy Clown Time* album. I am glad it's on the Roadhouse bonus feature, as the band's performance is great. They actually seem like they are having fun performing this track, although it is really funny when they cut to the audience dancing all uptempo. I'm not sure that cut is from this number, but maybe the crowd is all hopped up on Sparkle. This was used in Part 9 in the end credits sequence, but the band actually got to record three tracks. The last song is called "Sad Song." It wasn't used in the series, but it is the final song on the Roadhouse bonus feature. It was probably wise to not use three tracks from this band if you are going to use only one from Julee Cruise.

"Human" by Hudson Mohawke

Oh, now I get all the DJ jokes in sitcoms. I'm not sorry this song isn't on the vinyl release, thought technically it should have been because all the Roadhouse songs were selected and approved by Lynch. "Human" mostly sounds like someone is really enjoying a good sandwich. Maybe a sandwich Josie made with lots of mayo on it. (I am serious; all Mohawke does is grunt like he is enjoying an Arby's roast beef sandwich.) It is fascinating that both Part 9 songs were cut from the vinyl. This one plays before the booth scene in which the girl digs at her armpits like she is looking for hieroglyphics on Owl Cave. After that scene, the music goes into the "A Violent Yet Flammable World." Both were cut from the vinyl and both were included on the bonus feature of songs from the Roadhouse. This song plays when Chloe and Ellaare talk in the booth. I don't mind the idea of vignettes that tie the town together or show that there is more to the story of the town than Laura Palmer; I just wish they were more engaging and matched the music in the way the scenes did in the original series. But this is what *The Return* is about, and I can't change it. I will be honest and say this was the only song I didn't make it till the end of while writing this book, but also I am 100 percent certain Hudson Mohawke is not turning those knobs on stage for someone my age. That being said, I just don't see how this song brings to life the conversation that it scores; however, it does make me want to eat a really good Italian sub and say "Mmm." "Ahh." "Ooo." "Mmm."

The last missing song from this album is the Chromatics again, performing the instrumental "Saturday." This track was released on the other *Return* album. I get that the other album is billed as an instrumental-only album, but it does have "American Woman" on it, so that isn't true. It would have made the most sense for this song to have been on here. It would have been fine to have the Chromatics have two songs on it, just like Au Reviore Simone would have and should have.

One final thought: I absolutely adore this album. I know I have been hard on some of the choices, and the name is just ridiculous, but I do really love it. I love that they had all these songs from the Roadhouse. I am not being mean or disrespectful. I am being critical. The music of *Twin Peaks* is very important to me, and when the decision was made to lessen the score, that made the selection of these tracks all the more important. This is one of my main contentions with the current fandom of *Twin Peaks* and the internet in general. Back in 1991, we were allowed to make fun of Little Nicky or Evelyn and James. No one thought that meant we hated *Twin Peaks* or Lynch/Frost. But with *The Return*, there is such a love-it-or-leave-it attitude. I suppose part of it has to do with Lynch becoming so much more of a Godlike figure to a section of the fandom who believe he can do no wrong. As a true-blue Gen X-er, I was raised to look at everything with a critical eye and make fun of it. To mock is to love, and I love it all so much . . . except that Hudson Mohawke song. I'd rather watch *Hudson Hawk* with Bruce Willis than ever have to hear that song again.

TRACK 12

"Heartbreaking"

Twin Peaks Limited Event Series Soundtrack, 2017

"Because the directors coming in wanted to make it "Twin Peaks-y," they would do almost wall-to-wall music. They would get all the music cues and think, Oh, yeah, let's put this in, and put that in. And then when you see what David did with Season 3, you see that it really wasn't all music cues."
—Sabrina S. Sutherland. *Laura's Ghost* by Courtenay Stallings

It was only a few minutes into the combined screening of Parts 1 and 2 that I noticed the lack of a score. The absence of music was so loud I could hardly hear anything else. By the time we first saw the Red Room again, with no music playing, I knew things had radically changed. Dean Hurley explained earlier in this book that when Lynch rewatched Episode 29, an episode he had directed, he felt it was overscored. According to my calculations, 87 percent of that episode included music, which is the highest percentage of any episode of the series. It wasn't the directors coming in who were responsible; it was the boss. Lynch had a change of heart, and *The Return* embraced a new aesthetic: "Where we're from the birds better shut the fuck up because ominous woosh is coming to town."

Still, a record was released that was supposed to be the soundtrack to *The Return*. Just like the previous *Return* record, it has a horrible title that is impossible to remember and includes songs that conceptually it shouldn't. At the end of this chapter, I lay out which tracks should have been on which releases, again following not the rules I set up but the rules the albums set up. I would have liked to have seen just one large release rather than two mismatched

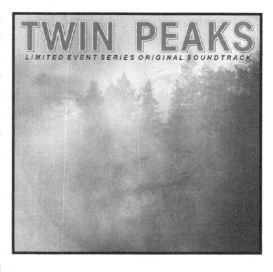

releases. But then again, it wouldn't be *Twin Peaks* if it wasn't a bit of a cluster release. The following tracks were released on the album whose cover features trees overlaid with Laura Palmer's homecoming picture.

"Twin Peaks Theme" by Angelo Badalamenti

Who is shocked this is where we start? No one. There is no earthly reason to have this on here. It doesn't even have Dean Hurley's "Intro Cymbal Wind" mixed in, which at least would have made it different and was how the theme actually aired. It would have been nice to at least have a different version. Better yet, just skip it.

"American Woman" (David Lynch Remix) by Muddy Magnolias

This track was most famously used in Part 1 as Mr. C heads to Buella's cabin. This is also used in Part 16. This set the tone for Mr. C and let viewers know immediately this was not the good side of Dale Cooper. This music, slowed to a snail's pace, fits the scene and sets the tone early in the series. How did it come to be? I'll let Dean Hurley explain:

Scott Ryan: Duwayne said he was editing in one room and you and David were working on music in the room next to him, and you were trying to mesh "American Woman" with "Falling." Do you remember that?

Dean Hurley: Sort of, vaguely. That's definitely one of those things where David would be like "Just try this. Lay it over top of it," kind of like with "Birds in Hell." He's looking for some magic. You have to see it through because that's how that whole usage of "American Woman" happened.

Sometimes my thinking pattern is not the best, and I recognize that there's a flaw in my instinct to kill something far too soon, where David will see it through to the end. It involved finding the Roadhouse acts. David's music agent at CAA is Brian Loucks, who's legendary. He was the one who orchestrated the original Warner Bros. *Floating into the Night* LP, and he's been with David ever since that. When we were working on music possibilities, he was sending me hot people he was working with. He sent a batch of stuff to me, and in it was "American Woman" by Muddy Magnolias. I listened to the song, and I didn't like it for the Roadhouse. I played it for David, who said, "Do me a favor and play it at half speed." All of a sudden what comes to the speakers is what's on the episode. It's just this extremely powerful, slow, David Lynch music cue. Again, David turned something where he's just trying all these random things that sound like bad ideas, or taking something that's dismissive and playing it backward, and then, all of a sudden, it reveals that there is a magic piece of music hidden within it.

"Laura Palmer's Theme" by Angelo Badalamenti

This is used in Part 4 when Bobby has his breakdown, a scene everyone involved in the making of *The Return* refers to as the example of how using the old music worked best. Whether that is true or not, I can't see why we need this song released again on vinyl when there are so many cues that have never been released. Are you keeping track of how many times I've said that? Good. That's how many times Lynch et al. have released the same stuff and not my precious "The Norwegians" or "Theme from FWWM (Sax)."

"Accident" / "Farewell" by Angelo Badalamenti

This is the first original Angelo piece on this album. It is used in Part 6 when the little kid is hit by a car. It is also used in Parts 5, 15, 16, and 18. The Part 5 usage is when Dougie cries at seeing his son in the car. The connections between cars and kids with this musical cue are interesting. It is a beautiful piece of music that certainly fits a very tragic moment of the series. Several people have told me this scene is too hard to watch. If it helps, nothing that happens in Season 3 is actually happening. Cooper is still sitting in his chair in the Red Room, so don't you worry about that little kid. He doesn't exist. Does that help or make things worse?

Dean Hurley: The song that was used in the Harry Dean Stanton scene, when the kid gets run over, was actually called "Accident" in the original session. It was one of David's trigger words, which was clearly for that scene. But the craziest thing is David basically just tells Angelo the scene. There's something really cosmic and fundamental with the way that they worked. It forces Angelo into this fumbling version of producing the gold on the spot. David says, "Okay, Angelo, there's a car accident. There's a five-year-old boy who's been playing with his mom in the park. He's running ahead. She's chasing them, and in the crosswalk of the intersection, after they leave the park, he gets ahead of her. At the last second, he sees this crazy fucking guy in a truck running through the stop sign." David gets elevated in the way he's telling it. Right now, you have to divorce yourself from the scene because you can picture it shot for shot from the scene. But imagine if you're Angelo and you're hearing just these words, you know what I mean? David goes on this tirade at the very end. He's like "You have to write this horror, Angelo. It's lost love! Horror! It's horror!" Like he'll get stuck on a repeating loop.

So Angelo, for a little bit, starts to say, "Okay, she's running. So maybe some percussion." But he doesn't have percussion available to him. All he has is his synth. So it's like it has to be made through his ten fingers—whatever he can do through that and maybe piano and strings, which is this piano patch and a string patch on top of each other. That's how he would do things like "Laura Palmer's Theme." So he's playing the piano, but the strings are shadowing everything. So it sounds like an arrangement, even though it's still just a single performance. Angelo plays the thing. And, Scott, it's just verbatim, exactly. No edits. Nothing. What ends up being in the original scene is what he played.

Scott Ryan: Incredible.

Dean Hurley: It gets better. Angelo stops. And David's just screaming, "That's so fucking beautiful, Angelo. It's so fucking beautiful. I saw the thing. I saw the scene." Angelo's like giddy, and says, "So did I, David." But the craziest thing is you skip forward to when Duwayne is piecing together that first assembly, he doesn't cut to music. He cuts to silence.

Scott Ryan: He mentioned that in his interview.

Dean Hurley: Duwayne tries to tune into that and find a rhythm to the scene—the scene's natural rhythm. Duwayne edited that whole fucking scene without any music. He'd never even heard what Angelo did. This is late in the game, when the music is finally laid in, and it lays in perfectly, Scott. The whole fucking thing just lays in there. I mean, I about shit myself because I'm the only person who knew how haphazardly it came together. I've never been in a situation where you wouldn't want to just make a nip tuck to extend something to have it suited for what's there. The only explanation I can have for something like that is this is what happens when you have all these practitioners working for a common goal. David is like this extremely loud, solid, strong, fundamental tone, and he gets people to sort of vibrate in harmony with that tone. So everybody is aligned to the same vibrational energy. I know I'm starting to sound a little new agey. But again, this is the only explanation I have for it.

It doesn't sound like an accident to me. I bet this track just moved up on your lists of favorites on this vinyl. It sure did for me. What a story. I love my job.

"Grady Groove" by Angelo Badalamenti

This track is used in Part 5 when Dougie goes to work at Lucky 7 and then again during the conga line in Part 13. With Grady Tate having passed away the same year that *The Return* came out, I figured this had to be an old drum track that was discovered and used.

Scott Ryan: Is "Grady Grove" an old track?

Dean Hurley: Yeah, it was just an unused *Twin Peaks Archive*. I remember early on, when we were gearing up for things, I was going through the library and pulling all the cues from the first series that I thought should return or that David would want to use for places. I had that one in there. David loved Grady Tate. He had this amazing anecdote about Grady when they were working on a song for *Wild at Heart*. Grady was coming in. This was after all the initial core tracks from *Twin Peaks* were recorded. They actually weren't using a real drummer. They had a drum machine for one of the *Wild at Heart* tracks. Grady walked in, and he heard this drum machine. He walks close to the speaker, furrows his brow, shakes his head, and goes, "Hey, that drummer has great time."

"Windswept (Reprise)" by Johnny Jewel

This cue was used in Parts 5 and 6 when Dougie is standing at the statue outside of Lucky 7 Insurance. You don't have to ask if I have gone to that filming location and stood there, pointing, just like Dougie, because you know I have. The statue and the red balloons weren't there, but the area certainly looked the same. I remember being sad when I discovered that this tune wasn't written by Angelo Badalamenti, because it really did seem like one of his pieces. Dean Hurley explained to me that when Johnny Jewel sent in some songs for the Roadhouse, he also sent in this track, and David Lynch thought it worked perfectly for Dougie. I always considered this track Dougie's theme song. It captures his loneliness mixed with a touch of goodness.

"Dark Mood Woods" / "The Red Room" by Angelo Badalamenti

This was used in Part 2 when Hawk walks in the woods. Not that anyone asked, but I believe that scene is the only moment in *The Return* that actually occurs in the Twin Peaks town that we knew from the original series. The rest is all in Cooper's mind. This cue was also used in Parts 3 and 16.

Good thing I worked on this book, because one thing I came to realize is that I had never captured this as an MP3. I always assumed it was the exact same as the *Season 2* version. I was always annoyed that this was on another recording. But now that I've done my research (with an assist from Josh Eisenstadt), I'm even more annoyed. This is just a shorter version of what already came out. Here someone remixed it and cranked up the volume, then they cut "The Red Room" part way down and played with that mix as well. The original is far superior. Who would have done this?

Dean Hurley: That would have been me who cut the length. Even though the track shares the same naming as the *Archive* release, they are different edits. I actually made the edit of the original archive release as well and combined the two tracks because I thought it was fitting to have those pieces together as a suite. When you're putting together a vinyl release, length of the individual sides is a big issue—if a side goes beyond twenty-one/twenty-two minutes-ish (depending on frequency content), the audio fidelity really goes noticeably downhill. So you really have to be careful about the length you load a side with. Without checking, I'm sure that's why it was truncated—the Red Room portion is too brief. Other than probably being slightly edited, "Dark Mood Woods" is the exact same mix. "The Red Room" in *The Return* is slightly different. I did make a different mix of that so it would be more of an atmospheric room tone without the prominent upright bass or guitar—specifically in *The Return*, that space seemed to big for just the essence of that environment, not the full-on ensemble music cue, each time it was visited. So there is the original "Red Room" cue, but in *The Return* it's almost like it operates as an ambience, not a distinct musical moment. But hundred percent I would have included more time on the "Red Room" portion on the soundtrack if I could have. I was just under timing constraints for the vinyl cut.

"The Chair" by Angelo Badalamenti

We are on the eighth track on this record, and we get the second original cue from Angelo. Again, this is a beautiful one. It has all the movements we expect from our maestro. This song scores my beloved friend Charlotte Stewart's scene in Part 9. Charlotte (Betty Briggs) has stated this will be her final scene as an actress, and what a beautiful one to go out on. I love that she is allowing Lynch to be her final director, as he allowed her to be his first actress, in *Eraserhead*, his first feature-length film. Charlotte is a dear member of my family now, and I have been so lucky to travel the United States with her. We've met up in more states than I can count. The fact that Betty Briggs gets to come back and talk about Major Briggs is meaningful because Charlotte loved Don Davis so much. Probably my favorite character moment in the entire *Return* is when Betty Briggs gives her emotional speech about the Major saying goodbye to her. Charlotte is such a free spirit and acts so naturally on screen; I appreciate that she got a meaty moment when so many original cast members didn't. I was surprised to find out that she didn't know what the scene was actually about.

Charlotte Stewart: I had no idea what the circumstances were. I was given no background. I didn't know if Major Briggs died of a heart attack or when he died. That is the way David works. He doesn't want you to have a lot of information. It is all very symbolic. All I could be was Bobby's mom. That was my whole motivation.

Scott Ryan: You had to wait till Part 9 before you showed up. What did fans think when they finally saw you?

Charlotte Stewart: The feedback I got afterward was "Thank God Betty's back" [Laughs], because Season 3 was so bizarre and symbolic. Then Bobby goes to his mom and needs her help. That is something I could do.

No doubt. Charlotte can do anything. She also had a great cue to score her work. Dean explained where that song came from. It wasn't from the work sessions for *The Return*, but somewhere else.

Dean Hurley: I found DATs upon DATs. On some of them, the synth was directly plugged in, so you wouldn't get the talking, but you can hear Angelo working out the music from "Silencio." You get all the raw footage. That is how I came across the cue "The Chair" for Season 3. I was going through those work tapes. That song was actually from a maybe Broadway show that they had an idea of working on about the life of Tesla. That cue was from some of the work tracks of *Tesla*.

Scott Ryan: So you were looking for different tracks that could be used on *The Return* and you found that?

Dean Hurley: Yeah. "The Chair" was so amazing. We were pulling from a wealth of material. There was a time-capsule quality of what they had been working on together across decades. Sometimes finding that cue in a bottle from years ago had a certain je ne sais quoi that was like "That is a classic Angelo cue."

"Deer Meadow Shuffle" by David Slusser, David Lynch

I bet you expect me to complain about this track being released on this vinyl? Nope, this is the only place this song has ever been officially released, so this is the kind of cue that should be released. Plus, it means I don't have to choose this for my vinyl box set because it is already released. This is such a classic song from *FWWM*, and it was always frustrating that it wasn't on the soundtrack to that film, but there were only so many tracks that could fit on a CD in 1992. One person who was really glad that the cue was reused in Part 9 to score the detectives in Las Vegas was David Slusser.

David Slusser: I got paid again. He dug a couple of things out and reused them, and David called me up and said he was going to pay me again. He has always been a great guy.

"Threnody to the Victims of Hiroshima" by Warsaw National Philharmonic

Part 8 is a masterpiece. It will go down in history as one of the most inventive hours on television. I can't really think of anything quite like it ever telecast. Sometimes I like to think about the Showtime execs, who had to be devastated that they had to play that Part on their channel. One of the things that truly sells the nuclear bomb explosion is that Lynch used a song was written for the victims of the American bombing of Japan. The cue plays for five and a half minutes of orchestrated nuclear annihilation. The visuals are mesmerizing, and the song is the second audible assault on the viewer's ears, "She's Gone" from NIN being the first one. Again, the Showtime suits must have been tickled black and white with this decision. This cue is also used in Part 11 and 15, so it became a recurring theme in the series, but I never want to listen to it, because the song doesn't quite sound the same to me on the vinyl as it does in the series. There is a reason for that.

Dean Hurley: David just cut up "Threnody" in Part 8. There's big phrases that go unaltered, but there's a lot of it used in the show where it's cut up. The version on the record is the original arrangement. You're kind of forced to put the original, unaltered thing on the soundtrack because you can't just cut up something and put it on the soundtrack unless you get permission from the original artist.

Scott Ryan: This entire book is about getting all the songs released, but this original version is not something I want to listen to when I'm in a *Twin Peaks* mood. I always skip it.

Dean Hurley: I do like the usage of that because he's using that for the atomic bomb test, and he's scoring it with the byproduct of what that catastrophic evil resulted in, which is somebody writing a lament for all the people who died.

Scott Ryan: Well, I love that it exists. I am glad it is used in Part 8. It's great to watch, but not so enjoyable to listen to on a Sunday morning with coffee.

"Slow 30s Room" by Dean Hurley, David Lynch

Part 8 isn't about just explosions; it also contains my favorite Dean Hurley composition ever. "Slow 30s Room" plays when the Giant/Fireman tends to the alarm as Señorita Dido waits patiently. (Anyone who lives with the Giant must have the patience of a saint. You know it takes him forever to bring the garbage cans up from the driveway.) This track starts and stops and has the feel of an old-time vinyl record. It has the kind of sound that we expect from a Lynch cue. But like a few other music cues from *The Return*, it originates from a different Lynch project.

Scott Ryan: Tell me about your composition "Slow 30s Room" that you worked on with David.

Dean Hurley: That originally was used in *The Air Is on Fire*, which was an art show that David did at the Fondation Cartier pour l'art contemporain in 2007. They built rooms that David designed on three-by-five cards. They were rooms designed as a real space that you could walk through. David said to me, "Do you have any ideas for what we want to hear in there?" And then he says, "Music for us; it'll be like a slow 30s room." And that just exploded in my head. I was really obsessed at the time, and still continue to be obsessed with these things called an optigan. It was in between a toy and an instrument made by Mattel in the early seventies. They had a big band disc, and you can basically hold these chord buttons down and play your own arrangement of a song. With "Slow 30s Music," I made this unusual progression with the optigan, because I'm just trying to make it sound as off-kilter as possible. The thing I liked about

it is it sounds like an authentic needle drop because it is actually an old optical sound. [Photo above courtesy of Keyboard Resource YouTube channel.]

Scott Ryan: So how did that get into Part 8?

Dean Hurley: The script described the scene as a far-off Latin sound. So at first I made a thing that sounded like this distant, far-off Latin music. David tried it in the edit. I didn't think it worked at all. I wasn't over the moon about what I'd made. When I saw the dailies, I immediately thought about "Slow 30s Room," because that's what it looked like to me. It was fucking black-and-white. It looked like an old Hollywood movie. I remember just softly suggesting to David that he should try it. And he's like "Okay, send it down." It just kind of marries perfectly. It almost seemed even more fitting for Part 8 than it did the exhibition.

"The Fireman" by Angelo Badalamenti

This is an over-seven-minute cue that sounds like something out of *Mulholland Drive* but with a little more hope. It is very much that signature created-on-the-synth sound that much of *Drive* contained. In the previous chapter, I talked about how important it is for Lynch to match the music to the scene; when he does that, the scene becomes a classic. That is why Part 8 is already thought of as a masterpiece. Every cue works exactly as intended. This cue, which starts out very mysteriously, explodes into hope and belief in the future, just as the Fireman creates the golden orb and sends Laura Palmer to Earth to battle Bob along with all the evil the bomb let slip into the universe. I love the movements within this piece. I could never hum it, but it sure does have a distinct melody that rises and falls along with the action in the scene.

Dean Hurley: "The Fireman" cue was part of that 2015 session with Angelo. The prompt was inspired by the Russian pianist Dmitri Shostakovich. Once David clings to an idea, he keeps repeating it. He probably first told Angelo to write something like Shostakovich in *Blue Velvet* because that's what he wrote that script to. He just loved that sort of timbre and the note choices of that kind of Russian world. When David was building that scene, he took some of that raw music that Angelo recorded and just chopped the shit out of it to make it work. He needed it to do a certain thing, especially with the sort of ritual of what was happening on screen.

The fact that David Lynch moved the pieces around to fit the scene is how he got away with not having Angelo score to picture. I always wondered if Lynch or Dunham did this because the cue really does match perfectly with what the Fireman does on-screen. This is the importance of the brotherhood between Lynch and Badalamenti. They completely trust each other, and there is no ego between them. I am not sure that another film composer would be so nonchalant about having a director just take their music and cut it up to fit, but it sure does work in this scene.

"Saturday" (Instrumental) by Chromatics

Dean Hurley: I wanted the Chromatics to do "Saturday" so David would have an instrumental to utilize. They filmed "Shadow" twice for the Roadhouse, and David said, "All right, are we moving on to the next one?" I was like "Well, they do have another instrumental track prepared if we can just do that." So we kind of just squeaked it in there.

Yes, this is an instrumental song, and this is supposed to be the instrumental soundtrack, but there really is no reason why this isn't on the Roadhouse album. This song closed out Part 12. One last thing I noticed about the performances at the Roadhouse, and why not say it here, when we have a song that should have been on that album? (I'm just trying to continue along with the nonsensical arrangement of these badly named collections.) If you watch the bonus feature of all the Roadhouse performances, you will notice the difference between the younger performers and the elder ones. No, I am not talking about wrinkles. I am talking about the enjoyment the performers are experiencing. A better word might be "emote." I don't want to single anyone out because I don't like that kind of criticism, but man, the younger bands just don't look like they are having any fun performing. Here is something someone should have told them: "You are in a David Lynch movie. Your music is captured for life. Have some fun." Maybe show some signs of life. Emote. Show us you understand the meaning of the song. It just doesn't work for me when a performer is on stage and acts like they are at the dentist's office rather than sharing the art they created. Now you can argue that maybe they were acting and it wasn't really them, but the point of all these scenes is that they are supposedly singing for an audience filled with the townspeople of Twin Peaks, so either way they are performing as an act. The older, seasoned artists either acted out their songs or at least let us know they were happy to be there. Just an observation. I leave here with no judgments, only an observation.

"Headless Chicken" by Thought Gang

This is an instrumental from Thoughtful Gang's album. The acoustic bass is a lot of fun. The entire song has an eerie mood synth that makes the song feel ominous. This track plays for the Mitchum Brothers in Part 10. If more Thought Gang music was like this, it would be a more listenable album. Knowing how Angelo and David work, I can see them writing this in one of their sessions and then not finding a place to use it until *The Return*. I am glad they finally did.

"Night" by Angelo Badalamenti

Dean Hurley: "Night" wasn't used in the series. Angelo did have a say in the soundtrack, and one of his notes was "Could we add this on the soundtrack?" It was recorded in that 2015 session. So it was for the new season. It just wasn't used.

I am glad this song was released, as any new Angelo music makes me happy. If Lynch couldn't find a spot for it on-screen, then he couldn't. And considering that he filled every moment of the screen with music throughout *The Return*, how could he ever have squeezed it in? It's not like more than half of Part 18 had scenes that took place at night.

The structure and synth really have a *Mulholland Drive* feel to it. I think this track could have been used in that film very easily. I know I have said that a few times, and what I really mean by that is that Badalamenti's compositions really started to change after 2001. The original *Twin Peaks* and *FWWM* really doesn't include songs with just synth sounds that move slowly and don't have a ton of other instrumentation. There were a few ("Dark Mood Woods"/ "The Voice of Love"), but mostly his compositions were flushed out by Grady Tate, Kinny Landrum, Al Regni, or Vinnie Bell. But after *Straight Story*, his work for Lynch usually was just a synth sound. This isn't a complaint, just a fact. I really like this track because it isn't just dark and spooky; it has a lot of light in it for a song called "Night." This would be a good track for someone to set Lynch lyrics to like they did with "The Voice of Love." Maybe they could use that wood poem he read at the *Missing Pieces* premiere.

I like that Lynch let a new song come out, just like he did with "Cop Beat" on *Season Two*. Knowing that only a small percentage of the music that Angelo and Lynch worked on has ever been heard means that once we get the *Twin Peaks* vinyl box set out, we need to start working on getting those unreleased tracks out before they also get tossed in the garbage because the next generation has no idea what the heck a DAT tape is.

"Heartbreaking" by Angelo Badalamenti

In Part 11, the suddenly wealthy Slot Lady finds her Mr. Jackpot in a restaurant. "Heartbreaking," which to me is the most beautiful piece of new music in *The Return*, plays in the background during this scene. Just like those *TPA* piano tunes that play in the Great Northern, this is played by a piano man in the restaurant. Lynch also used this song for the end credits of Part 11 rather than as a Roadhouse performance. I love this composition because the tune has such a connection to the "Laura Palmer Theme," which was used for most of the end credits in the original series. I really wish the piano music for this cue would be released; I would love to play it. It truly is a marvelous piece of music. I am so glad that Angelo lived long enough to have these new songs released and able to score *The Return* with his own music, however limited that ended up being.

Scott Ryan: With the track "Heartbreaking," I've always wanted to tie that song's chords or melody to "Laura Palmer's Theme," but I can't.

Dean Hurley: It's interesting because you hear it, and it immediately sounds like Angelo. Like how do you do that, even if there's no musical similarity? In terms of the notes, his performance is so distinctive that it immediately, a hundred percent, sounds like it's cut from the same cloth. "Heartbreaking" was a piano-only performance in the sessions from 2015. When we were working on the scene David said he wanted strings. This was late in the game, and everything needed to get done fast. I didn't have time to go back to Angelo and ask him to do that. So I just put the strings on myself. It was easy because the notes were all there. I was way too timid about it, because I felt like I was going into territory like touching up Michelangelo's stuff. I kept mixing the strings down because I was too ashamed that I did that part.

Scott Ryan: You shouldn't have felt that way, because it really does add something to it. And that's the classic *Twin Peaks* sound. You did a great job. There were two other piano pieces in that scene that were never released. Were those written by Angelo as well?

Dean Hurley: Yes, those are Angelo compositions that were done in August of 2016 as part of his new recordings for the third season. They were done by Angelo on his own, after and separately from the initial two-day 2015 remote sessions with David. One had a working title of "Generic Italian," and the other was called "Euphorically Happy." I believe the three Santini Restaurant cues were actually some of the very last cues to come from Angelo for the show.

Hmm, does anyone else smell a campaign for a *Twin Peaks Return Archive*? I mean who doesn't need more ominous woosh in our life? I really would like these other two piano tracks released. It would have been better to have them released than the next track.

"Audrey's Dance" by Angelo Badalamenti

Part 16 uses this classic theme from the original series to score a major plot point for Audrey Horne in *The Return*. But even so, there is no justifiable reason to include it on this soundtrack. Everybody has owned this track since 1990. At the end of this chapter, I have a list of the nineteen tracks unreleased on either soundtrack. I would submit any of those would be better than releasing what we already had. The song is listed as a remix, but it sounds exactly the same to me.

What makes the use of "Audrey's Dance" important in this Part is that just like in Episode 2, Audrey Horne dances to this track in public. Whether this takes place in someone's subconscious or in reality, I like that for the fourth time this track is heard by both the characters in the scene and the viewers watching on TV. Audrey hears the song she heard on the radio when she was eighteen and dances to it. I asked Sherilyn Fenn about performing this moment when she appeared on my live online COVID event, *Harold Smith Stay In/Play In*. She said, "I didn't like dancing because it was scary. We had to do it right on the same day that David told me I was doing it."

"Dark Space Low" by Angelo Badalamenti

The final song of the final soundtrack is called "Dark Space Low." Were you expecting a happy song? It is dark and low around these parts, my friends. There is no voice of love to be found. This short track sums up the mood of the limited series. I like that it has the typical Angelo synth sound but also this metallic sound that echoes through the track. I am sure it was chosen on Angelo's synth, but it really sounds like a piece of metal is vibrating. Maybe it is electricity? But it doesn't feel like normal instruments are creating this piece of music, and that adds to its mystery. This played during the end credits of Part 18, which starred Mary Reber and the Palmer house. [See picture below]

Proper Track Lists

Now that we have gone through both of *The Return* soundtracks, I want to present what the playlist for the two soundtracks *should* have been. Make no mistake; I am not asking for these two records to be released with this track list. I am not about getting things rereleased. I am here to promote the release of music in danger of fading away. I present these tracks so you can make a corrected playlist, reflecting how *The Return*'s soundtracks should have been compiled. And Lord knows, you can name your playlist anything you want and it will still be better than the original names for these two releases.

My final track list for the album that should have been called *Live from the Roadhouse*:

Shadow
Mississippi
Lark
Snake Eyes
Tarifa
She's Gone Away
No Stars
Human
A Violent Yet Flammable World
Saturday
Just You
Wild West
Axolotl
Sharp Dressed Man
Out of Sand
The World Spins

The second release, which should have been called *Twin Peaks: The Return Soundtrack*, is a collection of all the music from the series that wasn't performed at the Roadhouse AND hadn't been previously released. Just like normal soundtracks to films, it would have songs that played in the film and the instrumental score that played over top scenes. That list would be:

My Prayer
I Love How You Love Me
I Am
Viva Las Vegas
American Woman (David Lynch Remix)
Green Onions
I've Been Loving You Too Long (Live from
Monterey Pop)
Windswept (Reprise)
Accident / Farewell
Grady Groove
The Chair
Slow 30s Room
The Fireman
Night
Heartbreaking
Dark Space Low
Threnody to the Victims of Hiroshima

Now, I didn't add in any of the missing tracks from *The Return* because I will assume there were contract disputes that prevented putting them on a soundtrack to begin with. I could only rearrange what was used. I did delete the always-frustrating rerelease of the same songs we have on other albums to make room. If you wanna hear "Laura Palmer's Theme," listen to the original soundtrack; you don't need it here too. I did reluctantly leave "Threnody" on the list; I put it last because there is no way anyone ever actively wants to listen to this song, but still, it was on the soundtrack. I struggled with where to put the ZZ Top song but decided it should go on the Roadhouse album; even though it is not performed live, it makes the track lists more even. If these two soundtracks had been curated like this, the two-set release would have made a lot more sense. If you want to add the missing songs that weren't released on either album but were used in *The Return*, you could add these to your playlist.

Here is a partial list of songs unreleased on either soundtrack. I didn't list songs that are in the public domain or new Angelo, Lynch, or Hurley songs that are not released anywhere.

"Sub Dream" Dean Hurley and David Lynch (Parts 1,17)
"Frank 2000" Thought Gang (Parts 1, 5, 11)
"Take Five" The Dave Brubeck Quartet (Part 4)
"The Flame" Johnny Jewel (Part 5)
"Habit" and "Tabloid" Uniform (Part 5)
"Slow One Chord Blues (interior)" Dean Hurley (Part 6)
"Sleep Walk" Santo and Johnny (Part 7)
"Tone" / "Slow Speed Prison" / "Low Mood" Dean Hurley (Parts 7, 14)
"Interior Home by the Sea" Dean Hurley (Part 8)
"Slow Dreams" Johnny Jewel (Part 10)
"Red River Valley" Harry Dean Stanton (Part 10)
"Charmaine" Mantovani (Part 10)
"Angel Choir" Dean Hurley (Parts 5, 12)
"Seven Heaven" Dean Hurley (Part 13)
"Eastern European Symphonic Mood No. 1" Dean Hurley (Part 13)
"Forest" / "Interior" Dean Hurley (Part 14)
"Summer Night" Thought Gang (Part 15)
"Night Electricity Theme" Dean Hurley (Parts 16,17)

Most of the Dean Hurley tracks, except the 45-minute "Sub Dream," are included on Hurley's release *Anthology Resource Vol. 1:* △△. We also now know that "Generic Italian" and "Euphorically Happy" are also not on the soundtracks, but they have not been commercially released. Let's hope Dean feels frisky and slips them out to the internet at some point.

TRACK 13

The Voice of Love, 1993

Kevin Laffey: I worked hard on getting *The Voice of Love* done. It was a kiss of death to wait that long between albums. To get David and Angelo to do another record with Julee was a challenge, because David was already off onto something else. Julee got increasingly frustrated by not having her own voice. It's a hell of a long time to wait between albums. Julee was a handful. She fought with David all the time, and it was frustrating to be at the mercy of David and Angelo.

In 1989, when *Floating into the Night* was released, nothing but happy dreams appeared to lie ahead for Julee Cruise, David Lynch, and Angelo Badalamenti. In 1993, when Julee's sophomore effort, *The Voice of Love* was released, it was nothing but Bob-filled nightmares. *Twin Peaks* had been pulled multiple times and then canceled midcliffhanger. *FWWM* bombed at the box office and was treated like a pine weasel at a Great Northern fashion show. *On the Air*, Lynch and Frost's follow-up television series, was pulled even before all of its episode aired and has yet to be released on DVD or Blu-ray in the United States some thirty years later. David Lynch went from being on the cover of *Time* to being seen as a hack. This is when *The Voice of Love* was released. It was forgotten, unheard, never even given a chance. But I have placed it here in the final chapter because for me it serves as the exclamation point on all the wonderful music this trio created. These might be fighting words, but *The Voice of Love* is a far superior work to *Floating into the Night*. I love every song on it, and it is a bit more polished, well-rounded, and sophisticated. It is a great album, but my guess is that most of you passed on it or didn't even know it existed. Even Julee Cruise didn't love it.

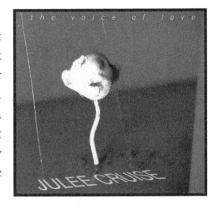

Julee Cruise: I didn't like how my voice was mixed, and I didn't like the songs "Movin' in on You" and "Friends for Life." There are certain songs from the B-52s I don't like, "Rock Lobster." I don't want to do it. I was too old to do it at forty; you look stupid.

Despite her feelings on her performance, which I respectfully disagree with, the album has some major connections to *Wild at Heart* with Julee's cover of "Up in Flames" and "Kool Kat Walk." It has connections to *FWWM* with "Questions in a World of Blue," "The Voice of Love," and "She Would Die for Love," my favorite "Theme from FWWM" with lyrics. As I've said over and over, I so wish Lynch had used this in *The Return* because I do believe this is Angelo's best written piece of music, and Julee's vocals on the album are angelic. Julee may not have praised herself, but she loved working with bassist Ron Carter on the track.

Julee Cruise: Ron Carter played the bass. We didn't have a stand-up bass on *Floating into the Night*; we just had a Fender Rhodes, and there is a big difference. He just makes you wanna hang yourself after hearing "She Would Die for Love." [Laughs.] You've achieved something. Ron Carter is a huge jazz star. It was an honor to have that kind of a band on the record.

So it isn't an album to ignore. Julee even wrote a song on the album, "In My Other World," which was a first for her. It became a bone of contention between her and Angelo and Lynch.

Julee Cruise: It was the apprentice bringing the song to the mentor. I wanted them to like it. Angelo made fun of it and said it sounded like a soap opera. I wanted him to critique it, not make fun of it. It is their record as far as writing and stuff of that. I don't think they liked that I had a song on there. I thought they produced it really well.

I always think of George Harrison when I think of Julee telling me how hard it was for her to share her music with them. Imagine poor George Harrison playing his tunes for Lennon and McCartney. It couldn't have been easy. Julee got the last laugh, though, when a major star picked her song to cover.

Julee Cruise: Martin Gore from Depeche Mode did a version of "In My Other World," and I really like that version. He phrases it differently, and I like his better. It was an honor.

I also placed this album in the last chapter because I believe the end of *FWWM*, when Cooper and Laura are in the Red Room and the instrumental version of "The Voice of Love" plays, is the end of all of *Twin Peaks*. I think this scene happens after *The Return*. To me, the end of *Twin Peaks* is captured in the music of Angelo when he wrote the song "The Voice of Love." Adding the lyrics and Julee's singing makes me feel the same way about the music. Yes, songs from *TPA* were released after this album. Yes, *The Return* came years after, but I like ending it all with Julee singing and whispering those words that I like to imagine Laura heard at the very end: "Listen. Listen. I hear the voice of love."

These lyrics are never heard in the series *Twin Peaks*, but they should be heard on your playlists. The music of *Twin Peaks* should be heard. It has to be protected with copyrights, vinyl releases, and official streaming on platforms that are heard around the world. Even *The Voice of Love*, which was not a commercial or critical success, although it was most surely an artistic success, has had at least two official vinyl releases. This album will be documented and found in the future. But so much of the *Twin Peaks* music is in danger of not being preserved. From my calculations, (and remember it's been a long time since I took a math class) 73 percent of the music that played in *Twin Peaks* has never been officially released. When people my age start dying and their children just toss our hard drives in the trash can, so goes the music that Angelo wrote to score Andy, Laura, Ben, Leland, Donna, Audrey, and Coop.

The majority of these songs, 212 out of 290, are not on Apple Music or Spotify. They have been released only through DavidLynch.com, and let's be blunt(I can be because we all know no one in power is ever going to read this book): releasing these songs was wholly and highly illegal. There were no contracts drawn up for the rehearsal piano part of the Miss Twin Peaks contest. The studio musicians got paid for their work that day, or Angelo just recorded something quickly on his keyboard and turned it over to Lori Eschler to drop it in the episode. So just like Lynch and Dean Hurley dropped these songs out on the internet in 2011, they could do it again on vinyl.

So why doesn't this happen? Is it better for them to just sit on a hard drive in David Lynch's closet under a severed ear from *Blue Velvet* and a lawn mower blade from *The Straight Story*? Corporations, lawyers, and executives cock block fans from releasing this kind of art more diligently than Doc Hayward standing in the kitchen doorway on James's first (and last) family dinner at the Hayward house. Not because they want to release them, but because, just like with the fan-run *Twin Peaks* festival, they would rather the music not be heard than miss out on someone making thirty-eight cents off something they didn't even know existed. If we are not careful, these songs will fade away into the jukebox in the sky as each of us original *Twin Peaks* fans slip into the cosmic drawer handles on the other side. If it wasn't for Daniel Knox, who kept screen grabs of what Dean Hurley wrote when the tracks were written and then shared them with me for this book, all that information would be gone. Dean shared lots of critical information about where this music came from, and before this book, it wasn't something anyone could read or future musicians could study. Just like the tracks. Let's do our best to protect them. Let's get a vinyl released of these tracks. Yes, I want them to do the list I curated, because I think those are the most important tracks, but I'd be happy with any or some, and even all of them. The music of *Twin Peaks* is so much more than "Falling," "Laura Palmer's Theme," and "Sycamore Trees." Oh yeah, I guess I owe you a bit more on that "Sycamore" mystery.

"And I'll See You"

This entire book started because of my desire to know how David Lynch improvised an episode that had a full song sung by a jazz legend in 1991. When was the song written? Throughout the book, I asked everyone what they knew about the song. We learned from Kevin Laffey that he was the one who introduced Lynch to Jimmy Scott. Josh Eisenstadt read me the scene from *Ronnie Rocket* with the dialogue that became the lyrics to the song. David Slusser thought the song was written for *Wild at Heart*, recorded by Koko Taylor. Duwayne Dunham remembered that there were plenty of scenes cut from the film. Lori Eschler said the song came in early, and she was told not to use it. Mark Frost said he knew there was a story there somewhere but couldn't remember what it was. Dean Hurley didn't have any information on it, but was intrigued by what I had found out. With David Slusser unable to find the Koko recording, it seemed like we would have to live with another unsolved mystery. But then I got an email from Dean Hurley, a few days after our third interview. He said he had a lead and asked me to call him.

Dean Hurley: Hey, Scott.

Scott Ryan: Is this the "Sycamore Trees" hotline?

Dean Hurley: It is today. I'm starting to build a timeline, because I think that's the only real way we can crack this situation. So I decided to just ask David.

Scott Ryan: Wow! What? I can't believe it. Something I have been wondering about for years is going to be answered by David Lynch. Okay. Life goals achieved.

Dean Hurley: Yeah. David said, "Koko just sang "Up in Flames."

Scott Ryan: Damn. So no *Wild at Heart* version of "Sycamore Trees."

Dean Hurley: I don't put too much stock in that, because he forgets things. All right, let me tell you the weird revelation that I found. I discovered a version of "Sycamore Trees" performed by Julee Cruise, a whole different version, and it was labeled BAM, which would be Brooklyn Academy of Music, seemingly intended for *Industrial Symphony*.

Scott Ryan: How does Julee Cruise sing "Sycamore Trees?" Was it like that ethereal vocal?

Dean Hurley: No, she does it in her lower voice, which she's naturally more of a . . .

Scott Ryan: . . . a belter. A Broadway baby.

Dean Hurley: Yeah, she's singing much lower than the classic soprano stuff. But it is interesting that both Julee and Koko sang "Up in Flames," and I'd have to verify this, but you can tell that "Up in Flames" is kind of the same backing track. It's just both of them are doing it. But this version of "Sycamore Trees" was an entirely different performance. But the most illuminating thing was it was labeled 1989.

Scott Ryan: Of course it was. It's like everything comes back to 1989. That is where this entire book started.

Dean Hurley: And didn't Lori say she got "Sycamore Trees" in a selection of music at the beginning of Season 2?

Scott Ryan: Yes, she got it and was told not to use it.

Dean Hurley: I found the original recording with the Little Jimmy Scott version, and I found evidence that it was take eight, and it was dated on the twenty-four track as February 28, 1991.

Scott Ryan: Which is the same day that is listed on the script of Episode 29 as the final revision from Mark Frost. Lynch started filming Episode 29 on March 4, 1991.

Dean Hurley: So I don't see how she could have that song as an early dump of music for Season 2. They also recorded "Dark Mood Woods" on the same exact date, February 28. So they're obviously doing that stuff for that last episode, sort of late into the season.

Scott Ryan: That totally makes sense, because the first time anyone hears "Dark Mood Woods" is on March 28, 1991, for an extended recap for Episode 24. They had Kyle MacLachlan voice-over an extended "previously on *Twin Peaks*" to catch viewers up because the series had been pulled, and the music that scored that recap was five minutes and twenty seconds of "Dark Mood Woods." That isn't on streaming services, so people watching *Twin Peaks* today heard "Mood" for the first time in Episode 29. But I first heard it on the recap. I remember loving it immediately. I can't believe they recorded both songs on the same day. Did they also record the track "The Red Room" that day?

Dean Hurley: The working title for "The Red Room" was "Composite," or something like that. The fact that I didn't mention the date doesn't mean it wasn't recorded that day. Everything is so chaotic that I don't have it all in a row. Let me try to find it. I couldn't find it on the first go. My guess is "The Red Room" was recorded that day because they both sound like the same arrangement. You've got the same organ. Some of the stuff has dates. Some of it doesn't.

Scott Ryan: Finding answers for these things can never be definitive, but this is all big news. Thank you so much for this.

Dean Hurley: When I was working on the *TPA*, there weren't dates on stuff because I wasn't looking at the original tapes. I was looking at compilations, like Lori was talking about when she received that dump of a bunch of new music. That stuff doesn't come with the original recording dates. But what happened was Angelo was basically sitting on a lot of the twenty-four-track and quarter-inch mixed down of the original magnetic tapes. In 2019 or 2020, he sent it all to David. It was transferred in October of 2020. So on all these transfers, we have whatever information was on the tapes. These tapes had lots of projects, but none of it was from *Wild at Heart*.

Scott Ryan: Of course, nothing is easy.

Dean Hurley: So February 1989 is when they recorded the demos. Then, the first official music sessions for *Twin Peaks*, where they recorded "Slow Cool Jazz" and "Fast Cool Jazz," was April of 1989, just a couple months later. The dates on the rest of the titles are a variety of dates. There are other bits of music recorded in December of 1989, January, February, and March of 1990. Then there's a huge gap, and you see September, October, November, December of 1990. You see

January of 1991, and then nothing until February of 1991 with "Sycamore Trees" and "Dark Mood Woods." So that's sort of the zone that things were being made. It is interesting to see the timeline of how everything is cross-pollinating because you got 1989, 1990, and 1991. You've got *Twin Peaks, Floating into the Night, Industrial Symphony, Wild at Heart*, and all that stuff is swirling together. I did find a demo version of "Sycamore Trees" as sung by Angelo.

Scott Ryan: Did that have a date on it?

Dean Hurley: No, unfortunately. That one the date is all fucked up because it's on a compilation tape labeled "Demos." So the date on it was late November 1991. But it had a ton of demos on there. It had "This Is Our Night," "Just You," "Movin' in on You," "Questions in a World of Blue." Also, an interesting tidbit that I found is that there was an early version of "Questions in a World of Blue" called "Your Hand Falls into Mine." It's the same tune, but totally different lyrics, and that was on there as well. So it was almost like at some point in November 1991, somebody had instructed somebody to put together all the demos of possible songs.

Scott Ryan: Well, all those songs but "Just You" ended up on Julee's *The Voice of Love* album. So that demo could have been created for that project. So one could extrapolate that "Just You," even though James sang it before November '91, possibly was gonna be a Julee Cruise song.

Dean Hurley: Well, it's hard to say. You don't want to jump to conclusions there. I think the overarching, bird's-eye view is that people were just thinking, "What songs do we have? And what can we use them for?" That's the key sort of mentality of all this.

Scott Ryan: We could do that, but my way is more fun. I like thinking of Julee singing "Just You." I love knowing that "Sycamore Trees" was written for Julee in 1989 and just didn't make *Floating into the Night*. There would have been no reason to put it on *The Voice of Love* in 1993 because Jimmy Scott had already recorded it in 1991. But maybe Julee would have also recorded "Just You" if it wasn't used in the series.

Dean Hurley: It is more likely that while writing an episode. David said, "James and Maddy and Donna could sing a song. What song do we have? Oh, they could sing that fifties song." Anything is fair game, as evident from "Up in Flames" and how David had Julee and Koko sing it. There's countless more examples of that. "Sycamore Trees" is one of them.

Scott Ryan: I love getting this information at the end. I am so glad I ended up covering all these offshoots from the music of *Twin Peaks* because they are all intertwined. Did you find any dates on when they finished *Floating into the Night*?

Dean Hurley: The twenty-four-track tapes for *Floating into the Night* had dates. The primary chunk of the album was recorded January 30, 1989. Titles like "Floating," "I Float Alone," "I Remember," "Into the Night," and "The Swan." Interestingly enough, "Falling" and "The World Spins" were dated June 21, 1989. Also, that New York City rat spot that I told you about was also recorded on January 30, 1989, and according to the label on the tape, Julee does abstract vocals on top of it. That spot is in that universe. It makes sense why that was pulled and slowed down for *Twin Peaks*.

Scott Ryan: Sure, they film the Pilot of *Twin Peaks* from February to March 1989. It is interesting that she sang "Falling" in the Pilot, and they had to have her lip-synch in that scene, and you are saying they hadn't finished the track in the studio yet. I wonder if they did a rerecord after they filmed the series and they realized it was going to be the single.

Dean Hurley: Yeah, I'm not looking at the actual boxes. So I don't know.

Scott Ryan: You did incredible. We actually solved it. I'd love to hear the Julee Cruise version of "Sycamore Trees." Want to send it to me?

Dean Hurley: NO.

Well you can't blame a James for trying, can you? So what is the final history of "Sycamore Trees"? As best as I can put together: David Lynch put the lyrics in his script for *Ronnie Rocket*, which he wrote back in the seventies after finishing *Eraserhead*. He had Angelo add music to it in 1989 when they were working on *Floating* and *Industrial Symphony* as one of the forty songs that Lynch said the two of them wrote at the time. It might have been considered for use in *Wild at Heart* in 1990, but we found no proof of that outside of David Slusser's and Kinny Landrum's memories. Lynch and Kevin Laffey go see Jimmy Scott in concert in winter 1990; then Lynch and Scott record the song on February 28, 1991, and it is used in Episode 29 in March 1991. It was released on the *FWWM* soundtrack in 1992 after being used as a brief instrumental in the film. That instrumental track was released in 2011 through *TPA*. The song was also performed by Jim James in 2016 on *The Music of David Lynch* tribute album. That is just one track of the 300 covered in this book. I'm not saying each track has that dramatic a story, but I wouldn't be surprised if almost every major song swirls in a nuclear bomb fever dream combining with atoms, creamed corn, and little Bob bubbles. You can't pull from just one place. You can't focus on only one project. They are all connected.

In the end, what I find so incredibly "Scott Ryan" is that I got interested in this because I said there was no way Lynch could have pulled this song together that week when they were filming the final episode, but he actually did. He may not have written the song that week, but they recorded it the day the script was finished, and he was filming with Jimmy Scott a few days later in the Red Room. Go figure. This is the best service I offer to the *Twin Peaks* community. I am never afraid to be wrong about a theory. But I sure love following them to the end. At least now we know the answer. Like all things associated with art and Lynch, it is more complex than it appears, and there is always a story about where that ear in the field came from. But hot damn, do I really want to hear that Julee Cruise version of "Sycamore Trees."

The work David Lynch and Angelo Badalamenti created is monumental, and the majority of it has not been captured for future generations. Yes, in 2024 a compilation of Angelo's greatest hits was released by Varese Sarabande records, but guess which *Twin Peaks* songs were on it? You guessed: "Falling" and "Laura Palmer's Theme." It is always the same old same old. How are new fans supposed to discover these tracks if they are never commercially released? They won't be found in parents' estate sales in bins of records or eight tracks. Some of them are on only MP3s, already an endangered format. It won't be long before Apple stops us from loading MP3s onto our phones. You may scoff at me, but would you ever have believed that it would get rid of USB ports or headphone jacks? Did you think it would take away your ability to hardwire your laptop to the internet? They don't want you to own your music. They want you to pay them for the right to stream what they want you to hear. "The Culmination" is too long and scary and doesn't have a beat you can dance to. So why would any corporation want you to own that song? The suits just want you to listen to "Falling"; the rights to that song has Warner Bros. behind it; therefore it matters to the lawyers.

It is up to us—the die-hard, original fans—to protect the art that Angelo Badalamenti left behind. I hope this book will light a fire under executives to preserve this art. Not for the sake of art. No. Never that. But so that they can make more money. Here is a money grab that could make a lot because there are so many tracks, and fans would pay top dollar to own them. As an aside, one of the greatest composer's life work would be saved. But please don't let that get in the way of the true purpose of the music industry: money.

We know that Ben Horne's heart wasn't really into saving Ghostwood, but my heart is really into saving the music of *Twin Peaks*. Julee Cruise gave so much of herself to bring us her art. Angelo Badalamenti became a legend after his work on this project. Kinny Landrum, Al Regni, Vinnie Bell, and Grady Tate changed television scoring forever. Lori Eschler curated these tunes and took them from songs to themes as she made sure that "Hank's Theme" was played only for Hank. Dean Hurley rescued these tracks once before and released them in the early days of music on the internet and curated them with a delicate touch. David Lynch and Mark Frost created a world that came to life with the beauty of music. Music truly was in the air for so many years. The birds really did sing a pretty song, and when I close my eyes, I don't have to imagine it. I just have to hit play. My fingers start to snap. I can feel the hair on one side of my head start to stand up like an antenna, and I wish I was wearing Cooper's blue pajamas. I want to scream to the world about the injustice of all this music being forgotten, but then I settle down for a second and ask myself, "Do I have to get these tracks released tonight?" That is when I remember: "No, it can wait till morning."

Special Thanks

Josh Eisenstadt. If you want your *Twin Peaks* book to have no mistakes in it, then you want Josh fact-checking it. I was pretty proud when one or two chapters came back with no errors. Josh dug through all his call sheets to help me piece together some of the mysteries of when things were filmed and in what order. I was grateful for all of his facts and knowledge. Plus, he is my friend, and that is even better. Is this a good time for us to announce we are working together on a new *Twin Peaks* book?

Brian "Dugpa" Kursar. Dugpa is the heart and soul of *Twin Peaks* fandom. No one did more for it than he did with his website and his work on getting the *Missing Pieces* released and on bonus features on a lot of the releases. He has been a silent supporter, but I won't be silent about what he has done for all of us. He really is the top. He also helped me get a few of these interviews, and that really helped the book.

Daniel Knox. Daniel is that completist fan that you need when you want to cover all of the music. Doing the David Lynch film fests with him has always been so much fun. He is a collector's collector and was able to send me lots of things for this book that made it better, including all the screen grabs from Davidlynch.com that Dean Hurley wrote.

Steven Miller. Is there a nicer *Twin Peaks* fan than Steven? Of course there is. But why would I want to know nice ones? I asked for one article from Steven, and he sent me a ton. Way to make me work twice as hard. His work on capturing the history of what actually happened is so important to the history of the series.

Brad Dukes. There was no one else but Brad that I considered to write the foreword to this book. His *Twin Peaks* book, *Reflections*, used to be the best book on the subject. Now this one is. WAIT. I say that because his foreword is so good. Brad and *Twin Peaks* have had ups and downs, but Brad and I have always been aces. I won't forget the circumstances under which he wrote this foreword. He is family to me.

Devery Doleman. Devery was kind enough to give me a sneak peak at Fuck You, Tammy!'s newest album. It really is a fun record. You should get it. So I asked her to share some thoughts on some of the songs she sings. It was great to have a singer comment on these songs. I hope she will duet with me someday.

Courtenay Stallings. If Steven is one of the nicest fans, then Courtenay is surely one of the worst. I mean, she is always yelling at me. She constantly bullies me on Twitter. No, maybe that is Melanie Mullen, who we might as well throw into Courtenay's thanks because she will never read this damn book. Why not just mention Brittyn Lindsey too? Either way, I have been working on *Twin Peaks* projects since I've known all three mean women, and their constant criticisms keeps me in check.

Em Marinelli. Em was very kind to listen to me talk about all the interviews and the songs I was working on. I couldn't have done this book without her constant support and friendship. I know you will always be my Cool Rider, even if you never subscribed to the *Blue Rose* magazine.

Becca Moore. All Becca has ever wanted was to have her name listed in a *Twin Peaks* book, but she never thought it would happen. But it did. I told you so. You are my huckleberry.

Sharon Parks. Sharon always texts me and catches up. We met at a *Twin Peaks* event and have been friends ever since, which is pretty much how I make all my friends.

Anita Dunning-Rehn. I thank her for getting me the Julee Cruise interview back in the day and for helping me get the facts right about

Julee's appearance at the festival. Anita is a sweetheart, and I don't know what I would do without her. She is the reason Julee performed at that final concert.

Katie Edgin. I miss you, and your spirit made the difference for so many people. Thanks for your bravery, and I sure wish I could give you a copy of this book. Shout out to Matt, as well.

Alex Ryan. Thanks for always listening to me talk about the books and for pretending it matters. I am very lucky to have a child who is also my friend. It's a pretty cool thing.

Joyce Ryan. Thanks for all the support and help. Whenever I have needed a boost, my mom has always been there to assist. That is how artists make it. Thanks, Mom.

Jen Ryan. Thanks for listening to more *Twin Peaks* music than anyone should ever have to. You have always been supportive of my work and helped me out in countless ways. Thanks for everything you do.

Dean Hurley. My favorite thing ever is to win someone over with my work. Dean was rightly skeptical of me, but I think we crossed that bridge. No one in the world of art ever did more for me than Dean did with his work on the *TPA* releases. I listen to them practically daily, and it inspired this book. I look forward to working with him on the vinyl box set. Thanks for writing such wonderful things about each Archive release. Dean is the hero of this book.

Kinny Landrum. All this and he loves Billy Joel too? Sign me up. Kinny answered every question I threw at him and helped me find Al Regni. Listening to him play Angelo's music live over the phone is something I will never forget.

Al Regni. The fact that Al actually answered me when I sent him a real letter through the mail is a first for one of my books. He had such great stories and created wonderful music. I am totally jealous that he played for Barbra Streisand and Sondheim.

Lori Eschler. I can't believe I'd never heard of Lori before working on this book. She is the most important interview in the book. Lori was the unsung hero of the music, but she is unsung no more. Fans will now sing her praises forever. She also is super nice.

David Slusser. Slusser sure sent this book on a fun mystery with his "Sycamore" claim. I am still hoping he finds the DAT tapes, and he better share them with me.

Tim Hunter. I had wanted to interview Tim since the 90s. I am glad that this was the book that allowed that to happen. He sure didn't disappoint.

Mark Frost. Mark has always been so kind to me. He has come through a million times, and he has no reason to. It is just because he is a nice guy, and it shines through in his interactions with fans. Also, the quote of this book comes from him saying that talking with me was the most he had ever talked about the music with anyone, ever.

Duwayne Dunham. Duwayne knows how to tell a story. He is always so entertaining. I have really enjoyed interviewing him a few times before and after Lynch screenings. I am so thankful that we have become friends, because his work is incredible.

Kevin Laffey. I was worried I wasn't going to find anyone to talk about *Floating into the Night*, and I ended up getting the person who made the album happen. He had so many memories, and he could probably do his own book. Thanks for the pictures too.

Julee Cruise. The fact that I got to talk with Julee Cruise and then got to sing Sondheim with her is a memory I will never forget. We can never really understand what artists go through to create their art. It is so easy to think they just sing the song, but we don't know what it takes for them to make those sounds or express those feelings live on stage. Julee was a nightingale and the answers in this world of blue.

Angelo Badalamenti. Man, do I wish I could have met Angelo. It will always break my heart that it never happened. We emailed back and forth, but I could never get him to commit to an interview. I wish I would have tried harder. His music will live on as long as I have an MP3 player that corporations allow me to play music on. He had an amazing knack for making musical sense out of the world. I have never written a book without listening to his art.

Thanks to David Lynch who passed after this book was completed. He created art that made me want to create art. That is a perfect legacy.

Before you go, I want to pitch you my religion. It's called kindness. The kindness that Dean Hurley displayed in this book should be a motivator. He was unsure at the beginning, and then saw the curiosity I had for the art of this music. This is how we should approach strangers, cautious and open. Be kind to someone today who you disagree with. Don't look for the reason to be upset with someone, look for the reason to bond.

If you have kind words about the book, feel free to email me at Superted455@gmail.com

More to read about David Lynch

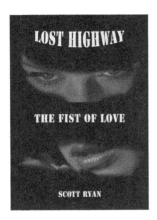
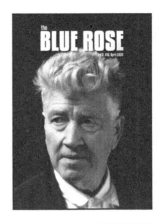
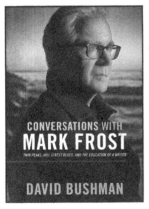

ALSO AVAILABLE FROM FMP/TUCKER DS

ORDER AT TUCKERDSPRESS.COM

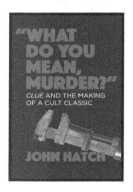

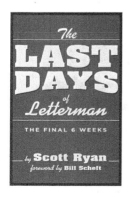